N.N.

On the Edge of My Seat

Test Highlights from Around the World

Henry Blofeld

STANLEY PAUL
London Sydney Auckland Johannesburg

Stanley Paul & Co. Ltd

An imprint of Random Century Group

20 Vauxhall Bridge Road, London SW1V 2SA

Random Century Australia (Pty) Ltd
20 Alfred Street, Milsons Point, Sydney 2061

Random Century New Zealand Limited
PO Box 40–086, Glenfield, Auckland 10

Century Hutchinson South Africa (Pty) Ltd
PO Box 337, Bergvlei 2012, South Africa

First published 1991

Set in Linotron Bembo by Speedset Ltd, Ellesmere Port
Printed and bound in Great Britain

A catalogue record for this book is available
from the British Library

ISBN 0 09 174872 0

For my wife, Bitten,
who gritted her teeth with true Swedish phlegm
when I wrote the first two chapters
on our honeymoon

Photographic acknowledgement

The author and publishers would like to thank Patrick Eagar, AllSport and the Hulton-Deutsch Collection for permission to reproduce their copyright photographs.

Introduction

When I began to write this book it was my intention to write at least one chapter about exciting moments I have watched in Test matches in every country in which Test cricket is played. I collected all my old notebooks and quickly realized that if I did that this volume would be about the same size as *Wisden*. I decided therefore that I would confine myself to Test grounds in England, Australia and the West Indies, but even that was too cumbersome and would have produced an indecently bulky volume. Accordingly, I have cut it down to three grounds in each country and have tried to relive the excitement and drama of games, some of which have for far too long been little more than a succession of historical facts deprived of their immediate flesh and blood.

If you happen not to agree with me that Colin Cowdrey's tour to the West Indies in 1967/68 was the best in the last thirty years, so be it. It is after all only a matter of opinion. But I now have up my sleeve a host of other exciting games played at venues which I have not touched upon in this book and which may in time fill another which would be a companion to this one. Bringing the past to life and indulging in severe bouts of nostalgia is surely the prerogative of all cricket lovers. I hope that the occasions that have left me on the edge of my seat may set off a similar reaction in anyone who reads these pages.

HENRY BLOFELD

1

LORD'S:
Strawberries and Mount Olympus

In his book, *Beyond a Boundary*, C. L. R. James described the Lord's pavilion as a cross between Mount Olympus and Canterbury Cathedral. It would be difficult to better that, for every time I have walked through the Grace Gates I have felt that I am taking part in a pilgrimage in white flannel trousers. The first time was on the Monday of the second Test match against Australia in 1948 when I was eight and I can remember bits of that day as if it had been a recent visit. I sat with my parents in Q Stand, now called the Allen Stand, and ate the strawberries they had brought up from Norfolk, picked from the small square field at Hoveton called Four Acres. I can still taste those strawberries and I've never had better since. We had two punnets full; one for the morning and one for the afternoon, and neither lasted out.

That was the day I saw Don Bradman bat for the only time in my life and, considering my age, I was pretty lucky to get him even once. I have two distinct memories of his innings. In the first, I can see him batting at the nursery end and receiving a no-ball. I cannot remember who was the culprit, but it must have been Alec Bedser (although I don't think it can have been him, for he assures me that he never bowled a no-ball to the Don, or anyone else for that matter), Bill Edrich or Alec Coxon. Whoever it was, the great man altered his stroke as you had time to do in those days when the no-ball was called in relation to the position of the bowler's back foot. He pulled it away through mid-wicket without any fuss and the ball sped straight towards where I was sitting. In those God-fearing days spectators were allowed to sit on the grass behind the boundary, and a chap just below us fielded it as it plopped over the rope (no advertising boards in those days). It had come close enough to make me feel that I had played for England.

The second memory is part joy, part tragedy. The Don was going along towards yet another Test hundred when Alec Bedser bowled to him from the pavilion end. I can't remember exactly what happened but I have a vague feeling he played it off the back foot. Anyway, the ball hit the edge and flew high to first slip where Bill Edrich leapt up and fell over and somewhere in between held the catch. For a moment there was a stunned silence, and then ecstatic applause; not that Bradman's wicket made the slightest impression on the state of the match for Australia were already winning by a big margin. My immediate emotions were mixed. Of course, I wanted an Australian wicket and Bradman's above all others, but it would have been lovely if I could have seen him score a hundred first. When Arthur Mailey bowled the immortal Victor Trumper in his very first over in a Grade match in Sydney, he later wrote that as he watched Trumper turn and walk away he felt like a little boy who had killed a dove. I think I must have felt something of the same as Bradman walked back into the pavilion that day at Lord's. I know I had nothing to do with it; I just felt that I had.

Another impression which has stayed with me was my first Lord's scorecard. How I wish I had kept it. I took it back to school at Sunningdale full of its and my own importance and I suppose that soon it disintegrated. There was too the exciting bagginess of the dark green Australian caps; the red ping-pong bat rubber on the palms of Godfrey Evans's wicket-keeping gloves was too good to be true; and then there was the feeling of awe and wonderment when my father told my mother that he was going to watch for a time from inside the pavilion. If Lord's was a temple, the Long Room was the sanctuary.

He brought that captivating red MCC membership card out of his pocket. It is something I still acknowledge with deference when it falls out of the brown envelope each April. It contains a magic all of its own. No other membership card confers upon you the same vice-regal status. I sat transfixed a minute or two later when my father came into view again, this time climbing the few steps that take one into the pavilion past the committee room window. I saw him wave his pass to a steward, and then he disappeared from sight. I had to be content with the small part of my Rover ticket which the stewards had allowed me to keep. In its original state it came in three parts held together by perforations, and on each part in red was a huge 4 which showed that it was for the fourth day. What a day it was, and when I returned that evening to Mr Fox's private school at Sunningdale I was pretty sure that I knew the meaning of life.

Lord's and I had made a good start, and our relationship has gone from strength to strength. I was lucky enough to play there half a dozen times and so I have a collection of both public and private memories; private from the games in which I played, public from the great deeds I have seen performed in the middle.

After that initial foray to London, NW8 in 1948, my long-suffering parents took strawberries and me to one day of the Lord's Test each year until 1957, when I spent the match unconscious in a hospital bed. Strangely, I cannot remember any of the later visits half as well as the first, although I can even now see Keith Miller, who took ten wickets in the match, having Peter May caught behind by Gil Langley playing back in England's second innings in 1956 in a match Australia won easily.

By then, believe it or not, I had already had the luck to play at Lord's. The preceeding year, when I was fifteen, I had somehow got into the Eton XI as the wicket-keeper and nothing in life since has in any way competed with the lofty feeling I had when I knew for about a month beforehand that I was going to play against Harrow for two days over the second weekend in July. I still have the letter inviting me to play, written by our captain, Clem Gibson, whose father had helped bowl out the Australians for Archie MacLaren's XI at Eastbourne in 1921. It was not the sort of invitation you refused.

Eton won the match by 38 runs and my principal recollection comes from my own appalling performance in our second innings. We had a reasonable first innings lead and on the second morning we were going for quick runs before making a declaration. Suddenly wickets began to fall and there was a mad scramble by the lower middle order to get our pads on. We were using the Middlesex and England dressing-room. Sitting on those leather sofas and thinking of the illustrious bums that had sat there down the years was quite something and made one feel even more nervous. Actually, the best part about the Lord's dressing-rooms is the smell, an assemblage of the rubber floor, linseed oil, Elliman's liniment, good old-fashioned sweat, musty cricket bags and moth balls. I can smell it as I write.

The comings and goings of our batsmen were frenetic. I was batting at number eight, and suddenly there was a yell from the balcony – it was magic sitting on the balcony – 'You're in.' I was just about ready and snatched my bat and gloves and set forth through the dressing-room door, meeting a slightly bemused Angus Wolfe-Murray who was making the same journey but in the opposite direction. I took guard at the nursery end and prepared to face Rex Neame, Harrow's captain who had been in their side for so long we suspected he was getting on for twenty-one. He purveyed a particularly crafty form of off-break. I had been urged by Clem to get a move on, and when Rex's arm came over I swung my bat in hope and the general direction of the old Tavern, and heard the ball hit my off stump. Whereupon I was engulfed in a crescendo of applause from the crowd and in delighted shouts from the fielding side. I walked back thinking harsh thoughts about Harrovian behaviour and feeling about six inches tall. It was a long walk. The attendant opened the pavilion gate for me and gave me a look which suggested that I might have been a rather low form of pond life. I didn't feel much taller when I reached the dressing-room where everyone looked at me before looking away and saying nothing although I am sure Clem Gibson would have said 'Bad luck' or something. I sat down and took off my pads and things, put on my blazer and left as quickly as I could. It was with great embarrassment that I joined my family in Q Stand. As I arrived, feeling that the gloss I had been given by my new Eton blazer, white with light blue bands round the edges, was now somewhat tarnished, my father looked up and said, 'You were a bloody fool to let him get a hat-trick.' And that was the first time I knew it had been a hat-trick. Rex Neame, now a considerable hotelier in the north of Scotland, has remained a great friend and has spent the last thirty-five years paying me back for my absent-mindedness. As I caught him in both innings, I suppose it was fair dos.

After that, Lord's grew progressively kinder. In 1956 I managed to slog a hundred there for the Public Schools against the Combined Services and three years later I nervously edged my way to my one and only first-class hundred, for Cambridge against MCC, who included Denis Compton. In the University match which followed I was less successful, scoring 2 and 1. In the meantime, I had been defeated yet again by the examiners and it was sadly my only University match.

Whenever I am asked to name my favourite Test ground I have to prefix my answer by saying, 'Lord's apart'. It is incomparable for so many reasons. It is the home of cricket. Wherever the game is played in the world, there is a thread linking it ultimately to Lord's. Marylebone Cricket Club are still the official lawmakers of the game and although the present site is the third ground opened by the

Yorkshireman, Thomas Lord, and cricket had begun long before he appeared on the scene, the ground gives off a strong feeling of being the birthplace of the game. The Grace Gates are themselves hugely evocative, and where else but at the centre of the cricketing universe would the greatest and most famous player of them all be celebrated? There is the cathedral atmosphere given off by the heavy Victorian architecture of the pavilion; the Long Room, where even to clear one's throat is a monstrous invasion of privacy, still has an almost sepulchral solemnity and stillness about it.

The names of the stands have a saintly ring to them, too. The Mound Stand, now the New Mound Stand with its delightful pagoda-like roof, the Grandstand with its solid balcony, its scoreboard and, on top of everything, Father Time wielding his scythe just over the heads of the scorers in their lofty perch, threatening them with violence should the books not add up at the end of the day. The Warner Stand was built in 1958 in honour of Sir Pelham Warner who was for years an unbending personification of Lord's Cricket Ground. It links the Grandstand with a pavilion which has for ever been an elderly Victorian matron constantly pulling down her skirts to make sure that not even the glimpse of an ankle can be seen. The committee room at the end of the pavilion nearest to the Tavern has something of the atmosphere of the Cabinet room at Number 10, Downing Street with a touch of Washington's Oval office thrown in. There is nothing in the least frivolous about any of it.

Q Stand, the scene of my early memories of Lord's, comes next although it has now been renamed in honour of Gubby Allen who for a long time was even more a part of Lord's than Father Time. His was always the face you saw if you had the audacity to look in through the open committee room window. He presided over the scene like a despot who was mostly benevolent but occasionally tetchy. Much of the Allen Stand has been glassed in giving it an unfortunate goldfish appearance and this is where the Test and County Cricket Board entertain their official guests at the big matches. For me, it will remain as Q Stand. The old Tavern has long since gone, making way for the Tavern Stand with its single row of hospitality boxes which would have been two rows if it had not been for the extraordinary parsimony of the MCC membership in the late fifties which forbade their committee to be so extravagant as to build two rows. That decision has cost Lord's and cricket an enormous sum of money over the years. Alas, contemporary behaviour has caused the disappearance of the open area in front of the long bar at the bottom of the Tavern Stand where it was possible to drink a pint, watch the cricket, shout a comment or two and indulge in lively conversation with your neighbour. The comments became too embroidered for comfort and the intake of pints too great, and so a permanent open stand has been built there. This has been the only one of the recent changes which has altered the character of the ground. All of this is quite simply Lord's Cricket Ground and for me there is no place on earth quite like it.

In this setting it is only natural that great deeds or, for that matter, misdeeds should assume even greater importance. It is one thing to score a hundred in a Test match; it is quite another to score a hundred in a Test match at Lord's. The phrase, 'He did it at Lord's', is either a cricketing absolution or else ample justification for a brisk journey to the game's condemned cell. And of course one of the great pleasures of spending half a lifetime watching cricket is to make sure that distance does lend enchantment. Memories would not be half such fun or so precious if they remained in the precise and unemotional persepctive in which most of them were seen in the first place.

I will take to the grave and I hope beyond the memory, still splendidly acute, of Ted Dexter's innings of 70 in England's first innings against the West Indies at Lord's in 1963. It was an innings of brilliant inspiration which combined technical perfection with guts of a high order. No cricket ball can ever have been bowled more fiercely or hit harder than it was that day, and to make it even more perfect, it was played by a *Boys' Own* hero. The only other person truly qualified to play that innings was P. G. Wodehouse's schoolboy hero, Mike Jackson, one of several brothers who turned out for Middlesex when they could and invariably hit hundreds when they did. The only other innings I have seen which can truly stand comparison with Dexter's that day at Lord's was the 110 made by Tony Greig against Lillee and Thomson at Brisbane in 1974–75.

Dexter was one of those magnificent athletes who commanded attention the moment he took his first step onto the grass. He was upright and handsome in the most patrician manner. His walk to the crease was always on the fast side of brisk, as if he could hardly prevent himself from running to the middle so keen was he to get at the bowling. Some batsmen make a meal of taking guard and then flutter up and down the pitch tapping here and tapping there. Not with Dexter. There were a few quick bangs of the bat to make his mark in the crease, a brief but thorough look around the field, and then he would settle into that easy, classical, upright stance and his look up the pitch to the bowler said in ringing tones, 'Let battle be joined'.

On this occasion, he came in during the second over after John Edrich had been caught behind first ball off Charlie Griffith. The atmosphere was electric. The two fastest bowlers in the world – Wes Hall had bowled the first over – were closing in for the kill, and although it was not quite David coming out to confront Goliath, it was Dexter, a cricketing James Bond if ever there was one, striding out, the personification of the amateur, to take on unequal odds. No wonder the full house crowd shifted nervously and onto the edge of its collective seat, at least that part of it which was not making its own calypso music and dancing the Jump-Up underneath the Grandstand.

The sight of Dexter's confident, businesslike swagger as he approached the wicket must have made even Hall and Griffith think for a moment. They had heard of Dexter all right, for he had played in all five Tests in the Caribbean in 1959–60 with some success. Now, when they pitched short Dexter moved behind the line and dropped the ball dead at his feet, and even those defensive strokes had about them an air of rare disdain. When they bowled to a good length or beyond Dexter unwound a series of glorious and unforgettable cover-drives. The ball sped through the off-side as if it had been fired out of a cannon. The fielders could only stand and watch and trot back to retrieve. I was sitting on the top tier of the Warner Stand immediately below the press box and I can well remember the split-second pause after the crack of bat against ball before the crowd erupted. Maybe no one could quite believe what they were seeing and had to have a second look and catch their breath before saluting Dexter. Those drives were not so much disdainful as contemptuous. A couple of hooks dispatched the ball to the boundary in front of square. There was a lot of horsepower in those strokes too. Dismissive in the extreme, they seemed to tell Hall and Griffith how futile their efforts were. Statistics could never on their own tell the story of Dexter that day although they would certainly make you think. He reached 50 in 48 balls and, in all, his 70 came in 81 minutes off 73 balls and he hit ten 4s. Hall and Griffith had never suffered such a dramatic counterattack.

Probably the only man in the middle who was appreciative and yet unmoved was Frank Worrell, whose calmness in moments of crisis had helped take the West Indies to their greatness. After a time he threw the ball to Gary Sobers, who came in from the pavilion end in that flowing, long-striding, elegant way of his. It was the run-up of a predator, fast but soundless and deadly. He burst into that lovely fluent action, left-arm over the wicket, and there was Dexter back on his stumps and lbw. I groaned at his dismissal. He walked off no less briskly than he had arrived. The ground stood to him, but he did not linger, seeming to take the pavilion steps two at a time before disappearing into the Long Room leaving us all to wonder if we could believe what we had seen. It is impossible to reproduce the magnificent challenge of Dexter versus Hall and Griffiths. One can only remind oneself of the atmosphere rather than conjure it up again. And I hope distance has lent just a little bit of enchantment. It would have been a unique innings wherever it was played, but because it was at Lord's the effect may have been heightened just perceptibly. But how lucky I am to have it as a memory.

There can never have been a better Test match at Lord's. Fred Trueman, who took eleven wickets in the match and can seldom have bowled better, Rohan Kanhai, Basil Butcher, Ken Barrington, Brian Close, 38-year-old Derek Shackleton, and Colin Cowdrey were other members of the cast. Cowdrey's arm was broken by Hall when he had made 19 in England's first innings and he came in later with it in plaster. When Hall began the last over England needed eight runs to win, the West Indies two wickets, and all four results were possible. Two runs were scampered, Shackleton was run out off the fourth ball, and now Cowdrey emerged. He stood dutifully at the non-striker's end while David Allen safely negotiated the last two balls of the match. Twenty-eight years on, it still leaves me limp with excitement.

Another brilliant individual performance, memorable for an entirely different reason, happened three years earlier. I was lucky enough to be present for some of it. Brian Statham took eleven wickets in the match and was the principal reason for England beating South Africa by an innings. I had taken my fiancée along on the third day as part of the process of breaking her by slow degrees into the gentle art of watching cricket. We had settled into our seats in the Grandstand balcony to watch the beginning of the South African first innings, and with high excitement we, or rather I, watched as Statham bowled Trevor Goddard. Jackie McGlew and Sid O'Linn were in all sorts of trouble and for a chauvinistic Englishman it was clearly going to be a great day.

My wife-to-be was less exhilarated. To relieve the general monotony she had a look at her engagement ring and was mortified to find that one of the small stones was missing. Panic rapidly developed and we had to leave immediately and make the journey to the shop in South Moulton Street where the wretched thing had come from. By the time the stone had been replaced and blame had been apportioned and we were back in the Grandstand, South Africa were seven wickets down and only just past 100. Statham had taken five of them, which made it one of the greatest pieces of fast seam bowling which I did not see. Statham was a wonderful athlete with not a single ounce of spare flesh and he reminded me of a sleek greyhound when he ran into bowl in that loose-limbed way before launching the ball at the batsmen so fluently, almost as if it were off the wrong foot. He will always be remembered as the lesser half of that great fast bowling partnership of Trueman and Statham, although as so often happens it is the conceived lesser partner who is responsible for so many of the other's wickets.

This second Test against South Africa was also memorable for a much less happy reason. The game finished in four days and on the Monday afternoon when it was over, the sides agreed to play an exhibition match to entertain the considerable crowd although these are never the most satisfactory of events. On the second day of the Test Geoff Griffin, one of the South African fast bowlers, who had been called eleven times for chucking by umpire Frank Lee, had taken a hat-trick when he had dismissed Mike Smith with the last ball of one over and Peter Walker and Fred Trueman with the first two of his next. In the exhibition match he bowled from the pavilion end. The other umpire, Sid Buller, was at square-leg and in his first over called him consistently for throwing. Griffin was forced to finish the over bowling underarm but because he did not notify the batsman that it was his intention to change style, he was called for his first underarm ball too. The whole situation was as acutely embarrassing for the players as it was for the spectators (I was playing truant from an office in the City). Buller has to be admired though, for he was a brave man who would never shirk what he saw as his duty and he had made up his mind that Griffin did not have a fair action and as far as he was concerned justice was being done. When, a few years later, I became a friend of Buller and occasionally met him with his golden labrador when I played cricket on the lovely college ground at Malvern, he never gave one the slightest impression of being the umpiring equivalent of Judge Jeffries.

The next time I saw Griffin was nine years later at Kingsmead in Durban where South Africa were playing Australia, and he was officiating behind a temporary bar which the sign hanging above it proclaimed to be 'The Bent Arm Inn', which showed that at least he never lost his sense of humour. He always said that the cause of all the trouble was a childhood accident which broke his arm in three places and gave it the apparent kink. It is ironic that some of those bowlers to be effectively hounded out of the game because it was thought that they chucked were characters who would never deliberately have cheated. I think especially of Australia's Ian Meckiff, a delightful man who to this day is sure he was legal.

I had one other visit to Lord's as an 'amateur' which will always stay with me, and that was in 1965 for the last Test match South Africa played there before their isolation. It was the first occasion I realized that brilliant fielding was worth the gate money every bit as much as individual batting and bowling performances. This was the year of Colin Bland who was a fielding perfectionist – a man who spent hours of his life doing nothing else except throw a cricket ball at a single stump from all possible angles, and who by this stage was hitting it more often than not. Bland gave a remarkable exhibition of his skill at Canterbury, repeatedly hitting a single stump in the outfield before the start of one day's play against Kent. Now, in the second Test he was to go one better and throw out Ken Barrington and Jim Parks when one had 91 and the other 32, which almost led to South Africa winning the match. Barrington surrendered his wicket more dearly than anyone I can think of, and on this occasion he played a ball to mid-wicket, called at once and set off for the other end. Bland was at wide mid-on, and running square he swooped on the ball, picked it up and all in one movement managed to hit the stumps at the bowler's end with Barrington easily short of his crease. It was little short of miraculous. In the mid-sixties players were still not given to violent and demonstrative outbreaks of emotion when wickets fell, but even by the standards of the day Bland's reactions to what he had just achieved were modest in the extreme. His execution of Parks was similarly carried out. Bland's fitness was a watchword as was his complete obsession with the game of cricket, and he was another whom one could watch with immense enjoyment even when nothing was happening because he moved and prowled in such a marvellously prehensile and predatory way. He was fairly tall, dark haired and slim and I wonder if there has ever been a better fielder. How sad it was that he fell in early middle age, a victim of cancer.

The first Test I watched professionally at Lord's was the one against Australia in 1975 when they stayed on after cricket's first World Cup. They had narrowly lost the Final of that competition to the West Indies after Dennis Lillee and Jeff Thomson's unlikely stand late in the evening in what may prove to be the best World Cup Final we will ever see. The first Test had been played at Edgbaston where Mike Denness got into a tangle with the weather forecast and enabled Australia to win by an innings. He paid the supreme penalty, and Tony Greig led England out for the first time at Lord's. This match was, in the end, a draw but there were some lovely self-contained moments in it.

It was the first Test match for David Steele, who was immortalized in the somewhat unlikely columns of *The Sun* by Clive Taylor, such a brilliant writer who was to live for only two more years. Steele, striding out to bat when England were 10–1, could hardly have been a more unlikely figure, with his glasses perched tantalizingly just above the bridge of his nose and below a most impressive head of prematurely grey hair the like of which countless women have been unable to achieve even with the help of the dreaded blue rinse. He looked studious, mildly scholastic, eccentric, and bulged with thigh pads and folded towels against the rampant Lillee. Clive got him to a T when he wrote the following morning that he had emerged from the pavilion looking like 'a bank clerk going to war'.

Steele dug himself in deep and defended with a heart-lifting courage and resilience. He kept prodding forward onto that front foot and swaying and ducking out of the way of the doodlebugs which hummed past his ears. Every now and then a deflection or a pushed drive brought him runs and he had a quite splendid fifty against his name when Jeff Thomson eventually got one past him. This had been an innings which had not only done wonders for the heartbeat of English cricket, it had also captured the minds and hearts of the nation in the same way as when an army private wins the Victoria Cross. People everywhere were able to identify with Steele and feel that if an ordinary bloke like him could do it, so maybe could I or even Bill up the road. Steele's success that summer seemed to bring the mysteries of Test cricket closer to the grass roots and the village green.

Before it all happened, however, he went through a most puzzling moment which could so easily have disturbed a less phlegmatic character. When England's first wicket fell he left the dressing-room and walked down the stairs to the Long Room level, but instead of pushing through the glass door into that hushed sanctuary he continued on down the stairs, went through another door, and found himself in the huge basement loo. He came out, had a worried look around, pushed at one or two more doors which held fast; it was an appreciable time before he realized what had happened and beetled back up the stairs. So the bank clerk nearly got lost on his way to war. He was an admirable hero, and of course the headline writers loved his name.

One of my favourite Australian cricketers, Ross Edwards, who was a cover fieldsman only marginally short of Bland's class, had the mortifying luck to be lbw to occasional bowler Bob Woolmer (his 4 wickets in 19 Tests cost him 74 runs each) when one run short of his 100. To his dying day, he will dream about it and maybe think that it was missing, although he told me he was happy with the decision.

Greig's leadership was more demonstrative than his predecessor's and in him England now had a captain who would lead by inspiration. The match will probably be longest remembered, however, for the appearance of Test cricket's first streaker. A strapping young merchant seaman from Marylebone appeared in all his nakedness from underneath the Grandstand and set off at a canter for the stumps at the nursery end where umpire Tom Spencer was presiding. I have to say that there was a certain novelty and therefore entertainment value in the performance of the first of what became an excessively tedious species. The young mariner jumped the stumps and Spencer peered at him through his specs in the manner of a man who knew he should do something but couldn't for the life of him think what. John Arlott was prompted to say that all was well for Spencer hadn't signalled 'one short'. Progress was interrupted near the Mound Stand by a policeman who hurriedly and in the interests of decorum put his helmet over the assembled nakedness. His colleagues then arrived and took the young man away for a night in the cells and a visit to the magistrates court in the morning. By the most happy of coincidencies Arlott was in full and inimitable flow at the time and his description was peerless and immortalized the occasion.

This was my first Test match in the BBC radio commentary box high in the pavilion at Lord's and in the course of it I learned one most important lesson – the hard way, of course. Fred Trueman and Trevor

Bailey were the two expert summarizers and I was quickly to learn the folly of attempting to put words into their mouths, in fact of trying to pretend to know as much about cricket as two men who had between them played in more than 120 Tests. On the last afternoon a draw was inevitable and I was on the air for the penultimate twenty minutes. Peter Lever, of the interminable run-up, was bowling to Greg Chappell who suddenly launched himself into the most perfect cover-drive. I wondered aloud if anyone could ever have played that stroke better and went on to suggest that in the ultimate coaching book, which was presumably to be found in heaven, there would be more photographs of Greg Chappell playing that particular stroke than anyone else. I then added, 'At the end of the over we will see what Trevor Bailey thinks.' Trevor started off by saying, 'Of course, the stroke Greg Chappell is best known for is the *on*-drive.'

In the late seventies Ian Botham made Lord's very much his own and I have many memories of him. He began his Test career against Australia at Trent Bridge in 1977 and in two Test matches in that series had twice taken five wickets in an innings. By the time Pakistan came to Lord's in 1978, which was Botham's first Test on the ground, he had scored centuries against New Zealand and in the first Test against Pakistan, and now he was to turn in one of his more remarkable all-round performances. He hit 108 in England's first innings score of 364 and had reached three figures from only 104 balls. It was an extraordinary display of controlled hitting. Then, after going wicket-less in Pakistan's first innings, he took 8–34 with his out-swingers in the second and in his last spell had 6–8 in 53 balls.

Statistics can be misleading, but not these. I shall talk about Botham, the batsman, in some detail in the chapter dealing with Headingley and the 149 not out in 1981. Botham the bowler was always a nasty proposition when he came running in from the Nursery end using the natural slope of the ground to help him move the ball away from the right-hander. When his figure lost some of its youthful fineness and he had to open himself up more at the point of delivery and the out-swinger disappeared, he was not the same bowler. As a young man starting out in Test cricket in the late seventies, there was something wonderfully infectious about his uninhibited boisterousness. He ran in to bowl with his mane of hair flopping all over the place and it was as if there was a large if slightly unrhythmical spring under each leg. One was rather reminded of a runaway lorry on a down slope. It was joyful, it was brimming with life and gusto and there was something marvellously and heroically uncontrolled about it. He was a primeval force as that final leap took him into his delivery stride.

He always bowled as if he was certain he could sweep away all remaining opposition. It was engaging that he should have seemed just as certain if his current figures were 0–120 as he did when they were 6–19. He never lacked spirit. He would take a wicket and was then almost impatient in his anxiety to snatch the ball back and make life undiluted hell for the next batsman. Sometimes it misfired and he was expensive, and then there was the slightly mystified expression of a labrador puppy who does not know his own strength as he vigorously wags his tail knocking a series of ornaments to the floor all round him. The ball would be hit for 4 and he patently could not understand it. Then came the quick walk back, the irritated gesture with one hand as he caught the ball, the militant run-up, the 'I'll get you this time' manner – and in those far off days he often did. Against Pakistan in 1978 he was irresistible. The out-swinger constantly found the edge of tentative Pakistani bats and Bob Taylor, Graham Roope and Graham Gooch hung on to the edges. It was all inevitable from the moment he was first given the ball in the second innings after the opening bowlers, Bob Willis and Chris Old, had not made much impression.

Botham's was a rhythm which did not easily evaporate and in the second Test match at Lord's that year, against New Zealand, he took six wickets in the first innings and five in the second. The wicket-keeper and the slips were kept constantly on their toes and again the batsmen could make little of him. This was only Botham's second season in Test cricket and yet he was already a veteran. The following year when he had Sunil Gavaskar caught at first slip by Mike Brearley in India's second innings he had taken his hundredth Test wicket – just two years and nine days after first playing for England. He had reached this landmark quicker than anyone else, and yet during the following winter Kapil Dev got there in one year and five days, which apart from indicating an extraordinary talent showed how thick and fast Test matches were coming along.

These were Botham's salad days and I wonder if there has ever been a more irrepressible cricketer than he was then. The sheer improbability of much that he did seemed to cock a snook at the well-balanced and manicured traditions of the game. There was a spectacular iconoclasm about Botham the cricketer, just as there was growing to be about Botham the man. He was a compulsive, enigmatic, warts-

and-all character, and small wonder that the British public took to him in a way they have not with a cricketer since Denis Compton scored all those runs immediately and so gloriously after the Second World War and glistened down from the advertising hoardings on behalf of Brylcreem.

The West Indies always proved to be a major sticking point for Botham, first as a player and then as a captain. He had effectively been nominated by Mike Brearley as his successor early in 1980 and had immediately to face the grizzly prospect of successive series against them, both of which were lost. He also lost the first Test to Australia at Trent Bridge in 1981, and so when England came to Lord's for the second no one was under greater pressure; he had shown himself to be something less than a genius as a captain and the responsibility of the job had been affecting his own form. As history knows, he succumbed, lbw on the back foot to Geoff Lawson in the first innings and, in the second, when all was falling down around him, he swept wildly at Ray Bright in an attempt to reach the Oval fourth bounce and was bowled round his legs. He had not scored in either innings. When the match was over – it ended in a draw – Botham anticipated the heavy knock of the chairman of selectors' knuckles on the dressing-room door and fell on his own sword minutes before it came.

This was drama of the highest sort and it was made so by the fact that no one was indifferent to Botham. To many he was the bust-a-gut good guy who had given pleasure and something to hope for to all those who were far worse off. He had infected a great many people with the same feelings as David Steele a few years earlier. They thought that he should remain captain for as long as he wanted, for he could do no wrong. Those at the other extreme were equally obsessional. There were those who kept their fingers crossed that every time he went to the wicket he would make 0, that when he bowled he would take none for plenty and that when he captained the side England would lose. The press box was garrisoned by troops from both camps as was every street and hamlet in the country. News of his resignation was greeted, therefore, as much with joy as with heartache. The man's own reaction was fascinating and was not for public consumption until the next Test match at Headingley, but geographically speaking we are moving ahead of ourselves.

There was an unforgettable Lord's command performance from Gordon Greenidge in 1984. Because he has played so much of his cricket in the shadow of Viv Richards, Greenidge has probably not been fully appreciated as the great opening batsman he undoubtedly has been. In this Test, David Gower's declaration had left the West Indies to score 342 to win in 78 overs on the last day on a worn pitch. By rights it should have been beyond even them. But Greenidge produced as memorable an exhibition of strokeplay as any that the ground has seen. He is not a large man but he is obviously strong and hits the ball as hard as anyone, combining power with a lovely sense of timing. There is a sharply etched decisiveness about his strokeplay. He is a batsman who never seems to be in two minds and on this last day he came up on England's bowlers like a pocket battleship against the wind.

One pulverizing square-cut followed another down to the Tavern boundary – no one can ever have played this stroke much better than Greenidge – and they were interspersed between a good number of cover-drives hit with clinical precision, and some most decisive hooks. At other times he helped himself off his legs as the West Indians love to do. It was breathtaking to watch, so much so that the result of the match suddenly did not matter. One knew one was watching a quite remarkable exhibition of artistry and however humiliated England's bowlers may have felt, it was a joy to see the cricket ball struck in this way. At 54, England had the consolation of running out Desmond Haynes who was later to make his own very considerable mark at Lord's as a Middlesex player. Haynes's departure now was to let in Larry Gomes, demure, fragile and almost inconsequential in appearance, but an obstinate and rugged left-hander with a formidable record who had himself played for Middlesex. On this occasion, he kept going unobtrusively at the other end to the tune of 92 not out, helping Greenidge in an unbroken stand of 287 in 236 minutes which took the West Indies to victory by nine wickets with more than eleven overs to spare. Botham was the main sufferer among the bowlers in the second innings and I'm not sure that his captain found it easy to prise the ball away from him. In the first innings he had had a rare moment of success against the West Indies taking eight wickets, and he probably felt that he could do it a second time. Greenidge's 214 not out was the first double century by a West Indian at Lord's.

We were back late in August that year for Sri Lanka's first Test match in England. After being put in to bat, a trifle patronizingly, the Sri Lankans made their highest score in Test cricket of 491–7 declared. Sidath Wettimuny showed in an innings of 190 over 636 minutes that his concentration was in good working order while his captain,

Duleep Mendis, scored a century in the first innings and failed by six runs to make another in the second. It was an impressive first appearance at Lord's although it was no help to them that a number of their senior players who had brought them into Test cricket were close to retirement. Although the Sri Lankans gained a first innings lead of 121, the match eventually ran out of time, but before this happened Allan Lamb had made his fourth Test hundred of the summer in another typically enjoyable and pugnacious innings. His first three were against the West Indies, a considerable achievement for a batsman who was always on the losing side. They don't come much tougher than Allan Lamb.

In 1985, Allan Border was the batsman to take Lord's over when he made 196 runs which played a big part in taking Australia to its only victory in that series. It was an innings which was typical both of the man and his style of batting. He first had to give the innings a base after the loss of two early wickets, and having done this he allowed himself to play with progressively more freedom. There are no frills to Border and neither does he bat like a back-slapping extrovert. He is one of the few left-handers whose batting is seldom an object of beauty, although his off-driving and square-cutting both have their moments. He is content to nudge and push and dab and generally soldier on until disaster is less imminent. There are too, few better players of spin bowling and it is a joy to see him use his feet to drive slow bowlers. There are many excellent reasons for wanting to see the return of the spin bowler to his rightful place in the game, and one of them is to be able to watch nimble footwork like this from a good batsman.

One tends to remember the facts of his big innings rather than to think back to their component parts, but I recall one exception to this, a century he hit in a one-day international against Pakistan in Sydney. I shudder to think what would have happened to Australian cricket if he had not been on hand to take over when Kim Hughes tearfully resigned his commission in the middle of a series against the West Indies the previous November. If I have a complaint against Border it is that for some reason he resolutely refuses to bat at number three which is where the best batsman in the side should be. The result of his determination to stay at number four has been that he has too often found himself committed to rearguard actions, whereas if he had gone in at the fall of the first wicket he might have been better able to seize the initiative from the bowlers and have taken Australia to rather more match-winning positions instead of having endlessly to dig them out

17

of a pit. The century he now made at Lord's was one of the rare innings he has played which has enabled Australia to win a match.

I remember him coming back to the pavilion that day after he had been out four runs short of a double century. There was no flicker of emotion, just a polite acknowledgement of the applause and doubtless inward seething at having got out; missing 200 would have been a lesser worry. One would like to think too, that there would have been an inner satisfaction that he had done his usual job with his customary efficiency. Border is a hard man to get out, a difficult man to beat, probably not that easy to please, and he never distributes smiles with any recklessness.

Australia's other hero at Lord's in this match was another naturally modest and unassuming man, leg-spinner Bob Holland who had come into Test cricket the previous year at the age of 38 and now took 5–68 in England's second innings. He is a roller rather more than a spinner for he sacrifices spin for accuracy although he now exposed England's shortcomings against a form of attack which is seen all too rarely these days. When he led Australia back into the pavilion after the fall of the last England wicket, he did it with his sleeveless sweater thrown over his shoulder and a slight but evident sense of embarrassment which suggested he would have been just as happy to be in the bunch of players behind him. It made a refreshing change.

The 1987 Test against Pakistan was not a collector's item. Play was possible for only two days and England never finished their first innings and so never took the field. It was cold too. The following year was repetitive of other West Indian Tests in many ways. Gordon Greenidge scored another fine hundred but this time only one, and Allan Lamb made yet another for the losing side. For this match England were captained by John Emburey after Mike Gatting's sacking for unspecified adventures during the rest day of the first Test at Trent Bridge. While Emburey's captaincy, like his bowling, was a little defensive, the English authorities had the consolation of seeing the receipts exceed £1m for the first time.

The Australians were back in 1989 and as had become their regular habit on the ground they won easily. This was a Test match which confirmed a mould that had been quickly established in the first Test at Headingley. England's batsmen had found themselves tied into all sorts of technical knots by Terry Alderman who continued to swing the ball away from the right-hander and cut it back off the pitch with devastating effect. But the ball which seemed to do most of the damage was the one which went straight on, and batsman after batsman played at it round his front leg with disastrous results. With the success of Leeds behind him, Allan Border was becoming a more adventurous, more commanding captain who was beginning to try and make things happen rather than resigning himself to a purely defensive role. While Alderman was the principal Australian weapon, he was well supported by the other bowlers and once again the Australians were fielding and catching as Australian sides are traditionally meant to. At Lord's, Steve Waugh's second score of more than 150 in successive Test innings underlined Australia's superiority as much as it drew attention to the plainness of the England bowling.

I find Steve Waugh a difficult batsman to fathom. The way in which he batted in these first two matches – he had made 177 not out at Leeds – suggested that he was about to become the second best batsman in the world. Yet by the end of the following Australian season one felt that it was the memory of these two innings more than anything else which was keeping him in the side. He was then looking as insecure as at Leeds and Lord's he had looked commanding. I daresay part of Waugh's problem lies in his mental make-up. Unlike his twin brother, Mark, who is one of the most outgoing of men, Steve is an introvert. He seldom shows any emotion in the middle and even when he is scoring runs you do not get the impression that he is particularly enjoying himself. When he hits one of those square-cuts in a manner which Gordon Greenidge would envy, there is a clinical impersonality about the stroke. At Lord's on the Saturday, England, principally through Neil Foster, had bowled themselves back into the match and at one point Australia were 265–6, but the following day the bowling went to pieces in a way I have not often seen in a Test match. Waugh led the assault in splendid style, although it was made easy for him. He and Geoff Lawson put on 130 for the ninth wicket in 108 minutes and for England and English supporters it was acutely uncomfortable and embarrassing. Besides the square-cut, Waugh drove beautifully, played the ball away powerfully off his legs and hooked and pulled. It was well-executed carnage and Waugh was in such form that he could have got away with anything against bowlers and a captain, David Gower, who had lost all control. Before the end of the year in Australia, this same Waugh was batting as if beset by dark and lingering doubts which affected his judgement, his footwork and his timing. Form and therefore confidence is a strange and elusive will-o'-the-wisp. For all that, Waugh's early form with the bat in

England played a big part in establishing Australia's superiority in 1989.

It was a Test which may be remembered longest for two incidents which only indirectly concerned the cricket. At the press conference which is always held after close of play on the Saturday, Gower, who arrived in a state of mild truculence, was not happy with the line or the tone of the questioning pursued by two former Test cricketers in their mantle as scribes, Phil Edmonds and Mike Selvey. It concerned his captaincy that day when, with the last four Australian wickets adding 263 runs, he never once bowled Foster from the Nursery end where the slope might have helped his out-swinger. In the end Gower could bear it no more and stormed out of the conference saying that he had a taxi meeting him to take him to the theatre. As captain he had a duty to take the conference and indeed to answer the type of militant questions which England's performance in the field had made inevitable. He did himself no good at all by walking out and only made it worse when he announced that he was going to a show. It was not the most clearly thought-out reaction to criticism, and if he was running late for the theatre, he should have accepted it, handled the press as best he could and have been prepared to miss the first act altogether. He had got his priorities a little bit jumbled up.

This was an incident which gave bounteous ammunition to Gower's detractors – a growing body – and may, illogically perhaps, have contributed to his not being chosen for the winter's tour of the West Indies. The incident left a nasty taste, and anyone not prepared to look too kindly on Gower would make sure that he did not forget it. If you are England's captain it is important to keep your nose clean at all times, especially if you are on the losing end of things. Gower, to some extent, made amends on the Monday when he scored an obdurate hundred in England's second innings, but by then it was common knowledge that he had been ticked off by Ted Dexter, the chairman of the selectors, and he had also made a public apology for his behaviour.

The second incident could hardly have been more different: the arrival from the Nursery end of the ground's first female streaker. A tall, dark-haired, and most attractive girl with the figure of an egg-timer came galloping across the ground in leaps and bounds and no one, players or spectators, was particularly keen to turn his back on her. Her joyful, bounding run took her down to the pavilion end where she performed a remarkable and much publicized somersault before disappearing into the pavilion and giving an essentially sober-minded membership the fright of its collective life. History does not relate whether a steward refused to allow her entry, purely of course on the grounds of her being female and thereby barred.

The scorecard for the Lord's Test against New Zealand in June 1990 included the name of cricket's brand new knight, Sir Richard Hadlee. He is another cricketer who is not given over to fanciful flights of emotion although there can be little doubt that this momentous mention in dispatches will have given him a quiet inner glow. The match was drawn but not before Hadlee had given yet another demonstration of the art of fast-medium swing and seam bowling delivered from close to the stumps with one of the most perfect actions imaginable. Hadlee ran in as if on egg shells and he controlled the ball like a puppet master. Even at the age of 39 he was wonderfully fit and he was bowling just about as well as ever. Every ball taught any aspiring fast bowler all the lessons he needed to learn. Hadlee was no mean batsman either, one of the finest strikers of a cricket ball, and unlike most fierce hitters he much preferred fast bowling to slow. In New Zealand's first innings he came within 16 runs of scoring his first hundred at Lord's, which would have been an extraordinary finale for him. It was a lovely piece of batting which contained any amount of clean, crisp hitting and the hundred looked a certainty. But then his nerve broke. He was facing some tight off-spin bowling from his former Nottinghamshire colleague, Eddie Hemmings, and was unable to get the ball away. Suddenly, in desperation he played a half sweep, half slog across the line and was comprehensively bowled. He walked back to a wonderful reception.

Although the focus had been on Hadlee throughout the match, one of New Zealand's bit-part performers came close to stealing the show. Opener Trevor Franklyn, a beanpole of a man who was on his third tour of England, scored one of those hundreds memorable only for the bare statistical fact. It took a long time and spoke wonders for his concentration and for his ability to play within the limitations of his technique; there are many better players than Franklyn who have not come near a Test hundred at Lord's. It is one of the unending joys of cricket that the nobodys of the game are able suddenly to seize their chance and leave an imperishable mark. There was a romantic twist to this innings too, for when returning to New Zealand at the end of the 1986 tour he had been struck by a runaway baggage trolley at Gatwick Airport and had his leg broken in several places. It was thought at the time that he would never play cricket again.

Lord's has an unending capacity for producing high drama and there was more of it in 1990 in the first Test of three against India. It began when their captain, Mohammed Azharuddin, completely misjudged the pitch and sent England into bat. Graham Gooch, badly dropped behind the wicket by Kiran More off Sanjeev Sharma when he had made 36, went on to score 333 which was by some way the highest score ever made at Lord's although, ironically, it was not the most commanding innings one has seen him play. He followed it with a small matter of 123 in the second innings and his aggregate of 456 was the highest by a batsman in a Test match. It was a phenomenal achievement by a man who, against all odds, had taken complete charge of English cricket. He had resigned from the Essex captaincy when he originally succeeded Keith Fletcher because it was affecting his form and he had not made much of a job of it, and became England's captain because Chris Cowdrey had been hit a painful blow on the toe by Derbyshire's Ole Mortensen in a county match just before the fifth Test against the West Indies in 1988. David Gower replaced him for the series against Australia the next summer and then Gooch, almost by default, took England to India for the one-day competition in 1989–90 and to the West Indies in the New Year where the side did wonderfully well and Gooch returned home knowing the job was his for as long as he wanted it. He is not a tactical genius, but by the end of this Test against India he had become a commanding figure. I wonder if he allowed himself to think back fifteen years to his first Test match, against Australia at Edgbaston, when he made 0 in each innings.

In between Gooch's two innings, Azharuddin made a glorious hundred which even if it did not atone for his decision to field first illuminated Lord's in a way few batsmen have been able to do. It was an innings which was all supple wrists allied to a ballerina's footwork and a bat which combined the lightness of a feather with the timing of a genius. If Gooch's innings had been a main course of roast beef and Yorkshire pudding, Azharuddin's was the most exquisite and delectable of savouries; and there was even better to come.

When he was out, India's innings became fragile and with one wicket to fall they needed 24 runs to save the follow-on. Eddie Hemmings, the scourge of Richard Hadlee, was bowling from the nursery end to Kapil Dev, an extraordinary all-round cricketer whose powers were now sadly on the wane. Kapil is a big man for an Indian, and has always been one of those exciting extrovert cricketers who so obviously enjoys himself enormously out in the middle. The first two balls of Hemmings's over were uneventful. The next four were all thrown up on a length pitching around the off stump. To each of them, Kapil Dev took a step forward and with his high backlift brought his bat down in a lovely powerful arc, and each time the ball most comfortably cleared the boundary behind the bowler. Twenty-four runs were scored and the follow-on was saved. After hitting three 6s I doubt if any other batsman in the world would have done more than push the last ball of the over for the single which would have given him the strike for the next. Not Kapil, and this ball disappeared in the general direction of the buses in the Wellington Road even more emphatically than the first three. I wonder if any other single stroke in the entire history of the game has spoken such volumes about a man's character. It was magnificent, and the sense of drama was heightened when Narendra Hirwani, the last man, was out to the first ball of the next over.   Of all the great deeds I have seen in Test matches on this unique cricket ground, I am not sure that this one of Kapil Dev's is not the one I would most have liked to have done. Or would I have preferred to have batted like Dexter that day against the West Indies?

2

SYDNEY:
Fans, Writs and Floodlights

In atmosphere as well as actual presence the Sydney Cricket Ground is very much the Lord's of Australia, but it is a ground which, sadly but inevitably maybe, has been 'sanitized' by progress over the last decade and more. When I first visited the ground in 1968 it had a charming and unsullied late Victorian feeling, the lovely pavilion with its green corrugated iron roof holding court at one end and the huge scoreboard behind the Hill at the other. Only the Noble and Bradman Stands at the Paddington end were of contemporary bricks and mortar, the rest bordering on the ramshackle.

The most significant step in the modernization programme came before the start of the 1978–79 season. Like several major cricket grounds, including Lord's, the SCG has for long suffered from the problems of having a ground authority which is separate from the two cricketing controlling bodies which operate there. The Sydney Cricket Ground Trust administers the ground, and both the New South Wales Cricket Association and the Australian Cricket Board have to watch their step. When Kerry Packer's World Series Cricket first became a fact the Establishment in Australia closed ranks and refused permission for WSC to play at the established centres. The one exception was the Gabba at Brisbane where the Cricket Ground Trust decided to go along with WSC against the wishes of the Queensland Cricket Association who were powerless. For the first year in Sydney, WSC were told by the Trust that they could not play at the Sydney Cricket Ground and instead they took over and converted the neighbouring Royal Sydney Showground into a suitable venue for a Supertest and the one-day internationals. Between WSC's first and second season the Trust had a rethink and decided that they would relent and allow World Series Cricket to use the SCG.

The showpiece of World Series Cricket was undoubtedly day/night limited-over matches and to play these floodlighting had to be put in. Packer and the Trust agreed to share the cost and by the time Mike Brearley's England side arrived at the SCG early in the 1978–79 tour six enormous black mushroom stalks had arisen round the ground each with a huge bank of lights perched on top. From the aesthetic point of view, it was impossible for a lovely old traditional cricket ground to live easily with such outlandish modern excrescences. But, as often happens, the pain grows less as the years go by and before very long the new comes to be more or less happily accepted. Once the floodlights were in place, however, it was only a matter of time before the rest of the ground was rebuilt in order that it should live with them and indeed provide the spectators with the comfort and the facilities they would expect. The new cricket was designed to attract a new type of spectator more than the traditional lover of the game who, round the world, seems perversely to regard the discomfort which he has had to endure for years at the older grounds as an irresistible form of masochism. The new spectator felt he had a right to expect the conditions that prevail these days at major tennis and golf tournaments and other equally prestigious sporting occasions which, considering the amount of money he had to pay to get in, was reasonable enough.

The result has been that much of the original character of the SCG has been slowly stifled by a succession of huge and magnificent stands with their banks of brightly coloured plastic seats and rows of luxurious hospitality suites which is where so much of the money lies these days. Cricket may have been a late starter in the world of corporate hospitality but now it pays obeisance to it as devoutly as any sport. It raises the eternal question of whether it is right to sell huge numbers of tickets to businesses who bring along clients and prospective clients who may not care in the slightest for cricket and spend much of the day, glass in hand, with their backs to proceedings in the middle or indeed in hospitality tents where their only means of visual contact with the game is through television sets; all this at the expense of the paying customer who is wanting to devour every ball that is bowled with his sandwiches and thermos flask at his feet, but is unable to buy a ticket.

One looks out from the top of the Noble Stand at the Paddington end across to the Randwick end where, in the sky behind, a constant stream of jets glide into or climb out of Sydney's Mascot Airport, seemingly held on a thread by a puppet master for they appear to be almost stationary. A small sightscreen is attached to the fence at that end, and to the right of it stands the new Churchill Stand. The ground was until recently used for rugger and this stand has been named after one of Australia's most distinguished performers. Moving round towards the pavilion comes the New Brewongle Stand, a magnificent structure with its refreshment facilities, the four tiers of seating including a row of private boxes, which includes that belonging to Kerry Packer.

The Brewongle joins onto the end of the Ladies Stand and then the pavilion itself and they both stand there with their prim green roofs, reminders of a bygone age. They are preserved buildings and one hopes they will always continue to be forbidden territory to the demolition gangs. Inevitably, they are dwarfed by the concrete jungles which rise up on either side, but if they went, the SCG would become just another sports ground. They may not have the comfort of their modern brethren, but those who are allowed to occupy them would far rather support tradition with numb behinds at the end of the day and a long walk for their drinks than give in to plastic bucket seats and the rest.

The Noble and Bradman Stands are effectively the two ends of the same stand. The Paddington Hill with its small patch of grass came after the Bradman Stand but that has now gone, submerged by more plastic seats, and then on the square boundary opposite the Brewongle Stand comes another huge modern edifice originally called the Pat Hills Stand after some bureaucrat who was chairman of the Cricket Ground Trust at the time it was built. This has now, most happily, been renamed the Bill O'Reilly Stand and neither Australian nor New South Wales cricket has had a much more splendid monument than 'Tiger' Bill O'Reilly. This stand has replaced the romantically named Bob Stand, a long small covered stand which joined the Bradman Stand with the Hill and had been called the Bob Stand simply because in the old days it had cost a shilling to sit in it.

If the Sydney Cricket Ground has acquired worldwide fame, it is more than anything because of the Hill where thousands of spectators sat on the grassy slopes packed in like sardines and glorified the action in the middle with loud, pithy and amusing comments. The Sydney Hill was the natural home of the Australian barracker, but alas it is no more. The lifestyle of modern sporting crowds is more to blame than any conscious desire to desecrate the ground. The days when crowds could be expected to behave themselves in a reasonable manner have long since departed. Sitting on the Hill was once a marvellous and entertaining way of watching the cricket, but it became a rather rougher world and at day/night matches in particular the behaviour was often appalling. Of course, alcohol played a big part in this and however much the police and stewards inspected the bags the spectators brought in with them, bottles of this-and-that escaped detection. The police found the job of controlling crowds on the Hill an almost insuperable problem. They have a control room on the top floor of the Brewongle Stand and officers watch the crowd on the Hill through field glasses from the first ball to the last. If they spot a miscreant they talk by direct link to the plain clothes officers scattered around the Hill and in no time two will find their way through the crowd, sit down on either side of the offender and suggest that he leaves quietly. I shall never forget one dreadful occasion when a drunk climbed up some television camera scaffolding at the Randwick end. When a policewoman arrived to bring him down he swung two enormous punches at her, but she was impressively quick on her feet and by the time her male colleagues arrived to assist she had taught everyone a thing or two about self-defence.

The Churchill Stand has encroached onto one side of the Hill while on the other, in front of the old scoreboard, the Doug Walters Stand has been built in honour of one of the Hill's greatest heroes, and so the area of grass has been greatly diminished and it is correspondingly easier for the police to keep control. The old scoreboard, also a listed building, still stands where it was, behind the Doug Walters Stand; its top is just visible but it can never be used again and sits there sadly like a beached whale. Those in charge of a ground have been faced with an almost unplayable lie for they have to try and please the young and the old but, all in all, they have not made at all a bad job of the SCG. If McDonalds hamburgers and members' badges are never likely to make happy bedfellows, at the SCG they can peacefully coexist.

The first series I watched in Australia was in 1968–69 when Gary Sobers's ageing West Indian side played five Tests. It was not an especially exciting series for after the West Indies had won the match in Brisbane thanks to the spin bowling of Sobers and Lance Gibbs, they were ruthlessly destroyed by Bill Lawry's Australians. Another great pair of fast bowlers, Wes Hall and Charlie Griffith (according to one's views on the veracity of his action) were now past it and the other senior players, Rohan Kanhai, Basil Butcher, Seymour Nurse,

David Holford and at times Sobers himself, were unable to find the will to fight back when things began to go wrong. For so long these West Indians had swept all opposition along before them without even having to pause and consider. Now that it no longer worked in the same way they all found it a little strange.

In those days they played two Test Matches in a five-match series in either Sydney or Melbourne because Test cricket was not played in Perth until 1970–71. The West Indies now played two in Sydney and lost both by huge margins, but the thrill of my first visit to the SCG has never faded even if there were almost a monotony about the way in which Doug Walters, Bill Lawry and Ian Chappell scored runs in both matches. Appropriately, Walters was the principal executioner. In the first match, he made a brilliant hundred, in the second he became the first batsman to score a double century and a single century in the same Test. His performances sent the patrons of the Hill into paroxysms of delight I shall never forget. There was something almost magical about some of Walters's strokeplay. When he was in this sort of form he made batting look as easy as almost anyone at any time.

He had burst upon the scene against Mike Smith's England side of 1965–66 with a spectacular innings of 155 in his first Test match, at Brisbane. Walters is on the short side but very strong and he hit the ball murderously hard. He was at once labelled as the new Bradman which must be a bad start for anyone as it is an impossible title to live up to, but for a while Walters was seen as the personification of Australian cricket. He had a humble start to life in Paramatta, an outer suburb of Sydney, and throughout his career Australian crowds seemed to identify more with him than any of his contemporaries until Thomson and Lillee blasted the life out of the Poms in 1974–75. There was a strong feeling of the-local-boy-makes-good about Walters. He was very human and always approachable; apart from his batting he was a brilliant fielder and a more than useful change bowler; a formidable smoker, an incessant card player and one who, if he turned away a can of beer, did so with the utmost reluctance. It was one of the mysteries of his career that he never came to terms with English conditions, and on four tours of England he never made a hundred in a Test match, although he was three times out in the eighties, and he was caught in the gully almost as a pastime. In these two Tests against the West Indies I was lucky to catch him at his very best.

The second of these matches was interesting for it spoke volumes about the Australian attitude to cricket in general and Bill Lawry's in particular. The West Indies came into that match 2–1 down and although by then they were demoralized they had, mathematically speaking, a chance of drawing the series. The Australians were put in by Gary Sobers. Lawry made 151 to go with Walters's 242, and Australia's 619 was then the highest score ever made by a side which had been put into bat. Lawry and Walters added 336 for the fourth wicket and it is not often that one sees an attack so destroyed. When the West Indies' turn came, their main batsmen all made a start but then got themselves out, which had been the pattern throughout the series. Australia had a first innings lead of 340 and with plenty of time to spare, for in those days the final Test was played over six days if the series had not been decided. Many captains would have been tempted to make the West Indies follow-on but not Lawry, who realized that that way a miracle might just possibly occur and they could give Australia an awkward task on the last day. He decided to bat again and by the time Ian Redpath and Walters had made hundreds Lawry's declaration left the West Indies to score 747 in the final innings. Sobers and Nurse made attractive hundreds but whereas once they might have battled it out, neither of them went far past three figures and Australia won by 382 runs.

I next came to the SCG six years later when England were being blown apart by the combined fire power of Dennis Lillee and Jeff Thomson. They simply had no answer to their pace and also to the constant stream of bouncers. Fast bowlers, especially when they come in pairs, have always had a profound effect on Test matches, and the losing side who have no effective means of reply invariably complain about the excessive amount of short-pitched fast bowling.

It was ever thus and raises a number of eternal and largely unanswerable questions. At what point does short-pitched fast bowling become intimidatory? Should bouncers be outlawed? Is it not unfair to remove from the fast bowlers' armoury one of their most effective weapons? Should not batsmen equip themselves better to play this type of bowling? The umpires have the power to decide at what point constant short-pitched bowling becomes intimidatory and have the powers to step in, first to warn the bowlers concerned and then to remove them from the attack altogether. Why are these powers not used more often? Why is it that umpires seem afraid to take a firm step in this way? Is it that they are afraid they do not receive enough support from the administrators who, after all, appoint them in the first place and ultimately stand in judgement over them?

In the best of all possible worlds, fast bowlers would be allowed to use bouncers sparingly, and somehow batsmen would not be hit. But those who are squeamish about bouncers would do well to remember that one of the most exciting moments in cricket comes when a batsman hooks a furious bouncer off his eyebrows for 4. The period of this book also covers the introduction of the crash helmet and other pieces of protective equipment which have become standard issue for those involved in cricket's equivalent of trench warfare. Does armour plating on the modern scale legitimize the use or indeed overuse of bouncers? I doubt these questions will ever be satisfactorily answered and that sides who continue to be able to put a pair of genuine fast bowlers into the field, to say nothing of the three or four which have become standard West Indian equipment, will continue to sweep all before them to the constant wailing and bleating about too many bouncers from the batsmen and supporters of the losing side. Fast bowlers and bouncers are a fact of life and we had better accept the fact and get on with it.

Thomson and Lillee were a great combination for they complemented one another to perfection. Thomson, long-haired and slightly primeval in appearance, had the reputation of being a rough and ready character who had once been dispatched unceremoniously from a football field by an unforgiving referee and who appeared to be none too upset if the batsman's body rather than his bat got in the way of one his bouncers. He was an out-and-out fast bowler who relied on brute force. In those early days especially there was not too much control but he was frighteningly fast with a dramatically physical slinging action which can only have made life a misery for the fainthearted.

Lillee was entirely different. He was very much in the classical image. He had a lovely fluent run-up, a glorious flowing action with his left hand high in the air pointing at second slip at the moment of delivery. His control was superb, he swung the ball away from the right-hander and was fast even if he did not convey quite the same outward menace as Thomson. He was helped too, by his obvious hatred of batsmen and in particular English batsmen. His appeal was the most ferocious I have seen as he ended up halfway down the wicket looking back at the umpire from a semi-squatting position and yelling his head off with both index fingers raised to the heavens. When the umpire denied him what he considered to be his due, he received the news with disbelief and astonishment so evident that all but the most resolute of umpires must have felt just about as small as the batsman whose life had recently been in the balance.

These two were backed up by some pretty considerable support bowlers in Gary Gilmour, Max Walker, Jeff Hammond, Alan Hurst, Len Pascoe, who all at different times will have profited from the pressures which Lillee and Thomson exerted on the batsmen.

Thomson and Lillee would, in their form in 1974–75 have beaten any side on earth; they were irresistible, but England's fall was all the greater because they arrived in Australia expecting to win and had dismissed all talk of Thomson and Lillee as Australian propaganda. After all, Thomson had played a couple of Tests against Pakistan with no success and less control, while Lillee had broken down the year before against the West Indies in the Caribbean with stress fractures of the vertebrae which would surely have ended the careers of most fast bowlers. The Poms underestimated Lillee. He returned home and fought and fought to regain fitness and eventually did so in the most impressive style.

England were two down when they came to Sydney for the fourth Test and in the state of disarray which comes to touring sides when their captain loses all form (although in this case Mike Denness can hardly be said to have found it in the first place) and decides to drop himself from the side. As a result, England were led out by John Edrich and just behind him trod the 43-year-old Colin Cowdrey who had been flown out to Perth as a reinforcement after the loss of the first Test in Brisbane. Cowdrey, it had been felt, was, at his age, expendable while a younger batsman might have been left with ineradicable scars after battling with these two Australian fast bowlers. It was a brave decision bravely accepted, and it so nearly came off. Cowdrey had shown exactly how bowling of this pace should be played and revealed a peerless technique, despite his reflexes which were not quite what they once were. But there is no doubt that when England came to Sydney their spirits were down in the basement. It was the situation in which the match was played which made it a memorable occasion. The game itself followed an inevitable course although England came remarkably close to escaping with what would have been an impressive draw. Only 4.3 overs of the match remained when off-spinner Ashley Mallett disposed of Geoff Arnold and Australia had regained the Ashes. It was an oddity for this series that an important wicket should have been taken by a spin bowler and Mallett picked up four in the second innings. The SCG had not yet turned into the spinners' haven it was to become in the eighties.

I was back in Sydney the following year when the West Indies made scarcely a better fist of coping with Thomson and Lillee. Their new captain, Clive Lloyd, made typically phlegmatic, gum-chewing runs but Australia bowled too well and too fast while Viv Richards had not quite arrived. My strongest memory of that match concerns Jeff Thomson, but as a fielder rather than a bowler. The West Indies first innings was in trouble when Deryck Murray, always a most difficult man to get out, took guard. He faced Max Walker who pitched one a little shorter than usual and Murray quickly swivelled and pulled it away to deep mid-wicket where Thomson, running flat out to his left held one of the most remarkable catches in the deep I have ever seen. It looked as if he had no chance of reaching the ball but at the last moment he dived forward, held it an inch or two above the ground and managed to hold on as he rolled over. It was one of those rare catches which I can still see perfectly in my mind's eye.

When England came to Sydney for two Test matches in 1978-79, controversy was raging as never before in Australian cricket. Kerry Packer's World Series Cricket had begun in direct opposition to the game run by the Australian Cricket Board, and now, for the second year, it was competing alongside traditional cricket on a mix of makeshift venues. In the first year, 1977–78, the Australian public were probably slightly bemused by the struggle, and the Cricket Board had brought back a 42-year-old Bobby Simpson to captain the Establishment side against the Indian tourists. Simpson had then taken Australia to the West Indies but now, with Mike Brearley's England side in Australia, he had resigned and the ACB had appointed the Victorian Graham Yallop to lead Australia. It was a decision which did not help the immediate future of Australian cricket. John Inverarity who had been such a successful captain of Western Australia and who had played a handful of Test Matches should have been chosen as Australia's counter to Brearley. He had the shrewdest of cricket brains and was a skilful diplomat. If he had been in charge a year later when Kerry Packer and the ACB came together, I have little doubt that the transition would have been easier and would have been conducted with less bitterness.

When England began their tour in Adelaide, I was asked by the sports editor of *The Australian*, Mike Jenkinson, if I would write a daily column for what was the only national paper in the country and was owned, inevitably, by Rupert Murdoch. Later, I was asked by ABC Television who were covering the Ashes series while Channel Nine devoured World Series Cricket if I would have a chat in front of the cameras every tea time during the Test matches with Peter Meares. Each day we laughed our way through about five minutes and it was all rather fun and apparently a few other people thought so too.

Of course, the protagonists of each form of cricket were all the time looking for evidence to support their hopes that 'they' were winning. Gate figures were eagerly scrutinized and neither camp had anything but contempt for the other. The new innovations of WSC were labelled cheap gimmicks by the Establishment who were in their turn thought of as so many pompous, old-fashioned fuddy-duddies. Both camps were sure that their cricket was all that the Australian public wanted and that salvation lay just around the corner. As usually happens, the truth lay somewhere in between. The razzamatazz and hype which went with WSC was already attracting a new and younger audience and the tremendous publicity it received meant that only the most traditional of the game's supporters refused to turn their television sets over – if only momentarily – to Channel Nine to have a look. I would bet that almost all the most devout traditionalists did too, but they were not letting on. Of course, there was a nine-day-wonder aspect to WSC but they also had most of the best cricketers in the world at their disposal. Against this, the traditional Tests between England and Australia for the Ashes attracted fewer people than they would have done normally, but all the same the crowds were not bad. One extraordinary aspect of all that was going on was that the England supporters who had come to Australia to watch the Ashes series, and who were almost to a man supporters of the traditional game, were hoping that Graham Yallop's Australian side would beat England and therefore create an increasing interest in this series among the Australian public. I never thought I would see Englishmen shouting for Australia at the Sydney Cricket Ground.

When the teams arrived in Sydney for the fourth Test match, England were leading by two matches to one and the general hope as everyone walked into the SCG for the first morning was that Australia would somehow level the series. But before the match came anywhere near a conclusion, the assembled company had to suffer an unusual diversion. The first morning's play had been in progress for about an hour and I was sitting in the press box which is high up at the back of the Noble Stand at the Paddington end of the ground. Tom Prior who laboured unremittingly on behalf of the Melbourne *Sun* walked behind me and said. 'Blowers, have you seen what's on the pylon on the Hill?' There was a good crowd on the Hill, where one of the customs is for spectators to drape flags on which they have written messages over the boundary railings or on the wall at the back or anywhere else that is suitable. A sheet had been tied round a floodlight pylon and something was written across it in bold red letters. I looked through my binoculars and read, 'The bespectacled Henry Blofly Stand'. It took me a moment or two to realize that it referred to me.

My initial reaction was one of great embarrassment and of course my leg was pulled all day, but gradually it began to dawn on me that it was a tremendous compliment that the denizens of the Hill had actually bothered to write a message to me when people like Doug Walters and Thomson and Lillee were the usual well-deserving recipients. The next day *The Australian* carried a photograph of the sign and I suppose I arrived at the ground feeling something of a hero and rather hoping that it would still be there. To my relief it was, but when I looked more carefully I saw that it had been changed. It now read, 'Come on over Henry and have a pint'. That day I had been asked to lunch by the SCG Trust who live in a certain degree of luxury at the bottom of the Noble Stand. I was wearing my I Zingari tie, an impressive combination of orange, yellow and black stripes signifying out of light, through fire and into darkness: not a tie to accompany a hangover. I received a good deal of ribbing during lunch and there was no doubt that I had to go across and visit my newly won friends on the Hill. After lunch, and I cannot remember whether it was in the Trust or back in the press box, Jack Fingleton said to me when I told him I was going round to the Hill, 'Blofeld, I bet you won't dare wear that tie.' That was a challenge I could not ignore. The only concession I made was to undo my collar and loosen the tie. And then I set off, going down to the bottom of the Noble Stand, round the back of the Bradman Stand and then through the passage and along in front of the Bob Stand.

As I went it began to dawn on spectators who I was and my progress was accompanied by applause and yells of 'It's Henry Blofly.' Nothing much was happening out in the middle and even the players turned round to see what was causing the noise. When I reached the pathway which leads along the front of the Hill, bedlam was breaking loose and the guys and girls who had put up the signs on the pylon had seen me and were contributing their own welcome. I threaded my way over the grass between the spectators and when I arrived at the foot of the pylon I found myself in the middle of a notable drinking session and I was handed cans of beer from all directions. A lovely girl who can't have been more than sixteen told me that she wanted to marry me and then, to my horror, added that the chap she was really after was Geoff Boycott; which only goes to show that there is no accounting for taste. It was terrific fun and while I was there I was told that they were forming the Henry Blofly Club. Eventually I had to leave because work called and my walk back caused another embarrassing crescendo.

Of course the next day I found the event had been much photographed and, sure enough, there was yet another sheet on the pylon: 'Our Henry can even outdrink Keith Miller.' (At the time of going to press Keith has not sued for libel or defamation.) At the end of the match which England won, my friends, who were mostly students at Sydney University, streamed across the ground carrying the original banner and in front of the Noble Stand the sheet was presented to me. I still have it in my house in Norfolk although I doubt it will ever fly again. The Blofly Club went on for a year or two and we even got together for a party one evening at the Sebel Town House. The banners kept coming too, and the most amusing said, 'Our Henry is to cricket what Tony Greig is to limbo dancing'. I was not quite sure how to take that, and I don't think Tony was either.

Nowhere was the battle between WSC and the ABC joined more keenly than in the pressbox. Those who had set up World Series Cricket were particularly quick to look for an insult perceived or intended, and I daresay libel lawyers were scanning the papers daily. Nothing upset the WSC people more than when articles implied that although the standard of the Establishment series may not have been the equal of the standard of play which the Australian, the West Indian and the Rest of the World sides could produce in WSC colours, the battle for the Ashes was at least fair dinkum cricket played with a purpose, while the others were really only exhibition matches. I had written a column along these lines for *The Australian* and I don't think that my cause was helped by the headline writers.

At some stage of this fourth Test match I was having a glass of beer at the bar in the bottom of the Noble Stand. Alan McGilvray, the famous Australian commentator was there and so was Robin Marlar who was writing for the London *Sunday Times*, and I think the former Australian Test player, Ken Archer, was in the group, when a most attractive girl bearing a pen and a piece of paper bore down on us. She asked me if I was Henry Blofeld and while replying in the affirmative, I took a pen from my pocket, grasped her piece of paper and was about to sign my name – after all the publicity the Henry Blofly Stand had brought me, a few people had wanted my autograph. But this young lady tore the paper away from me, drew herself up to her full height and told me that she was serving me with a writ for libel and defamation which had been issued by World Series Cricket in view of the article I had written. Those standing around thought it was highly funny but this was the first writ with which I had ever been served and I was most uncomfortable about it. Proceedings were not taken any further and I daresay it was what appears to be known in the trade as a stop writ. I think this means that it would have been stupid if not fatal for me to have continued to comment along the same lines.

The match itself was not one of the most memorable I have watched. Popular demand was not satisfied and the Australians were beaten. One of the main reasons for this was an innings of 150 from Derek Randall who, at his best, was a brilliant player but who was too often seen at his most irritating worst. A batsman who had played as well as he had in Melbourne in 1977 when he made 174 in the Centenary Test should have been much more consistent. This 150 at Sydney was not such a good innings as at Melbourne but it was still a useful reminder of what a good batsman he could be. There were some marvellous strokes, an inordinate amount of frenetic movement at the crease which made him look a little like a circus clown who had just put the plug in the wrong hole and received the most enormous electric shock. He tugged at the peak of his cap, rolled his shoulders, played around with his shirt sleeves, set off up the pitch or away to square-leg after every ball with that exaggerated walk that Groucho Marx would have envied. Then there were the moments of downright clowning and in my experience there has been no one more naturally funny than Derek Randall. One of the drawbacks of watching cricket is to suffer players who are naturally quite stultifyingly unfunny trying to imitate, say, Randall. I shall always remember with great embarrassment, Bob Woolmer's efforts at putting on a funny walk to entertain a big Indian crowd at some distant venue. Mercifully, the Indians also forbore to laugh. When a playful Randall had frogmarched a policeman round the same boundary it brought the house down.

In England's second innings there was a bizarre moment which at least one of the bemused participants will have eventually put down as an act of God. This was the series which saw the appearance of another successful if moody Australian fast bowler, Rodney Hogg. In the first Test, which was also his own first, he had taken five wickets in each innings and went on to take forty-one in the series. Now, he bowled the first ball of the England second innings to Geoffrey Boycott and it was very much a warm-up ball, delivered at half pace from a run up which was hardly an animated stroll. It caught Boycott in the middle of a dream, cut back into him, hit him on the pad and he was palpably lbw, to his obvious dismay and the equally apparent amusement of several others.

The sixth Test of the series was also played at Sydney and Australia's captain Graham Yallop played a remarkable innings when he scored 121 of his side's first innings 198. Yallop was a lanky left-handed Victorian who was not a great captain or batsman, but he was capable of the occasional brilliant innings of which this was one. He was a powerful square-cutter, he picked the ball up off his legs in the way of so many left-handers and he had a thumping off-drive which was effective rather than beautiful. In spite of this innings he was unable to save Australia from another defeat and the Ashes returned to England even if it was an unreal victory with the Chappells, Lillee, Marsh and the rest otherwise engaged.

By the time England had returned to Australia for a three-match series the following year – Lord's refused to agree to this series being played for the Ashes – a fragile peace treaty had been worked out between Kerry Packer and World Series Cricket on the one hand and the Australian Cricket Board on the other. England had answered the ACB's call for assistance and once again Mike Brearley took a side to Australia. The West Indies also played three Test matches and then there were a possible twenty one-day internationals for the World Series Cup which was very much the flagship of the WSC operation. In the Sydney Test, which Australia won, Derek Underwood and Greg Chappell fought a fascinating duel which Chappell won in the end most conclusively. These battles within battles are always an absorbing by-product of Test cricket.

From the next two years when first India and then the West Indies came to the SCG almost nothing has stuck in the mind although I remember Larry Gomes, a vastly underrated batsman, scoring a hundred for the West Indies in 1981–82. Over the years when the main

West Indies batsmen had failed, Gomes consistently succeeded and he had an impressive record in Test cricket. It would be hard to imagine a more modest or unassuming performer. He had a lovely off-drive but in the main he was one of those players who accumulated runs unnoticeably and unglamorously and it would come as a surprise to discover when you looked at the scoreboard that he was already in the 40s.

The following year, England under Bob Willis returned to Australia and when they played in Sydney runs came from a much more unlikely quarter. Off-spinner Eddie Hemmings, whose career was to have a most prolonged and glorious autumn, did duty as nightwatchman in England's second innings and stayed on the next day to take his score to 95. A series of cheerful, ginger-haired buffets consistently sent the ball to the leg-side boundary interspersed with one or two pretty decent off-drives, and much bustling between the wickets kept his score mounting until the approach of a century was finally too much and he was caught behind off fellow off-spinner Bruce Yardley.

The next two Test matches I watched at the SCG will probably stay in my memory longest of all, not entirely for deeds committed on the field but because they were matches which saw different eras draw momentously to a close. In 1983–84 Pakistan were Australia's opponents and this was the final Test for those three great Australian cricketers, Greg Chappell, Dennis Lillee and Rod Marsh. I have dealt with the occasion at some length in *One Test After Another* and I can only reiterate that it was the ultimate in nostalgia. It was appropriate that they should all have made important contributions to Australia's ten-wicket victory. For Chappell, it was the perfect end. His innings of 182, as handsome a piece of batting as ever he can have produced, took him past Don Bradman's Test aggregate and he reached 7,000 Test runs. He then held two catches, the first enabling him to beat Colin Cowdrey's record of 120 which was the most in Test cricket by a non-wicket keeper. Lillee took four wickets each innings taking his aggregate in Test cricket to 355 and becoming the first bowler to go past 350. Marsh held on to six catches and took his total of dismissals to 355, another Test record. When he caught Abdul Qadir off a skier from Lillee late in Pakistan's second innings, it was the 95th time that 'c March b Lillee' had appeared in a Test match scorebook. For five days this match was an extraordinary and unforgettable valedictory procession. With the departure of these three great cricketers, not surprisingly the course of Australia's cricket changed considerably.

The West Indies were back at the SCG the following year (1984–85) and this was another sad farewell for it was the final Test appearance of Clive Lloyd who had among many other things been their longest-serving and most successful Test captain. But this was a much more remarkable match, for the West Indian fast bowlers cut a devastating swathe through Australian cricket that season and had already won the Frank Worrell Trophy. For a year or two now, the Sydney pitch had been helping spin bowling which in itself was an excellent thing in an age when Test cricket was becoming more and more dominated by phalanxes of fast bowlers. Before the match, rumour had it that this pitch would be vastly different in character from the others in the series and the Australian selectors had included two spinners in their side and both were New South Welshmen, leg-spinner Bob Holland and othodox slow left-hander Murray Bennett.

The West Indies selectors refused to listen to rumour and actually dropped specialist off-spinner Roger Harper who had played in the two preceding Tests. They went in with their usual complement of four fast bowlers. Viv Richards and Larry Gomes were left to produce occasional off-spin, and in Australia's only innings they were allowed nineteen overs between them; this argues perhaps that Lloyd's captaincy did not leave Test cricket in a blaze of imagination. After a typically boring innings of 173 by Australia's domiciled South African, Kepler Wessels, it was a question only of whether the West Indies batsmen could bat through for rather less than three days to save the match. This they comprehensively failed to do, losing in four days by an innings and 55 runs in what was Lloyd's eleventh defeat in 74 Test matches as captain. The main damage had been caused by the 38-year-old Holland, in only his third Test. He and Bennett knew all about the Sydney pitch and they tormented batsmen who had little idea of how to play the turning ball. It was a joy to watch, considering the constant battering fast bowlers give contemporary Test match batsmen at unforgivably slow over rates. Holland, not naturally a big spinner of the ball, took six wickets in the first innings and four in the second whilst Bennett managed only two and three. As so often happens though, they complemented one another perfectly and I doubt if Holland would have taken so many wickets otherwise. Nothing was more splendid than the delight the means of this Australian victory gave to that great Australian leg-spinner, Bill O'Reilly who was in the press box on behalf of the Sydney *Morning Herald* and who had been fighting a lone battle in print for spin over many years.

The fact that the much-vaunted West Indian batsmen made such a poor fist of playing spin was alarming evidence of the way in which the balance of the modern game has become so distorted. Even in the 1960s when Frank Worrell's and then Gary Sober's sides carried all before them, they still fielded a balanced attack with Sobers himself on hand to bowl orthodox or unorthodox left-arm spin and Lance Gibbs to bowl the off-breaks which brought him 309 Test wickets. Lloyd's side in the eighties invariably contained four fast bowlers and often, as on this occasion in Sydney, no specialist spinner. Any criticism of recent West Indian methods whereby they have used fast bowlers to dictate the course and the tempo of the game has met with furious objections from the West Indians themselves who rightly say that they are playing within the Laws of the game. The desire to win is surely the controlling factor in all of this, just as it was with Douglas Jardine when he formulated his plans to beat the Australians in 1932–33. This desire to win has become an increasingly potent factor with the financial rewards for victory forever climbing. This is probably truer in the West Indies than in some other parts of the world where the concentration of their youth on developing their cricket talents is controlled more strongly by the socio-economic factor.

I find it hard to blame the West Indies for playing cricket the way they do and often it appears that their greatest crime is to go on winning. In the best of all possible worlds it would be nice if cricket's crown of excellence could be spread around more liberally, but it is up to the other countries to develop players who can knock the West Indies off their pedestal. If I have one objection to the way in which they play their cricket, it concerns their lamentably slow over rate which is used as a thinly disguised tactical weapon. Their argument is that crowds all over the world have come flocking to see their dramatic fast bowling and the strokeplay of Richards, Lloyd and Greenidge. That argument cannot be faulted. But if they bowl their overs at eleven or twelve an hour with quite a few bouncers off which the batsmen are unable to score, the other side is not receiving enough balls an hour to leave itself time in which to gain a lead and then bowl their opponents out twice. This, I believe, is stacking the odds in a way which was never intended and is where action should be taken. Only the most naive can surely claim that a slow over rate does not, in this sense, become a tactical weapon.

Before I leave the Sydney Cricket Ground and the fifth Test against the West Indies in 1984–85 I would like to come back to where I began, which was with Clive Lloyd's last Test match. In the first innings he had made 33 which was the highest score for his side before he too, fell to the wiles of Holland. In the second, he came out of the pavilion with that long-striding lugubrious walk, slightly stooping at the shoulders, a white floppy sun hat pulled down improbably almost over his eyes, chewing rhythmically all the while. It was an identical picture to an entry he had made many years before which had prompted John Arlott to say that he looked like Paddington Bear.

Although spectacles provided the antidote to short-sightedness, there was always something slightly myopic about Lloyd's appearance as he peered down the pitch at the bowler, especially early on in an innings. When he took guard now, the West Indies were 93–4 and he must have known that there was nothing he could do about staving off defeat. Nonetheless, he was clearly determined and of course the fact that the SCG was a ground on which he had never scored a hundred may have acted as an extra challenge. He started off by swinging Bennett rather thoughtfully to mid-wicket for 4 and then, having as it were cleared his throat, he thumped that huge right foot down the pitch and drove him far over long-on for 6. When he leant in his angular way into a pushed off-drive which brought him 2 runs to extra-cover and took him past 50, one began to wonder if that elusive hundred might not appear to round off a spectacular career in the best possible way. Allan Border who had taken over the captaincy when Kim Hughes resigned after the second Test in Brisbane, now brought back Craig McDermott from the Noble Stand end.

Lloyd celebrated with a scything square-cut for 4, a stroke which took one back to the start of his Test life, for I can well remember one or two such strokes in that hundred he made against Colin Cowdrey's Englishmen in Port of Spain in 1967–68. This square-cut was followed by another classic Lloyd stroke, this time off the front foot which sent the ball racing through the off-side field to the pavilion rails. When he drove again the ball found the outside edge and went away to third-man for 4 more. Later in the same over he almost played a splendid yorker into his stumps and with a nice gesture he raised his hand in appreciation to McDermott. Lloyd needed 28 more for his hundred when McDermott ran in to bowl his next over. The ball was up to the bat, but not quite as far as Lloyd thought. The front foot came forward, the huge, heavy bat followed and struck the ball a satisfying blow out of the middle. But Lloyd had not been quite to the pitch and although the ball went fast it was a foot or so above the ground and straight to extra-cover where Border took the catch without fuss. Lloyd sloped off, angry with himself at first with his jaw thrust out in front of him, and with some impatience he rehearsed the stroke before collecting himself as the applause rose from all round the ground. Looking at his feet and waving his bat he trudged off a Test ground for the last time as a player and into the pages of the history books.

It is always a sad moment when a great cricketer leaves the scene and Lloyd's final departure was no exception. He had exerted an influence over his players that maybe only Frank Worrell had achieved before. His had been a noble reign for all except those who held him solely responsible for the ruthless way in which the West Indies had developed and used their pace attack. Certainly, Lloyd presided over a cricketing machine which changed the mechanical balance of the game at this level but it is hard to argue that he did more than allow the forces of nature at his disposal to take their course. Victory was important to Lloyd although not more so than it was to all the other Test sides of the world. This controversial aspect of Lloyd may always remain. Yet what cannot be argued was that a great batsman with a prodigious record, who had kept going for almost twenty years in spite of possessing the most operated on pair of knees in the game, departed the scene that afternoon in Sydney and the game was the poorer for it. His departure also left a biggish question mark over West Indian cricket which was: what sort of a job would Viv Richards make of succeeding him?

A year later Bob Holland had another haul of ten wickets in a Test, this time against New Zealand in a match which Australia won thanks to a most determined innings by David Boon which enabled them to score 260 in the fourth innings to win by four wickets. New Zealand's two experienced spinners, John Bracewell and Stephen Boock did not use the conditions especially well. What Test drama there was at the SCG that season came from the bat of Kris Srikkanth while scoring his first hundred for India. Srikkanth has been one of the three or four most exciting batsmen in the world over the last decade and to find an opening batsman who hit the new ball as hard one probably has to go back to the Barbadian, Cammie Smith, although he did not often go on to make a big score.

In this innings Srikkanth reached his hundred in 97 balls and because of a muscle injury had to bat for most of the innings with a runner. If the first ball of the innings was a half-volley he drove it for 4, if it was short he either hooked or cut it and for him a defensive stroke was only the last despairing resort. He was quick on his feet and wonderfully entertaining to watch. Any batsman able to take an attack apart as Srikkanth did on the first day of that Test in Sydney is a match winner, and his value to India was even more firmly underlined by the fact that his partner was no less a performer than Sunil Gavaskar. In fact, towards the end of Gavaskar's career, some of Srikkanth's ebullient methods had rubbed off on the great man and there were times in this innings – Gavaskar made 172 – that I had to look twice to make sure who it was who had hit the ball. By the time Gavaskar's career had ended he had become positively skittish at the crease and his most memorable innings of all which I was lucky enough to see was played against New Zealand at Nagpur in a qualifying match for the 1987 World Cup Final. He made 103 not out reaching a hundred in 85 balls with three 6s and ten 4s: in order to qualify for the finals, India had to win in 41.5 overs or less and they achieved 224–1 in 32.1 overs. It was quite a contrast with his innings for India in the 1975 World Cup at Lord's when, for some extraordinarily perverse reason, he batted throughout the 60 overs while making 36 not out after England had made 334 for four declared. But Gavaskar has always been his own man and sometimes a trifle obstinate with it, as was shown in England in 1990 when he refused to accept honorary membership of MCC on the grounds that on one occasion a steward had failed to recognize him.

Test matches at the SCG never seem to be wholly dull and the one against England in 1986–87 was remarkably similar to that against the West Indies two years before. It was England who had now won the series and the Ashes, and they came to the SCG more than aware that they would have to do battle on a turning pitch. This fifth Test match had been given a bizarre start when the Australian selectors, in announcing their side, had included a certain Peter Taylor, an off-spinner from New South Wales who had played only one first-class match that season and only six in his entire career. His selection was an emphatic vote of no confidence in the regular New South Wales off-spinner Greg Matthews who had for a few years been in and out of the Australian side. But Matthews, extremely punk in appearance and behaviour, was by no means everyone's cup of tea and I daresay that included the new cricket manager of the Australian side, Bobby Simpson who had for a few years managed New South Wales. From the boundary Matthews was a great irritant as he went about his work in the field as a sort of professional gee-er upp-er which involved constantly clapping hands and shouting, 'Come on lads' or words to that effect and when fielding within reach of the bowler taking the ball to him as he walked back to his mark and giving him a couple of hearty slaps on the behind once he had given him the ball. It was like having a wasp buzzing around all the time.

Taylor's selection had invited the perhaps inevitable newspaper comment of 'Peter *Who?*' and one or two even went so far as to suggest that the selectors had got the initials wrong and had chosen the wrong Taylor and that they were really after Mark Taylor who was shortly to make his impact in Test cricket although at the other end of the batting order. Of course, they had done no such thing and with his off-spin delivered with a run which ends with a kangaroo-like leap, Peter Taylor took 6–78 in England's first innings after Dean Jones had given Australia a most important advantage scoring 184 after Border had won the toss. Taylor is fair-haired and unassuming, and cricket has never had a more whole-hearted performer. I have always felt that he would have been a better bowler if he had had the courage to give the ball more air; maybe he would have tried to do so if he had not played his first-class cricket at the SCG where you can bring your arm over and wait for the pitch to do the rest. He is also a fine fielder especially in the deep where he has a lovely arm, and he is no mean batsman besides, as he now showed in Australia's second innings when he made a crucial 42, putting on 98 for the eighth wicket with Steve Waugh – the decisive runs of the match. It is very seldom that the Australians produce a bowler who understands no more than the basic rudiments of batting. England failed by 56 runs to score the 320 they needed to win and just as it had done two years before, an unsuccessful Australian season ended on an optimistic note for the future thanks largely to Peter *Who*.

The one-off Test match which England played at the SCG the following year as part of Australia's bicentennial celebrations ended in a boring draw and never looked much like doing anything else. The only reason it will be remembered was the shocking behaviour of Chris Broad who scored his fourth Test century in Australia – he had made three on the 1986–87 tour – after Mike Gatting had won what looked like being a decisive toss. Broad, in his tall left-handed way, had made 139 efficient and uncomplicated runs when he pushed defensively at a ball from Waugh which bowled him off his body hitting the leg stump. As he turned to go, Broad, in his annoyance, swung his bat at the stumps knocking one of them out of the ground and sending the remaining bail flying. It was appalling behaviour and against almost everything that cricket stands for and was made even more unaccountable by the fact that England had only just completed a most unhappy tour of Pakistan which had seen the dramatic on-the-field row between Gatting and the umpire, Shakoor Rana. On their brief return home before going on to New Zealand and Australia, the players had been spoken to in the strongest terms about the importance of good behaviour on the field of play. Broad's act was something that was done on the spur of the moment but a Test cricketer's behavioural reflexes should have been honed to a satis-factory condition after the usual apprenticeship in county cricket. In short, banging the stumps with his bat was not an option Broad should even have considered. The management of that tour took a strong line on the incident and Broad was fined £500. One sad, off-the-field highlight was that this was the last Test match which Bill O'Reilly reported for the Sydney *Morning Herald*. He was 82 years of age. His pithy comments, usually in support of spin bowling and against the modern prevailing attitudes both out in the middle and in the corridors of power, have already been much missed. There was a short ceremony in the press box to mark the occasion.

The dramas of the SCG took a most unexpected turn in January 1989 when Australia salavaged yet another spinning victory after the series had been lost, once again to the West Indies in a match which saw the introduction to Test cricket of the other New South Welsh Taylor, Mark. Australia's hero was their captain Allan Border, but in the unlikely role of an orthodox slow left-arm spinner. Border had always been an occasional Test bowler and in a career which began in 1978–79, he had taken a total of sixteen wickets in his first 100 Test matches. Now, in his 101st he took 11–96, including 7–46 in the West Indies first innings. He bowled well and found a fair amount of turn but would be the first to admit that he was helped by the curious ways in which some of the West Indians found to get themselves out. Not content with this remarkable bowling feat, he went on to score the slowest Test fifty ever made by an Australian. It took him 262 balls and 310 minutes and played an important role in taking Australia to a decisive first innings lead of 177 while David Boon, who loves the SCG, made a typically pugnacious 149 at the other end.

When Border decides to bowl, which he does all too seldom, there is an apologetic air about him which almost seems to say to the batsman, 'Well, come on, let's get this over quickly', and when he takes a wicket you feel that no one is more surprised than he is himself. For those of us watching, a spell by Border starts off more than anything as a form of comic relief.

The decade ended with another visit to the SCG by Pakistan, under the captaincy of Imran Khan surely for the last time in Australia, although he flirts with retirement in a way which would make Dame Nellie Melba envious. While he was no longer the force he had been with the ball, which was hardly surprising at the age of 37, this three-match series heralded the arrival of what may easily turn out to be one of the most deadly fast bowling combinations of all time. Wasim Akram was already well established in Test cricket and had been carefully nurtured by Imran himself. Tall and powerfully built, Wasim, who bowls left-arm over the wicket and was already close to being the fastest bowler in the world, was now joined by Waqar Younis who was only eighteen and already genuinely fast. He has remarkable control and the ability to move the ball both ways in the air to the right-hander although his late, dipping in-swinger is his most dangerous delivery. As a third seamer they had Aaqib Javed who was also only eighteen. In a year or two, especially if the doctors can find a satisfactory answer to Wasim Akram's recurring groin injury, this will be an attack which even the West Indians will face with something approaching trepidation. They did not bowl Pakistan to victory in this series, but before long they will be irresistible.

3

HEADINGLEY:
Yorkshire and
England Expects . . .

I doubt if any group of people in the world feel as passionately about their cricket as Yorkshiremen. For many years Yorkshire cricket was the heartbeat of English cricket and their main ground in the Leeds suburb of Headingley is the ancestral home of the White Rose cricketers. It is a ground which is as redolent of Yorkshire grit and determination and pithy good sense as it is of the industrial north of England. It is a ground without frills set in amongst tree-lined roads and red brick Victorian houses. Until the mid-1960s, it was always something of a surprise if Yorkshire failed to win the County Championship and although they have had little success since then, they have still won the Championship more times than any of their rivals. For a long time England sides were packed with Yorkshire players and it was always said, and rightly, that a strong Yorkshire meant a strong England. The same was said of New South Wales and Australia. The dedication of Yorkshiremen to their cricket and their obsession with their own county side was marvellously summed up in a story told by Neville Cardus. Watching cricket at Scarborough in the 1920s, Cardus was sitting behind two middle-aged Yorkshiremen who were engaged in the time-honoured game of being amateur Test selectors. An England team was to be announced the following weekend and they produced a pencil and paper and began to pick their own side. They had a long debate and thought most carefully before writing down each name, and at the end of it they had picked the entire Yorkshire side. Cardus lent forward and said to them, 'But you've left Hobbs out.' They both looked at each other and their list of players and thought for a moment before one of them turned and replied, 'But how could we fit him in?' No cricket team at any time can have had a greater expression of loyalty than that.

The three Ridings have produced a line of cricketers which has stretched from Wilfred Rhodes and on to Len Hutton, Fred Trueman and Geoffrey Boycott. They were all Yorkshire to their bootlaces. Lord Hawke was one of the very few to have played for the county who was actually born outside the county boundary – he was born in Lincolnshire. The rule until 1990 was that no one from outside the boundaries could play for the county. There are many instances of expectant mothers being rushed home just in case it should be a boy and have an aptitude for cricket. Unhappily, in recent years Yorkshire cricket has been in a turmoil essentially about how best to get back to the habit of winning. There has been much internal bickering and characters such as Brian Close, Ray Illingworth and Geoffrey Boycott have all had their say and their supporters, while Trueman too has never been afraid to express an opinion. The latest controversy concerns the employment of an overseas player and while liberal views have triumphed to the extent that the birth qualification has been relaxed for English players, the membership voted heavily to reject the case for overseas players. Close and Boycott were on opposite ends of that argument and Trueman has said that if Yorkshire resorts to overseas players he will drive to Headingley, in his Rolls I hope, and personally hand back his membership to the club.

No ground anywhere is more heavily steeped in the tradition of cricket and it is sad that there are those who want to move the headquarters of Yorkshire cricket. The problem with Headingley is that Yorkshire do not own the ground. It belongs to the Leeds Football and Athletic Club, an august body which seems to identify more with the Rugby League played on the adjoining football ground which employs the back of the main cricketing grandstand as its own grandstand. It is the Cricket, Football and Athletic Club which collects the revenue from the advertising boards which circle the cricket ground and as a result neither English nor Yorkshire cricket benefits from any of it.

Headingley is not a beautiful ground, and although it is gradually being brought up to date it is still strongly reminiscent of a bygone era when life was more of a struggle and, of course, in the old days, Yorkshiremen being what they are, would not have considered comfort an important ingredient for watching their cricket, as the old photographs of countless thousands packed into the ground watching Yorkshire win the County Championship suggest.

Our Test Match Special commentary box is perched at the top of the Rugby Stand and gives us a fine view behind the bowler's arm, although it is somewhat cramped. There is not much covered seating at Headingley and steeply banked open terracing stretches round the Kirkstall Lane side of the ground which is to our left as we peer out at the cricket. The new electronic scoreboard stands at the back of the terracing by the entrance to the ground on that side. At the far end, the Kirkstall Lane end as it is known, there is a new stand with a row of hospitality boxes which is to the left of the sightscreen. This stand is one of the ground's concessions to the modern commercial age. The open seating then stretches round up to the new modern red brick pavilion diagonally across to our right as we commentate. It is a neat building which is now almost thirty years old although if it was built again today it would be considerably enlarged. The players' changing rooms are on the top floor which has a balcony with outside stairs at each end. The players' dining-room is on the ground floor and so too are the offices of Yorkshire's redoubtable secretary, Joe Lister, who died while this book was being written. At the back of the open seating at the Kirkstall Lane end, there was once a row of handsome elm trees but sadly Dutch elm disease accounted for them revealing the red brick houses behind, the owners of which were the only people to be pleased about it for it has meant that they can sit on their balconies and enjoy an uninterrupted view of the cricket. More open seating links the new pavilion with the old which stands in the right-hand corner of the ground as we look out of our box. The top has been given over to the press while the Yorkshire committee hold sway on the middle floor; the Leeds Cricket, Football and Athletic Club offices are there as well. The ground floor of the old pavilion is obscured by more banked open seating. It has been turned into a huge bar and there are also a couple of hospitality suites. Between the two pavilions, on the lawn behind the seating is a complex of about twenty temporary hospitality suites built on scaffolding to house corporate customers.

Another of Headingley's problems in recent years has been the state of the pitch. Too often pitches have been produced which have made batting something of a lottery in the later stages of a match. In 1972, the Australians were the victims of a pitch which took a huge amount of spin from the first morning and Derek Underwood picked up ten wickets in the match. All sorts of reasons were put forward for its condition. It had been flooded by a violent storm five days before the match began and the weather had not allowed the groundsman to use the heavy roller. There was very little grass on it too, and this was said to be the result of the efforts of a fungus called Fusarium. The Australians shook their collective heads in disbelief and Jack Fingleton, the former Australian opening batsman who wrote for the *Sunday Times*, went to his grave certain it was all part of a sinister plot.

The Australians were particularly unlucky, for when they returned to Headingley for the third Test match three years later, they went to bed on the fourth day at 220–3 needing 225 more to win and fancying their chances. When the players reached the ground in the morning they found that the pitch at the Football Stand end of the ground had been vandalized during the night. The friends and supporters of a certain George Davis had attacked the pitch with knives and oil in the hope that they were making a case for the release of their hero who they felt had been wrongly imprisoned. Davis let his supporters down badly for when he was eventually released he was immediately had up on some other charge and sent back inside. Sadly, an intriguing game of cricket had to be abandoned as a draw, although consistent rain during the day would almost certainly have come up with the same answer.

Although Australia were beaten twice, the 1980s was not a happy decade for England at Headingley with New Zealand, India, Pakistan, the West Indies and finally, in 1989, Australia all winning Test matches there. The pitch certainly played its part in these defeats, but in the last, against Australia, there was a strange twist to it. The groundsman was sure that he had at last solved his problems and that the pitch for what was the first Test against Australia was a beauty. It looked full of runs but the England management were not prepared to believe their eyes. They left out their only spinner, John Emburey, on the morning of the match and decided that it would be best to bowl first. David Gower won the toss, invited Australia to bat and watched while they compiled 601–7 declared. Thanks to a fine hundred from Allan Lamb, England saved the follow-on, but when Australia's declaration on the last morning left them to bat for about five hours to save the match, they were destroyed by Terry Alderman who took ten wickets in the match, and lost by 210 runs. This was one of the most damaging defeats that I can remember, for it seemed to knock the stuffing out of the England side and set the precedent for a series which Australia went on to win 4–0.

Since taking over the Australian captaincy in 1984, Allan Border had had a most difficult job and for a while in the eighties Australia was as weak as it has ever been. Bobby Simpson was then made coach of the Australian side and he and Border gradually rebuilt the team. When this 1989 side was chosen, it was generally felt that the greater experience of the Englishmen would be decisive and in their early games against the counties the Australians did not hint at what was to come. They even lost their three-day match against Worcestershire. Border himself had been an efficient captain without ever showing any great flair for the job, but he had one important piece of luck. He had played two seasons for Essex in the County Championship, the first under Graham Gooch who then resigned the captaincy for he felt it was affecting his own cricket, and then under Keith Fletcher who took back his old job the following season. Fletcher had for a long time been regarded as the shrewdest of captains on the county circuit and by his own admission, Border learned a great deal from him. Fletcher had two important attributes. He was brilliant at working out opposing batsmen; he was very quick to spot strengths and weaknesses and to plan accordingly. In one match, a young batsman came to the crease and Fletcher said that he couldn't remember his name but he knew he needed a second gully – who took the catch an over or two later. Fletcher was also good at getting the best out of his players knowing who would be best served by the sympathetic approach and who would react better to the sharp side of his tongue.

These two years in England had also given Border the chance to look at all England's cricketers at close quarters and none more so than his own county colleague, Graham Gooch. In this first Test match at Headingley, Border began to put his plans into action. For the first time Gooch found when he faced Alderman that there was a short mid-wicket as well as a forward short-leg for the bat pad catch. Gooch likes to play the ball off his stumps to wide mid-on and often sent the ball skimming above the surface for the first few yards. Seeing the short and straight mid-wicket, Gooch began to try and hit the ball squarer on the leg-side and was therefore playing further across the line. Gooch was lbw playing round his front pad five times in the series, and three times to Alderman.

This was one example of Border's planning, and he was now very much a captain who tried to make things happen rather than one who simply waited and hoped for something to turn up. He was, of course, greatly helped by Bobby Simpson who was himself an able tactician.

This Test established the pattern for the series and also saw the emergence of Mark Taylor as a considerable Test player. He made 136 in his first match against England and went on to make 839 runs in the series. This match also produced Steve Waugh's first Test hundred, a thrilling innings full of brilliant strokes, the best of which was his square-cut which the England bowlers gave him far too much opportunity to play. It was an infinitely sobering Test match for England and I still wonder whether if those in charge had accepted the pitch at face value and batted first the series would have followed the same course. Once the Australians had gained this initial burst of confidence they were unstoppable although I believe they would, in any event have won back the Ashes, but not so easily.

Headingley has seen many outstanding Test matches and some extraordinary individual performances. On no ground in the world has Don Bradman left a deeper mark. When he first came to England in 1930 at the age of twenty-one he made 334 in the third Test at Headingley and four years later he made 304 in the day in the fourth Test there after Australia had lost their first three wickets for 39. In 1948, when Australia scored 404–3 in a day to win by seven wickets, Bradman contented himself with 173 not out. This was the highest score in the fourth innings to win a Test match until India made 406–4 to beat the West Indies in Port of Spain in 1975–76.

When South Africa played at Headingley in 1929, Tuppy Owen-Smith made 129 in their second innings in a remarkable rearguard action which almost stood comparison with Ian Botham's efforts fifty-two years later. He came in when South Africa were 73–5 still 119 runs behind. On the third day of a three-day Test he became the only South African ever to score a hundred before lunch in a Test, taking his score from 27 to 129, and he also had a tenth wicket stand of 103 in 65 minutes with Alexander Bell. In the end, England needed 184 and won by five wickets. It seems astonishing today that in those three days 372.1 overs were bowled. When Australia beat England over five days at Headingley in 1989 a total of 410.3 overs were bowled.

On the second day of this earlier Test South Africa had seemed so well beaten that Neville Cardus left Leeds for London to go with a friend to a concert. He wrote his account of the heavy defeat on the train and before meeting his friend checked the score on the tape machine at his club. He was horrified to read of Owen-Smith's innings. He at once cancelled the concert and the girlfriend and settled down to write a most fulsome account of Owen-Smith's innings which he had not seen. He was lucky that Owen-Smith could only bat one way, and he had seen him make runs before. He took the account round to the offices of the *Manchester Guardian* at a time which would have coincided with the arrival of the last train from Leeds. It was printed in full and Owen-Smith himself and a number of others who had seen the innings later congratulated Cardus on his brilliant description.

Headingley will be remembered longest by many for the astonishing events on the last two days of the third Test against Australia in 1981 when first Ian Botham and then Bob Willis destroyed Kim Hughes's side after England had been forced to follow-on 227 runs behind. It was a game which had been given a dramatic twist even before it began by the decision of the England selectors to bring back Mike Brearley to the captaincy following Botham's resignation at Lord's. Brearley had always handled Botham well and although at times they had formidable arguments there was a strong mutual respect; indeed Brearley's appointment may have decided Botham to continue playing in that series. It was not the least of Brearley's triumphs that he was able to create an atmosphere within the England dressing-room which enabled Botham to relax and regain the form which had fallen away so alarmingly in the twelve matches of his captaincy.

England were one down in the series when they came to Headingley and for three days everything suggested that they would leave two down. Hughes won the toss and batted and Australia spent most of the first two days compiling a total of 401 which looked to be a good insurance against defeat. Brearley stood at first slip and directed operations and to his evident delight Botham took six wickets in this innings. It was the Botham of old who was once again running in as if he didn't have a care in the world, and this performance took him a long way down the path of rehabilitation. Each time Botham took a wicket, no one was quicker to congratulate him than Brearley, but at the end of the second day I would be astonished if either had had hopes of achieving anything but a draw from the match. At the end of the following day, when England were 6–1 in their *second* innings, they would hardly have dared to think even of a draw. Alderman, Lillee and Lawson had worked their way through the England first innings taking full advantage of some poor strokes, and it was only thanks to some typically robust strokeplay from Botham, by now well on the way to a full recovery of spirit as well as form, that England made as many as 174. The day had begun with Gooch being out lbw as he tried to work Alderman off the front foot wide of mid-on, a dismissal which gave one a preview of the recurring nightmare of eight years later. It looked that evening that brave as Brearley had been to answer the selectors' cry for help, he was more likely to be involved in a four-day defeat than a miracle cure.

It was not surprising that the fourth day's play began in front of something much less than a full house crowd, and those that came will have felt like going back home for lunch and not returning. There was just a glimmer of early hope as Brearley, looking like a Victorian explorer in that homemade crash helmet of his, on-drove Lillee for 4 with a stroke which did not please Australia's fastest bowler. It was the briefest of glimmers for later in the same over Brearley played forward to Lillee and Alderman took the catch at third slip; the bowler reacted as if he was not certain if it was adequate repayment for the mortal insult of a few balls earlier. It was now Gower's turn to raise and then dash our hopes as he seems to have been doing almost ever since. A glorious, almost liquid square-cut off Lillee rippled to the fence and later in the over he forced him with time to spare through mid-on for 3. In the over after that he faced Alderman and played a loose forcing stroke off the back foot with his bat away from his body and was caught by Border at second slip. This made England 37–3, and very soon afterwards Mike Gatting played back to Alderman and was very lbw: 41–4.

At the other end, Geoff Boycott had been defending dourly with the odd nudge and the occasional pushed drive bringing him a slender income and he was now joined by Peter Willey, one of the most stubborn of fighters. Without ever having us sitting back comfortably in our seats, these two restored some sort of order and took England into lunch at 78–4. The deficit was still 149 but at least they suggested an air of slight permanence which was more than could be said for the others. After lunch, Willey played one resounding square-cut off Lawson but while we were still relishing it he tried to cut a bouncer from Lillee and was caught by Dyson at short third-man. In the circumstances it was a dreadful stroke. To loud applause, Botham took his place, and at once produced a powerful off-drive against Alderman which thudded into the boundary. While Botham was prepared to chance his arm, Boycott eschewed even the faintest of risks and it came as a nasty shock when he reached forward to a ball from Alderman which cut back into him and had him lbw. The Yorkshire faithful cheered him off after he had been batting for 215 minutes in which time he had hit a solitary 4. The score was now 133–6 and the deficit 94, and salvation was further away than ever. Two runs later Bob Taylor popped a short one from Alderman into Ray Bright's hands at forward short-leg. At the other end, Botham was 23 and stamping around while Graham Dilley walked out to bat.

In such circumstances one of the most famous of all sporting bets was struck. In the Ladbrokes tent, a red and white striped affair tucked in by the corner of the football stand to our left as we commentated, the former England wicket-keeper Godfrey Evans, who was in charge of these things, quoted an England victory at 500–1 against. The full story was given to me by Rodney Marsh himself. At the tea interval on the fourth day when their coach driver told Dennis Lillee the odds, Lillee found his wallet and pulled out a £50 note telling the driver to put it on England. Marsh heard this, snatched the note and told Lillee that he was not going to allow him to waste his money. Lillee protested but in the end was persuaded to settle for a bet of £10 which the driver was asked to put on.

The players took the field after tea and Marsh, standing back at the football stand end of the ground, saw the coach driver walking round towards the Ladbrokes tent. He attracted his attention and then held up one hand with the fingers outstretched to signify a fiver and then pointed at himself to show that he wanted to put on £5. The driver shook his head to say that he would not do it for Marsh, whereupon Marsh repeated his instructions and again received a negative answer. Finally, Marsh went through it all again and then held up a clenched fist and pointed towards the driver indicating the punishment he would receive if he did not put on that fiver for Marsh. Of course, he did put it on and the two Australians collected, although Marsh reckoned it was the most expensive bet he ever won because it seemed that he was buying drinks for his side for ever afterwards. It may seem strange to bet against your own side and Australia has no two greater patriots than Lillee and Marsh, and certainly there was never the slightest question of them pulling the horse. It was just a bit of fun, a larky way to waste a bit of money. I cannot think of many others who would have bet against themselves in this situation but thank goodness they did for it provided a splendid story. It also gave Ladbrokes unparalleled publicity.

With Dilley as his partner, Botham went rather more on the offensive and as that front leg came stamping down the pitch those thunderous drives rang off his bat with a noise which did the heart good. At least it meant that England were going down fighting, and when Dilley suddenly square-drove Lillee for two 4s it even seemed that they might avoid the indignity of an innings defeat. Botham chased these two strokes with a lofted cover-drive which was brimming with contempt and a delightful late-cut off Alderman. A loud cheer erupted when the follow-on was saved and eight runs later there was another when the 100 stand was posted. It all seemed highly improbable. Botham's 50 was the next landmark, and he celebrated by taking 16 in one spectacular over from Alderman who was always the bowler most likely to break through. By now, this stand was becoming a severe irritant to the Australians. No one on the ground and certainly not Mr Marsh, Mr Lillee or Mr Ladbroke had any inkling that the match would end other than in a massive defeat for England. There is something intensely frustrating about a big stand late in the innings just when you think you have got the other side on the ropes. In this instance, the Australians may have been guilty of letting-up fractionally when the scoreboard reached 135–7, knowing that it was simply a matter of waiting for the end and that with Botham chancing his arm it was only a question of time before he gave someone a catch.

Dilley's 50 was the next to be saluted, but we were all brought back to earth with a big bump when, after he had made six more, he suddenly decided to have a wild swing at Alderman and was bowled all over the place. He had done a noble job, batting for eighty minutes for the 117-run stand and hitting eight highly respectable 4s. To relieve his feelings Botham immediately stepped out and straight drove Alderman for a thumping 6. As every over went by he was batting better and better and there was hardly a false stroke except for one or two mighty swings and misses when all our hearts were in our mouths waiting to see if Marsh would throw the ball aloft and claim a catch. Chris Old had taken Dilley's place and he too was soon hitting the ball well through the off-side. Then, Botham found himself on 99 and there was a hush round the ground as Geoff Lawson ran in to bowl to him. The ball was well up and wide of the off stump, Botham played another flailing drive but this time he did not get it quite right. The ball flew off a thick edge to third-man for 4 and the cheers which greeted the stroke combined relief with pleasure. Botham's statistics were irresistible. His hundred had taken 155 minutes, he had faced 87 balls and hit one 6 and nineteen 4s which meant that 82 of his runs had come in boundaries. Remarkably, he had hit only two singles. By now I am sure there was a general realization that something quite extraordinary might just be going to happen. Of course, logic still pointed unerringly to an Australian victory, but before the end of this fourth day I began to detect a definite feeling of 'Well, having got this far it may just be that the momentum of Botham's innings will carry over into the bowling if we can get another fifty runs.'

Botham clearly considered this was a serious rescue operation, but when he had got to 109 he had his first major piece of luck. He hooked at Lawson, got an edge to the ball and for once Marsh, a wicket-keeper with a voracious appetite for anything that flicked the edge of the bat, dropped the catch. If that one had stuck Australia would have won. But I doubt if that miss worried Marsh unduly and I daresay it didn't give Mr Ladbroke a sleepless night either, but it did add to the general sense of frustration among the Australians. Hughes was now walking more quickly between overs and was looking around anxiously, perhaps, and unusually, for someone to give him some advice. When the 300 came up England's lead was still only 73 and there was no cause whatever for Australian alarm and even less when at 319, Old made room for himself to drive Lawson and lost his leg stump. England now had only Bob Willis to come. Willis was the owner of the longest forward lunge in the game, at any rate since Wes Hall's retirement, and it was a stroke which he played to bouncers and full tosses and anything in between. Botham did his best to keep him away from the strike but when he had to face the bowling that trusty left leg came stamping yards down the pitch and it kept him out of harm's way. Botham continued to strike the ball magnificently off the front foot and in these closing overs I remember a sweep off Ray Bright which he deliberately played very fine and which brought him four runs. At the close of play Botham was 145 not out, Willis had a single and at 351–9, England had a lead of 124.

It had been a nerve-wracking day for English supporters and while one knew that Australia should still do it easily, there was the lingering thought that perhaps, just possibly, we could be in for a fifth day to match the fourth. The next morning, however, wiser counsels prevailed and one realized that it was absurd even to consider that England might continue to surprise the Australians. Botham hit one more 4 before Willis, who had doubled his score, found that the forward lunge did not always provide the answer and he was caught by Allan Border low to his right at second slip off Terry Alderman, who finished with 6–135, figures which bore testimony to his skill as well as the power of Botham's 149 not out. Australia needed a mere 130 to win; Messrs Marsh, Lillee and Ladbroke were the epitome of calmness and the only question was how soon would we all be able to start the journey home.

Not surprisingly Brearley gave the new ball to Botham, for when a player is on a roll anything can happen. Botham started from the Kirkstall Lane end and his first over did nothing for English nerves when Graeme Wood played him strongly off his legs through mid-wicket for 4 and then hooked him for another with a most decisive stroke. It was then Willis's turn to come bounding in from the Football Stand end. Five more runs had been scored when Botham again bowled to Wood. The left-hander drove hard at one which was pitched up outside the off stump and Bob Taylor in his white floppy sun hat threw the ball high into the air. Australia were 13–1 and it was general jubilation in the middle while spectators took nervous glances at each other as if they were too frightened to suggest that this might be the start of something. John Dyson was joined by Greg Chappell and without hurry or concern they began to pick up runs with a disconcerting ease and, in all honesty, too many bad balls were being bowled. The fifty came up and the mood round the ground had now changed to one of reluctant but quiet resignation. On the last two days of this match the mood of the ground sometimes changed dramatically as many as three times an over.

By now, Willis had moved to the Kirkstall Lane end and at once he looked to be running in to bowl with a greater rhythm. Australia had reached 56 when Chappell played back perhaps a trifle carelessly to one which lifted sharply onto him and the ball lobbed off the top of the bat to Taylor. Now there were scenes of even greater glee. Australia needed only another 74 but at least 'we' were making them fight. Two runs later Willis, now coming in to bowl like a man possessed bowled another short one to Kim Hughes who hurriedly played back and Botham caught him cleanly low at third slip. It was 58–3 and everyone sat up a little straighter. Graham Yallop took Hughes's place and immediately played back to another from Willis which lifted on him and Mike Gatting held a quick, low catch at square short-leg. Australia 58–4, still 72 short, and the ground really humming; a miracle seemed more than just an outside chance now.

Border joined Dyson who had been looking completely in control while all this was going on, but facing Old was less of a problem than facing Willis. Or so it seemed until, seven runs later, Allan Border played back to one from Old which came back into him, found a gap between bat and pad and knocked out his leg stump. That made Australia 65–5 and looking to Dyson to get them out of trouble.

In the radio commentary box it was all we could do to remain impartial and keep up the good old BBC balance. Three more runs were scampered and now Dyson faced Willis who came roaring in as if his whole life had been a preparation for all this. The ball was short, Dyson hooked and Bob Taylor threw aloft another catch and he and more particularly Bob Willis were submerged by triumphant team-mates. Willis seemed in a trance and probably didn't take in anything that was said to him. In his next over he bowled short again and Rod Marsh hooked and the ball steepled away to fine-leg where Graeme Dilley stood about three inches inside the boundary. His concentration never flickered, he kept his eyes on the ball and clasped it in both hands in front of his chest. Not many catches in the deep come with as much pressure as that one. If he had taken a half shuffle backwards it would have been a 6. Instead of which Australia were 74–7 and even the most sanguine of spectators had begun to realize that England were going to win an astonishing victory. This feeling was strengthened one run later when Lawson played back to Willis and Bob Taylor clung to his fourth catch.

It is at moments like this that party poopers have a habit of appearing and while Mr Marsh and Mr Ladbroke were considering their likely wealth at the end of the day, Mr Lillee was striding purposefully to the crease and began to bat as if his greatest friend in the world was Mr Ladbroke. He and Ray Bright made batting seem a possible art once more. The half-volleys were dispatched and suddenly it was the turn of England to grow nervous again. Runs came with ease off both Willis and Old. It was now that Brearley's calmness really counted. Throughout the day he had remained much the coolest man on the ground. He certainly never panicked. When Botham began to wave his arms, he quietened him down. He gave his bowlers just the right encouragement and advice and when he walked up to talk to them his whole demeanour helped take the tension out of the players. Now he walked up to talk to Willis in the middle of an over; then it was to Old. While the ninth wicket pair were together and putting on 35 runs, each one as valuable as a gold bar, it was Brearley's example which held England together. Never for a moment did one feel that he did not know what he was doing.

The hundred came up and was greeted with the most perfunctory applause. The score reached 110 with only 20 more runs wanted and the mood was now one of dark despair as Willis ran in with one last effort. The ball was well up on the leg stump and Lillee chipped in a gentle arc towards mid-on. It hung tantalizingly in the air and Mike Gatting came racing in, dived forward despairingly and somehow came up with the catch. I don't remember another single incident which produced such an incredible feeling of relief. People laughed and smiled and wiped their brows. Terry Alderman was the new batsman and hardly the man for this sort of crisis. I was lucky enough to be commentating at this particular moment and another single brought Bright down to face Willis who came galloping in to bowl, giving it everything he had got. His arm came over, it was the perfect delivery, a straight, fast yorker, Bright was hopelessly late and the ball smacked into his middle stump and by 18 runs England had won the craziest game of cricket maybe I shall ever see.

It will be remembered as Botham's match, but in the end it was every bit as much Willis's match, although of course Botham's innings gave him the chance. As a cricketer Willis sometimes seemed a remote, almost unapproachable figure. When he was bowling he seemed to switch himself off from all outside influences and never did he do it more than he did that day at Headingley. He is said to have used hypnotherapy to help him concentrate while bowling and in Australia's second innings it was as if a spell had been cast over him. Willis is a tall, rather ungainly man who is not a natural athlete and has had to work for his success and in his own way adopted an approach which was best suited for him as a tally of 325 Test wickets illustrates. No one has bowled his heart out more for his country than Willis. He was never a great communicator on the field of play as was evident when he took on the England captaincy. Off the field, there is a great transformation. He is great fun and one of the friendliest of people, with a lovely sense of humour and a genius for giving people amusing and appropriate nicknames. His own was Goose and I can only imagine it was because of his appearance. I shall remember Willis coming in to bowl from the Kirstall Lane end that last afternoon just as long as I shall remember Botham's spanking drives and Marsh and Lillee's adventure with Mr Ladbroke. Willis is a cricketer who may never be given full credit for what he did for England and this is maybe because he captained the side at a time of uncertainty, although in all honesty, he was not the most inspirational of captains. He would never have sought the job but was given it by Peter May who, when he became chairman of the selectors, was determined to see England make a fresh start and, to make way for Willis, kicked out Keith Fletcher who had taken the side to India in 1981–82. I feel Willis would have been best served if he had never been burdened with the captaincy.

This was not the only time Botham made his mark at Headingley. There was a blistering 137 against India in 1979 in a match which was ruined by rain. He made 99 runs before lunch on the fourth day and at the time it would have been impossible to think such a display of controlled hitting could ever be bettered. His first Test on the ground was against Australia in 1977 when he took 5–21 in eleven overs in Australia's first innings in a match which England won by an innings.

Yorkshire will never forget that match. Geoffrey Boycott scored 191, his hundredth first-class hundred and the only instance of a batsman reaching this landmark in a Test. This was an extraordinary summer for Boycott who, half way through the series, emerged from the tent of his self-imposed exile from Test cricket. Boycott's problems had come to a head in 1973 when, after the third Test against the West Indies, Ray Illingworth was sacked as England's captain and Mike Denness, who had not been in the England side that summer, was asked to take England to the West Indies the following winter. Boycott was not happy with the choice of Denness and would have liked to have been asked to do the job himself. He was chosen for the tour, however, and had a good series. Ironically, his scores of 99 and 112 in the final Test in Port of Spain were an important contribution to a victory which enabled England to share the series and which may have helped keep Denness in the job.

On returning to England, Boycott found himself in the side for the first Test against India at Old Trafford and he was out for low scores in both innings, first to Abid Ali and then to Eknath Solkar both of whom were military medium at best. Scores of 10 and 6 may have been more the reflection of an inner turmoil than of bad batting. The result was that after the match Boycott announced that he was no longer available to play for England. The following winter he missed Denness's tour to Australia when England were blown apart by Thomson and Lillee. He has been accused of not wanting to go on this tour because of Australia's explosive fast bowling, but this is an absurd suggestion because the side itself had no idea they would be facing such a formidable combination until they actually came face to face with it in the first Test in Brisbane. No one has suggested that Boycott has unusual powers as a crystal-ball gazer.

England lost that series as they would have done under any captain, for Australia, thanks to Thomson and Lillee, were much the better side. The next summer Denness was replaced by Tony Greig, a decision which will almost certainly have given Boycott second thoughts if he had been contemplating a return to the colours. Greig's reign lasted almost two years until it became known that he had embraced Kerry Packer. Mike Brearley was appointed to lead the side against Australia in 1977 and Boycott's feelings about Brearley were apparently not so strong and after the first two Test matches he declared himself once more available to serve England.

Boycott is nothing if not a complex character. I well remember watching one of his first games for Yorkshire, in 1962 at Northampton in a match which saw Fred Trueman make a rare hundred. The reason I remember Boycott in that game is that for a long time he fielded on the boundary near the main scoreboard where I was sitting. He was wearing his dark blue striped Yorkshire Second XI sweater and was a callow, bespectacled youth. Was this just another Yorkshire colt destined to play a few matches and to cherish his second XI sweater for ever, or was he heading for greater things? His single-minded determination was clear to see, although his batting was wholly unmemorable.

The history of the game can surely not point to a batsman who was more dedicated to success than Geoffrey Boycott. He was not a naturally gifted player, which meant that he had to work hard for everything he achieved. He was intelligent, he watched carefully, listened intently and questioningly, harked to advice, sought help from good players and methodically perfected a batting technique which could seldom be faulted. Within two years of first playing for Yorkshire he was opening the batting for England against Australia and all he ever wanted was runs, runs and more runs. He had the ability to concentrate without wavering for hours on end, and he was able to compartmentalize his life so that nothing got in the way of this endless, relentless quest.

For Boycott, it was as if big scores provided the self-justification for his very existence. Centuries enabled him to hold his head high. With mountains of runs behind him he could look the rest of the world in the face. In his view, runs meant acceptance and he never lost sight of what runs on a large scale would do for his life and where they would lead him. They got him out of the village of Fitzwilliam, out of Yorkshire, out of England and onto a lengthy run-making voyage around the cricketing world. His huge aggregates made him a local, a national and finally an international hero, and I would not be surprised if they have made him a millionaire as well. Throughout his career Geoffrey Boycott seems to have been driven on and on by a powerful socio-economic factor and it is enormously to his credit that he achieved all that he set out to achieve. He has never knowingly taken a risk.

But all of this has a downside. Obsessive ambition on this scale is usually fuelled by an innate sense of insecurity and therefore lack of self-confidence. The constant striving to achieve can produce a mind unable to countenance failure and consequently an inability to cope with it. A by-product of all this can be to create a mental process which is certain that it knows the answer to everything and which produces forcefully expressed views on almost anything. It is a sort of assumed ability to score mental runs against intellects both big and small.

To a great extent this must be a matter of conjecture, but why did a man who regarded the business of scoring runs, especially runs for England, as the sole purpose of life, suddenly run away from his power base for thirty Test matches? It must have been that he perceived his continuation in the England side under a captain or captains, he did not respect as a weakness and maybe a threat to the public perception of Geoffrey Boycott. He was unable to tolerate playing under a captain he considered to be inferior to himself. One thing is sure, and that is that Boycott must have gone through considerable mental agony before electing to pull up the anchor on himself in this way.

We have come a long way from his hundredth hundred at Headingley, an innings which epitomized the ruthless determination of Boycott with a cricket bat in his hands. He had re-established himself in Test cricket with a century at Trent Bridge, the first match of his return, and he now wanted to go one better and make his hundredth hundred in a Test match and only an act of God was going to prevent him. I would not be surprised if he considers these runs now as a justification for his abdication as well as being a sharp reminder to the selectors of what they and England had missed by their decision not to make him captain. The 1977 Australian side had undoubtedly been affected by the uproar which had greeted the news that World Series Cricket had been formed in Australia. Boycott knew his chances were good at Headingley.

Another Headingley occasion which I shall never forget happened in 1983 when New Zealand won their first Test match in England at their twenty-ninth attempt. It was also a match in which Richard Hadlee did not take a wicket in either innings. My memory is not of the match itself which was far less noteworthy than the result but of the reaction afterwards of Richard Hadlee's father Walter who had captained New Zealand in England in 1949 and was chairman of the New Zealand Cricket Council. When the game was over I had to go over to the pavilion to interview the captains for BBC radio and Walter was one of those on the players' balcony. The joy on his face was wonderful to see. He had seen New Zealand cricket develop over fifty years as a player and then an administrator, and his feelings at this moment having seen his country put it over England in England was worth the journey. He said to me out of a face of sheer delight, 'You know, I never thought I would live to see this day.' It was so easy to understand how he felt.

The following year the West Indies swept all before them, winning all five Test matches, and at Headingley they required only four days to win by eight wickets. This match was remarkable not for the result but for the fact that Malcolm Marshall, who was then the fastest bowler in the world, took 7–53 in England's second innings and bowled with his left thumb in plaster after it had been broken in two places. In recent years there have been few more dramatic sights than Marshall running in to bowl. That sprinter's run up to the wicket produces a real sense of urgency. Then comes the fast, smooth action and although Marshall is not a tall man who bangs the ball down into the pitch to achieve bounce, he has the ability to make the ball lift almost from a good length and it is this which makes him so dangerous. He was an inspiring sight at Headingley and it was extraordinary that he should have been completely unaffected by the broken thumb. One would have thought that every running stride would have jarred the bone and that soon the pain would have been unbearable, but he got through twenty-six of the most hostile overs anyone could want to see.

In 1987, it was Imran Khan's turn to take Headingley by storm when Pakistan won by an innings. Imran took ten wickets in the match and 7–40 in the second innings and when he took the wicket of Jack Richards he became the eighth bowler to take 300 Test wickets. Imran has always been one of those cricketers who commands attention the moment he walks out onto the field. His patrician bearing is as noticeable as his obvious athletic prowess. There is an easy, relaxed grace about all his movements. He has been a brilliant fast bowler who, at his best, would compare with anyone. He has a strong and irresistible run up and you can almost feel the build-up of power as he approaches the crease to launch himself into a lovely classic action. Born a Pathan, he is a man of great national pride even though he lives for much of the time outside Pakistan and figures high in the social scene of the Western world. If cricket had not been his strength, he would have served Pakistan well in other fields. He is irresistibly good looking and his pursuit of the opposite sex has kept gossip columnists busy for getting on for two decades.

On the field Imran was in every sense a Colossus. He captained his side skilfully and should have captained Pakistan for longer than he has. He is the one leader they have had who has never allowed himself to become involved in the petty power struggles which often seem to be going on in Pakistan cricket. He is perhaps the only captain Pakistan have had who has gained the complete respect of all his players and is able to get the best out of them on the field of play. I have seen a number of outstanding bowling performances by Imran Khan but I do not think that I shall remember any of the others for as long as his performance in this Test match. He bowled at his best. He was fast and accurate and his control was magnificent as he moved the ball both ways, and the England batsmen could make little of him. The one other memory of that match was of the delicious strokeplay of Salim Malik who failed by one run to reach a hundred.

These are my main memories of Headingley. I doubt there will ever be another Test there to compare with 1981, but I have no doubt that this formidable home of cricket will continue to throw up great Test performances and one hopes that it will not be too long before big crowds are once again cheering on a winning Yorkshire side. To end on rather a sombre note, you may have noticed that I have not referred to a Test match at Headingley in 1990. The reason is that because of the doubtful surface and the lack of support in recent years, Headingley has lost the automatic right to a Test every year and in 1990 had to be content with two one-day internationals. It seems sacrilegious that Yorkshire should be deprived of their annual Test match, but just now in a cricketing context they are not a happy county.

4

TRENT BRIDGE:
The Hand of Friendship

Lord's apart, I have the greatest affection for Trent Bridge of all Test match grounds in England. Visually it may not be the most exciting of venues. In fact, one could say that it is in some ways a fairly ramshackle ground where only slowly are the old open stands giving way to greater comfort, although most years now some small addition has been made. The reason I love the ground so much is that I find it the friendliest Test ground of any in the world. I have never *not* enjoyed a Trent Bridge Test Match and even the rain seems more bearable there than anywhere else.

I must come clean straightaway, for being a member of the BBC's Test Match Special team I am in a privileged position, as indeed are the television commentators. For years the committee at Trent Bridge have thrown open their rooms to the broadcasters and for every Test match which is played there we are given the freedom of the committee rooms. From the first cup of coffee an hour before the start to the final glass of wine long after the close of play – and our wives too should they be with us – we are welcomed into the holy of holies. On almost every other ground the committee room is a sort of a sanctuary into which outsiders like us broadcasters are welcome under sufferance, by special invitation. There is a certain formality which is never there at Trent Bridge. The atmosphere of the committee room embraces the entire ground. Unlike some grounds, the gatekeepers appear positively anxious to welcome you and in my experience everyone has a smile. The present chairman, Cliff Gillott, carries on the splendid tradition in the committee room itself where Test selectors, committee men from all round the country, famous players of the past, important visitors from overseas and all other friends of the committee who have been invited, mix happily together in most relaxed surroundings.

Unfortunately, Trent Bridge is these days dominated by a large and most unattractive office block in the far right-hand corner of the ground as you look out from the pavilion. Some years ago that corner of the ground was sold to keep the county club ticking over, and the building that has gone up is far from being an architectural gem. The old stands with the open upper deck still survive at the Radcliffe Road end of the ground although to the left of the sightscreen the old press box has now been converted into hospitality suites. In the other corner at that end of the ground is the new press box stand which has replaced the ancient and most uncomfortable seating which stretched round from the old press box to square-leg where Parr's Tree used to stand. There are more hospitality suites on this side of the ground next door to the lovely old pavilion with its Long Room which positively reeks of cricket history. Then come the president's room recently presided over until his death by Jack Baddiley whose kindness and good humour and chuckling laugh helped to make Trent Bridge what it is today, and the main committee room.

On the other side of the pavilion there is a restaurant in what used to be the Ladies Stand and then more open seating goes round to the scoreboard in front of the office block. For Test matches and one-day internationals the car park of the office block usually houses a temporary stand of hospitality suites which on these big occasions is an important source of income. The radio and television boxes are situated on the top deck of the pavilion and we have a wonderful view of the cricket even if space seems to become more and more cramped each year.

My memories of Trent Bridge go back to 1956 when as a sixteen-year-old I played there for Norfolk against Nottinghamshire Second XI in the Minor Counties Championship but without any great success. The next time I came to Trent Bridge was in 1959 when Cambridge University played Nottinghamshire in a game which I am never likely to forget. Although he had officially retired at the end of the Australian tour of England in 1956, Keith Miller was persuaded by Reg Simpson, then the captain of Nottinghamshire, to turn out against us. Keith came to England each summer and wrote a column for the *Daily Express*. He was a legendary figure, and obviously there was a good deal of publicity given to his appearance. On the Saturday, the first day of the game, there was a goodish crowd which had come to watch him and he did not let them down. In the first innings he made a hundred for which I was in a way responsible, for when he was in the sixties he played a massive pull-drive at our off-spinner Alan Hurd. The ball seemed to go about a mile up in the air and descended exactly where I was standing at wide long-on in front of the Ladies Pavilion. To the great delight and relief of the crowd I dropped the catch. To this day the list of players in *Wisden* who made a hundred for their county on their debut includes K. R. Miller.

In the second innings he contented himself with sixty-odd. As I opened the batting I was lucky enough to face him with the new ball and apart from the fact that he was still pretty sharp, I was completely foxed when he suddenly ran in off about six yards and bowled a quick leg-break. Luckily it was not straight. He did not get me out in either innings although I am not quite certain why not, although it may just have been that the bowler at the other end got me first. When Simpson declared Nottinghamshire's second innings we were left an impossible target and our only hope was to bat through for a draw on the last day. By a great fluke I stayed in for most of the third morning and was not out at lunch, when I found myself sitting next to Keith. I had been scoring very slowly and really had been batting pretty badly and I more or less said to him that it was a pathetic way to bat.

'You want to ask yourself one question,' came the reply. 'Are you better than the bowlers or are the bowlers better than you? You've only just started this game and of course the bowlers are better than you. If they weren't you'd have fifty or sixty on the board. You've done well to stay in.'

I am afraid I did not for much longer but it is a remark I often think of when I am watching a batsman who is just starting in first-class cricket. What may seem a thoroughly boring and unimaginative piece of batting may have rather more to recommend it. When Keith was over in England in 1990 we spent a few minutes during the Lord's Test reliving that game at Trent Bridge and he reminded me of one incident I had forgotten. When play began on probably the last day, he was not out overnight and when the hands of the clock showed five minutes to eleven – the third day began half an hour early at eleven o'clock in those days – Keith hadn't arrived and Reg Simpson was worried. Suddenly the door to our dressing-room which was on the floor below the home side's room, burst open and there was the great man somewhat dishevelled and out of breath. He threw his bag down, borrowed any gear he hadn't got with him from us and just made it to the crease in time for the first ball and with borrowed boots, bat and the lot thrashed us to all parts of the ground before the declaration.

I suppose only twenty-one other people can actually say that they played in Keith Miller's last game of first-class cricket.

Trent Bridge was immortalized long ago by the Gunn family and all those lovely hirsute characters who played for Nottinghamshire in the last century. It was the home too of Harold Larwood and Bill Voce of bodyline fame or, as Larwood would always say if anyone used the word bodyline to his face, 'You mean my leg theory.' It was at Trent Bridge in 1938 that Stan McCabe played his famous innings of 232 against England. During the course of it, his captain, Don Bradman, called all the Australians in the dressing-room out onto the balcony telling them that they would never see the like of it again. The one innings at Trent Bridge I would have given anything to see was Graeme Pollock's 125 for South Africa in 1965 when he became just about the only batsman ever really to destroy that cleverest and most accurate of seam bowlers, Tom Cartwright. In that innings Cartwright had figures of six for 94 and Pollock's superb driving was mostly responsible. In seventy minutes after lunch he made 91 out of 102. I remember listening to snatches of the innings on radio while playing in a Minor Counties match against Buckinghamshire under Bill Edrich, who returned for a few years to captain his native Norfolk when he had finished playing for Middlesex.

The Test I shall remember as long as any that I have seen at Trent Bridge was the third against Australia in 1977, not because it was a particularly dramatic game of cricket, for England won by seven wickets and were always in control, but a lot of interesting things happened. It was Ian Botham's first Test match and on the very first day he stamped his mark on the game by taking the first of his twenty-seven hauls of five wickets or more in a Test innings. He was less successful with the bat making only 25, but there were one or two of those drives to give us a preview of so much of what was to come later.

It also saw the return to England colours of Geoff Boycott from his voluntary thirty-Test exile. When England began their innings late on the first day I have never seen a man more determined to make a hundred and, if need be, to bat for ever in order to do so. In fact, in this match Boycott became only the second player to bat on all five days of a Test match. Of course, it was the perfect comeback for Boycott but it should never have happened for early on he was badly dropped at first slip by Rick McCosker.

It did not take Ian Botham long to get into the action. The

Australian openers had put on 79 on the first morning when Ian Davis mishit a drive against Derek Underwood and Botham with a great surge of triumph threw the ball aloft at mid-on. Then, after lunch he came on to bowl to Greg Chappell who played back and tried to force the ball away through the covers and succeeded only in edging it into his stumps. A little later the two gullies which were obligatory when Doug Walters was batting in England were in place and he shuffled across his stumps to Botham, pushed defensively and was caught by Mike Hendrick, the finer of the two. The score was still 153 when Rod Marsh played half forward to Botham and was lbw to what was an in-swinger to the left-hander. Australia were out shortly before the close on the first day and Botham led the side off for the first time. It had been a remarkable effort.

England began disastrously the next morning. The worst moment came when they had reached 52–2 and the local hero Derek Randall was partnering Boycott and had made 13. Boycott pushed a ball from Jeff Thomson back towards the bowler and set off for a run. With the ball so close to the bowler, Randall was unable to move immediately, but Boycott raced past him and Thomson picked the ball up, lobbed to Rod Marsh with an underarm throw and Randall was run out by yards. Boycott had always been a bad judge of a single but this was an appalling piece of running even by his own standards, and after a moment of stunned silence the crowd got after him in a big way. Typically, he was entirely unmoved by them and continued to grind his way on. When the fifth wicket fell at 82 in mid-afternoon Boycott's score was still only nineteen, but he was now stung into action by probably the best innings that Knott ever played for England. It began with a delicious cover drive off Max Walker and it was now that Boycott should have been caught by McCosker. Knott carried on cutting and square- driving Walker for eleven in one over and now Boycott, whose only other boundary had come from his 115th ball, cover-drove Walker for his second and followed with two more in an over off Pascoe. When Knott turned Thomson off his toes for 4 the 50 stand had come up in only 46 minutes. Knott's batting was a delight and he transformed the game.

When Boycott square-cut Kerry O'Keeffe for 4 it took him to his 50 in 232 minutes; when Knott late-cut O'Keeffe to reach his 50 he had been batting for only 111 minutes and he went on to overtake Boycott who by then had been batting for 171 minutes longer. The batting was as fascinating as it was perverse. The next morning Boycott was again dropped in the slips and it was actually Knott who reached his hundred first, in 202 minutes. Boycott's came two overs later in 378 minutes and when he was eventually caught by McCosker at slip off Thomson he had been batting 419 minutes for his 107 and so he can hardly be said to have let his hair down when he reached three figures. It was an extraordinary innings and although it served England's cause well, it was difficult not to think that it served his own interests pretty well too. If it had not been for Knott's splendid example, Boycott's innings could have ended by being entirely counterproductive to England's needs.

Knott was the most delightfully impish of batsmen who based his batting on his quicksilver wrists and his ability to improvise. He was a lovely late-cutter, he was always using his feet to give himself more room, he loved to come down the wicket to the spinners and played his own brand of sweep when he stayed at home in his crease. To look at, he seemed a frail chap, almost as if a gust of wind might blow him away, but this was far from the case. When towards the end of this innings he cut and drove Thomson for three 4s in an over there was nothing the slightest bit frail about any of the strokes. His darting improvisation made him, for me, one of the most exciting I have watched. He always provided tremendous entertainment.

In the second innings McCosker made a thoroughly workmanlike hundred – with his handsome upright stance he always suggested that he would be a classical strokemaker, but he never quite managed it. The two strokes I remember were both hooks, one for 4 off Bob Willis which brought him to his 50, the other for 6 which took him to 100, but he never quite made up for that dropped slip catch from Boycott. The other excitement in the Australian innings was a brilliant diving catch in his right hand by Tony Greig at third slip which brought Marsh his second 0 of the match as he played forward to Willis.

England needed to score 172 to win and it was settled by a fine opening stand of 154 between Boycott and Brearley who played one of his best innings for England. Just when it looked as if he might get the Test century which always eluded him, he tried to drive Walker through the covers off the back foot and edged the ball into his stumps. Boycott ground remorselessly on and was 80 not out at the end when his partner was once again Randall whom he avoided running out on this occasion. This was England's first win against Australia at Nottingham since 1930.

The following year it took Boycott almost seven hours to score 131 against New Zealand in an innings of great technical efficiency and it was another of those innings which one remembered for the ultimate size rather than the beauty of its component parts. It was quintessential Boycott. The next highest score was made by Clive Radley who had got his chance as an England player the winter before when he joined the England party in Pakistan and New Zealand after Mike Brearley had broken his arm in Karachi. In his second Test match, in Auckland, he had made 158 and played in all six Tests the following summer. Like several distinguished cricketers before him, Radley played Minor Counties cricket for Norfolk before moving to Middlesex. He was an excellent county cricketer who was probably unlikely to play for England but, having got his accidental chance, made the most of it. It makes one wonder how many other good county cricketers over the years would, if given the chance, have succeeded in Test cricket. Radley, fair haired and like a terrier, was no great stylist but he was a busy batsman who pushed his drives without any great backlift, scampered between the wickets and held some splendid catches close to the wicket. He was lucky to get his chance against New Zealand and Pakistan rather than Australia or the West Indies. He was a brave batsman too but his England career was effectively ended later in 1978 at the start of the England tour of Australia. Playing against South Australia in Adelaide he was hit a nasty blow on the head by Rodney Hogg and was never seriously in contention for another England cap. That day at Trent Bridge though, he coped manfully with the young and fast Richard Hadlee on the ground which was to become Hadlee's home for many years after he joined Nottinghamshire. Above all, Radley was a cheerful cricketer and one who I shall remember for this reason while many who have been more successful have not seemed to enjoy themselves so much and have been more easily forgettable.

In 1980, three years after making his first appearance for England on this ground, Ian Botham now captained his country for the first time in a thrilling Test match against the West Indies, who won by two wickets. It was not a match which contained any dramatic individual performances, but it was one of those absorbing games where every ball counted and there was never much between the two sides. The West Indies became a bogey team for Botham and he was unlucky enough to play his first two series as England's captain against them. He had been made captain largely, one heard, through his predecessor, Mike Brearley's advice for he felt that Botham at the age of twenty-four was ready to take on the job. He was perhaps unlucky not to chalk up a victory in his first match as England's captain and one could not help but wonder if Brearley himself might have been able to winkle out those last two batsmen. Botham was never very successful with the bat against the West Indies, but in this match he made his only score of more than fifty in twelve Tests as captain. His eleventh was at Trent Bridge the following year when Kim Hughes's Australian side won another tight, low-scoring match by four wickets. This was the first Test for the young, demure and fair-haired Terry Alderman who took nine wickets in all, looked innocuous enough, but bowling from close to the stumps used his out-swinger with telling effect and went on to take a record 42 wickets in the six-match series.

Modest and unassuming and never indulging in histrionics, Alderman is an unusual Australian cricketer. He simply gets on with the job he does best of all, which is bowling out English batsmen. Few bowlers have hit the pads as frequently as Alderman. In 1989 in England 19 of the 41 batsmen he dismissed were lbw, and yet when he has an appeal turned down he does not stand full of resentment at the decision but walks quickly back to bowl the next ball. Alderman, of course, missed the 1985 tour of England because he had gone to South Africa with Kim Hughes's rebel side and was disqualified for playing for Australia for three years. He also missed a number of Test matches after badly injuring his shoulder in trying to rugger-tackle a streaking spectator who invaded the WACA ground in Perth on the second afternoon of the first Test against England in 1982/3. But over the years Alderman has not changed in any way. There is not the slightest side about his cricket and he has gone on to disprove the theory that he can only take wickets in Perth and England. I am writing this chapter in Brisbane in 1990 the day after Alderman had taken 6–47, the best figures of his career, and Australia had beaten England in three days by ten wickets.

I went to Trent Bridge in 1983 for the opening of that year's World Cup and watched a thrilling day's cricket which ended with Zimbabwe beating Australia most convincingly and in the process showing that if they had more exposure to top-class cricket there is no reason why they should not soon be elevated to Test match status. It was a day which had a most amusing start. I drove up from London in the morning and when I turned off the M1 at the South Nottingham exit where the road, in a mile or so, runs past the Radclyffe-on-Soar power station, there was a queue of about twenty cars stretching back almost to the motorway. As we edged forward up the slope towards the roundabout at the top I saw a policeman was poking his head into every car. My first thought was that someone had escaped from prison and they were checking the cars, and then I remembered the miners' strike which was in full swing, and the Yorkshire miners in particular who were extremely militant especially in regard to the Nottinghamshire miners who would not have any part of the strike. Eventually my car arrived at the top and the young policeman bent down and asked me if I was a miner's picket for apparently a good many had been coming down from Yorkshire to menace the Nottinghamshire miners. I smiled and gave a resounding, 'My dear old thing', and the look of amazement on his face was alone worth the journey. It was a second or two before he remembered to wave me on.

By 1983, Richard Hadlee and Clive Rice had made Trent Bridge their own and Nottinghamshire were winning trophies most years. Hadlee now found that the combined might of England was too much for him to cope with single-handed and New Zealand lost the fourth Test by 165 runs. There was a typically robust hundred from Ian Botham which is always good value for money and then after Hadlee had become the first bowler to take 200 Test wickets for New Zealand, he delayed the end of the match with a marvellous exhibition of straight hitting and when the last man was out he was left eight runs short of his hundred. Hadlee did not know how to play a dull innings and if his bowling had allowed him to concentrate more on his batting he would have ended with a formidable all-round record.

In 1985 against Australia, David Gower played one of those exquisite innings which makes one wonder if any man at any time could have made batting look easier. His bat was all middle, his footwork was quick and daring, the arc of his bat was an object of beauty and his strokeplay was out of this world. It is these innings which make Gower so infinitely infuriating on those days when he goes in to bat, plays a couple of perfect strokes before getting himself out and walking off the ground as if he hasn't a care in the world. On those occasions I could throttle him. On this occasion he made 166 in a high-scoring draw and although Graeme Wood and Greg Ritchie made hundreds for Australia they suffered greatly in comparison with Gower.

The New Zealanders were back in 1986 when, at the tenth attempt, they won their first series in England by dint of their eight-wicket victory at Trent Bridge. Inevitably Richard Hadlee took ten wickets and made a most entertaining contribution of 68 with the bat to round off another prodigious all-round performance. But the real surprise was provided by New Zealand's off-spinner John Bracewell who, batting at number eight, made 110 and drove off the front foot with enormous power and frequency. The English bowling was not good, for little attempt was made to stop Bracewell coming on to the front foot and indeed when the ball was dropped short, it was usually much too short and he went back and dispatched it where he wished either hooking or cutting. The game had a most unusual end for when New Zealand needed one run to win Mike Gatting gave the ball to David Gower who deliberately threw his first ball to Martin Crowe who hit to the boundary. A no-ball was called and it was later decided that the runs scored from it should stand although I cannot see any good reason why they should not have done.

Two years later in 1988 the Trent Bridge match against the West Indies produced unlimited scandal and drama off the field and brought England the unexpected luxury of a draw, for they had lost their last two series to the West Indies by five matches to nil. Brave innings from Graham Gooch and Gower enabled England to avoid defeat after the West Indies had built up a big first innings lead, but by the time that the game ended the cricket was of secondary importance to the scenes which had been acted out over the weekend at the team's hotel.

The story as told to one of the popular papers by a young lady who was employed in the hotel was that Mike Gatting, the England captain, had been much impressed by her physical attributes and all sorts of fun and games had ensued. It was perfect ammunition for the tabloid press and there were thoughts that one paper had planted the girl and that it was therefore a set-up. Perhaps Gatting's greatest crime was that he had not been more careful and that he had been rumbled, but whatever the morals of the story, it undoubtedly brought the England cricket team unwelcome publicity. It was obviously most damaging to Gatting himself, who had managed to keep the captaincy after his public row with the Pakistan umpire, Shakoor Rana, in the middle of the Faisalabad pitch the previous winter. The long and short of it was that Gatting was removed from the captaincy, which brought screams and yells of moral indignation of the 'of course, everyone has been doing this for ever' sort. What may have happened is that those in power had blamed themselves for not taking a firm stand and removing Gatting after the incidents in Pakistan, and therefore found this opportunity a heaven-sent chance to get rid of him. I wonder if Gatting would have been sacked if that on-field squabble in Faisalabad had never taken place. At all events the captaincy now passed to John Emburey for two Tests, Chris Cowdrey for one and Graham Gooch for two and the game and its administrators became something of a public laughing stock.

The 1980s ended at Trent Bridge with an innings defeat by Australia and a record opening stand of 329 between Geoff Marsh and Mark Taylor. England failed to take a wicket on the first day and with the Ashes already lost this was the low spot of a desperate summer for England's cricketers. Robin Smith made a marvellously attacking hundred for England, but once again Alderman caused the problems and took seven wickets in the match. Gower had almost resigned the captaincy after the defeat in the fourth Test at old Trafford but had apparently been persuaded by Ted Dexter to see the summer out. Ironically, it was Gower who produced the one moment of humour in a match which from the English point of view was exceptionally unfunny. With about an hour of the first day left he was fielding at a deepish mid-off and suddenly turned to the England balcony and waved on the twelfth man. At the end of the over Greg Thomas ran out to Gower and they had a long conversation before Thomas went off, his shoulders heaving with laughter. In the commentary box we speculated on what might have happened, but we had to wait until the following day before the truth was known. When Thomas arrived on the field, Gower had told him that he wanted him to go straight up to the press box. He told Thomas that each morning during the series as he lay in bed reading the papers, he had read what he should have done the day before if Australia were to have been bowled for a manageable score rather then letting them get well past 400. 'There is an hour to go today,' he added with a smile, 'and I want you to go and ask those clever buggers what they are going to tell me I should have done in tomorrow's paper. You can then come back and tell me and I can do it now.' It is a splendid story which said a great deal for Gower in that it showed that in spite of the endless defeats and the searching criticism he had received he had not lost his sense of humour.

5

MELBOURNE:
One Hundred Years On

I am constantly amazed at how much of my cricketing life has been conditioned by my earliest contacts with the game. Every time I set out on that delightful walk through the Fitzroy Gardens, past Captain Cook's cottage, to the Melbourne Cricket Ground I am lured on by the attraction of a ground which has seemed huge, dramatic and exciting – a sort of Colosseum of cricket grounds – ever since I was first acquainted with it in 1950–51. I was only eleven but cricket was already an obsession and the only reason I had the faintest idea about the MCG was because I was even then an avid listener to the cricket commentaries on the Ashes series which hissed and crackled their way across the intervening 12,000 miles. They were, without any shadow of doubt, the most exciting broadcasts I have ever listened to. They beat *Dick Barton, Special Agent* into a cocked hat.

When I was away at school, Pauline, the under-matron, kept me up-to-date with the scores and occasionally let me listen to her wireless – no 'radios' in those days. At home during the Christmas holidays I was allowed as a special treat to have a wireless by my bed during the Test matches, and I shall never forget the anticipation of the half past five start in the morning. It was far more exciting than trying to stay awake for Father Christmas. There was the agonizing suspense once the wireless was turned on to see if the chap in the studio was going to be able to make contact with Australia. He told us the latest news from the ground, which on that tour was often pretty desperate for English ears, and then he would hand over to commentators already talking to their Australian audience. There would be several seconds of crackling and hissing which was rather like the sound of distant gunfire. While this was going on one imagined technicians frantically twiddling knobs in Australia as well as England. Then the miracle occurred, the static would die down and, wonderful to relate, the Australian voice of, say, Alan McGilvray would come floating into the dark, cold bedroom. For me, there was a certain magic about the Australian accent for it meant cricket and with all the background interference this really was a pioneering adventure. I wish there was a little of the same snap, crackle and pop about today's broadcasts for it would heighten the perception, but they are so infernally good it is as if the voices were talking to you from just down the road.

I was magnetized to every audible ball while Freddie Brown's gallant side fought hard and honourably but lost the 1950–51 series. I have never doubted for a single moment that they suffered the cruellest of luck in the first Test at Brisbane when it rained after England had bowled out Australia for 228 on the first day. The only blot on my personal horizon in that series, which I have to admit considerably tempered my overall enjoyment, was the unaccountable and incredible loss of form of Denis Compton who was the only true hero I have ever had in my life although I do remember a little later being particularly moved by the not inconsiderable qualities of one Cyd Charisse. Compton had begun the tour with a series of magnificent hundreds against all and sundry in the build-up matches and I was convinced he would continue to plunder the Australian bowling. But when the Tests came round he managed to score only 53 runs in eight innings which included three ducks. At school I had been very public about my support for Compton and I felt I had been deeply let down. To make matters worse my main cricketing comrade-in-arms at school, Edward Lane Fox, enthusiastically followed the progress of Len Hutton who scored a small matter of 533 runs in the series.

I can still feel the tingling excitement of waking up in the pitch dark and groping feverishly for the switch terrified that I might miss a ball of the second Test match in Melbourne which Australia won by 28 runs. The commentators, Alan McGilvray, Johnnie Moyes and Vic Richardson were there and I think that they were joined by Rex Alston and Arthur Gilligan from the BBC. How could one ever forget the thrill as they described Freddie Brown winding himself up and hitting Ian Johnson or was it Jack Iverson for 6. The commentators brought home to one the hugeness of the ground which even in those days must have been more of a sports stadium than a cricket ground. A crowd of more than 50,000 was mind boggling for I thought that life had nothing more to offer than a full house at Lord's which would have numbered less than 30,000. Eleven years later, by which time the reception was much better, I can still hear the excitement from Melbourne as Ted Dexter neared his hundred before being caught at slip off Richie Benaud. The crack of Dexter's cover-drives even penetrated the atmospherics. In between, I remember listening to England's victory by 128 runs in 1954–55 and particularly the description of Godfrey Evans's fantastic diving catch to send back Neil Harvey on the last day from an authentic leg-glance off Frank Tyson. Tyson took 7–27 in Australia's second innings, and again lying in bed on a winter's morning one could feel the pace he was generating on the other side of the world. Thanks to these magnificent commentaries the Melbourne Cricket Ground acted on my youthful imagination as no other ground, and then there were the wonderful mental pictures which with the help of some photographs I built up for myself.

When I first visited the ground in 1968–69, its sheer vastness took my breath away and I saw that in those mental pictures I had badly underestimated. The capacity of the ground had been enlarged for the 1956 Olympic Games and it was able to hold a crowd of 130,000 at the Australian Rules Football Grand Final. Cricket crowds take up more room for they bring with them things to eat and drink and the largest cricket crowd ever to have assembled at the MCG was the 90,800 on one day of the fifth Test against the West Indies in 1960–61, the series which produced the famous Tied Test match at Brisbane. As I write these words, the next stage of development at the MCG is under way and when a third tier has been added to the Southern Stand a crowd of more than 100,000 will be able to watch cricket in comfort, although the additional capacity is being put in to cope with bigger football crowds.

The MCG is curious in one respect in that the members' pavilion and the players' pavilion, although side by side, are two separate entities. The old members' pavilion is a handsome throwback to the last century and has an atmosphere which suggests that one still may be liable to come across butterfly coats and winged collars. I was once refused entry because I was wearing a pair of new jeans. The Long Room, even though ladies are now admitted, is every bit as sepulchral as its counterpart at Lord's. On either side huge stands with goodness knows how many tiers climb towards the heavens and the players' pavilion is situated at the bottom of the stand on the right of the members' pavilion as you look out towards the middle. At the far end of this same stand and on the topmost tier is the huge electronic scoreboard which is Mitsubishi Mark II as opposed to Sydney's Mark I. The vast Southern Stand stretches in a semicircle round that half of the ground. The Southern Stand is known as the Outer, and part of it is the equivalent of the Hill in Sydney. In bay eleven of the Southern Stand the most vociferous elements in the crowd gather to glorify their heroes or to vilify their opponents. Fielding in the deep is not a job for faint-hearted young men and if a fielder drops a catch in the deep in front of a 70,000 crowd, it is quite an experience. The ancient Christians who did battle with the lions in the Colosseum would have been the best qualified to handle it. Even when there is a crowd of perhaps only 4,000 for a state game the MCG is still a remarkable if somewhat eerie spectacle. When it is more than three parts full it defies description and when the Englishmen are being pulverized it is, quite frankly, terrifying.

The MCG can also be one of the coldest grounds in the world although the new stands have made life more bearable on the worst days. The first day's Test cricket I watched there, on Boxing Day in 1968, produced a wind which had touched nothing since it had left the Antarctic. It made for a bitterly cold day and a rather surprising day's cricket. In the old press box, which was draughty on the hottest of days, there were a couple of huge electric fires suspended from the wall and although they both glowed promisingly, the wind blew away the heat before it could make any difference to our discomfort. Gary Sobers's West Indian side had spun the Australians to defeat in the first Test in Brisbane where a tall, lanky, bespectacled and rather unlikely looking young man called Clive Lloyd had hit a spectacular hundred. The West Indians came to the MCG for the second Test full of optimism and will not have been unduly disturbed when Bill Lawry won the toss and put them into bat.

While the West Indians will not have found the temperature to their liking, the Australians will not have relished the prospect of fielding first on such a day. On the other hand Graham McKenzie, that robust fast bowler who had such an unusually amiable character for one of his sort, will have been delighted by the tinge of green on the pitch. While the left-handed Roy Fredericks, playing in his first Test, stood firm at one end, McKenzie ran in with the wind helping him and destroyed the West Indies with a wonderful exhibition of out-swing bowling. McKenzie was a strong man with a lovely fluent run-up and a formidable delivery stride which enabled him to extract any help that was going from the pitch. He was backed up by some splendid close fielding and one felt that some of the older, more experienced West Indians did not relish the fight as they once would have done. Fredericks thwarted the bowlers throughout the first day before McKenzie picked him up the next morning. It was a gutsy innings by Fredericks but, as we were to discover over the next few years, it was wholly out of character with his natural inclinations. The best and most spectacular innings I ever saw Fredericks play was in the second Test of the 1975–76 tour of Australia in Perth when he made 169 off 145 balls hitting one 6 and twenty-seven 4s. That was much more his form than the way he played on his first day's Test cricket.

After that first day the weather warmed up and although Australia were one Test down, Bill Lawry and Ian Chappell took the series by the scruff of the neck in a superb second-wicket stand of 298 to set up an innings victory in three days. The West Indies never recovered from this and went on to lose the series 3–1. Lawry was essentially an obdurate left-hander and one of the few who batted this way round who did not have a touch of elegance. He pushed his drives and was a great nudger and deflector who loved more than anything to occupy the crease, a job he did outstandingly well even if his runs tended to be noticed more by the scoreboard than the spectators. Chappell, like Lawry and Doug Walters, scored a lot of runs in this series and batted very much according to his rather abrasive character. He always sold his wicket dearly and was a great pragmatist at the crease. He drove, he hooked, he pulled and really had all the shots although he never turned them into objects of beauty as his brother Greg was to do. There was always something slightly unsatisfying aesthetically about Ian's batting, although if I wanted a man to bat for my life I would always have chosen him. The best innings I ever saw him play was the 156 he made in the same Test match in Perth that Fredericks scored his 169. In that game Andy Roberts and Michael Holding got it all together for the first time and gave warning that the West Indies were on the verge of becoming the best side in the world.

The next time I walked through the Fitzroy Gardens from the stately old Windsor Hotel to watch a Test match was on Boxing Day in 1974. Jeff Thomson and Dennis Lillee had already destroyed England in Brisbane and Perth; England had suffered injuries and a batting reinforcement had come out in the person of Colin Cowdrey. Denness, the captain, was struggling with his batting form, John

Edrich and Dennis Amiss had both suffered painful blows on the hands and morale that Christmas was not high, but against all odds we were to watch a game of cricket which was as good as anything one could wish to see.

Ian Chappell won the toss and put England in, a decision dictated more by the presence of those two fearsome fast bowlers in his side than any great expectancy from the pitch. When you are two matches up you hold a powerful psychological advantage. It was a slow pitch and Thomson and Lillee got much less out of it than they had in Brisbane or Perth. They picked up four wickets on the first day and Ashley Mallett who was ever present in the Australian side in that series, took two more with his off-breaks. After Amiss had gone, brilliantly caught right-handed by a driving Doug Walters at third slip in the first over of the day, bowled by Lillee, the 76,000 crowd gave Colin Cowdrey a tremendous ovation as he walked his well-padded way to the middle.

For 48 overs he did his best, revealing a splendid technique and moving into the line of everything the fast bowlers gave him. In its way, it was one of the most stirring performances I can remember. He waited and watched and had been in fourteen overs before he indulged himself in the luxury of a beautifully played hook off Max Walker. Ten overs later he square-cut Walker for another 4. Maybe he felt his reflexes were a little too elderly to attempt much more than defence against the fast bowlers, but five overs later he cut Thomson most gloriously to the square-cover boundary. It was slow progress on a pitch on which it was never easy to score runs for the ball did not come on to the bat. Cowdrey's first moment of trouble came when he had reached 25 and a ball from Walker lifted on him, hit his glove and carried to Ross Edwards at forward short-leg who juggled with the ball but could not hold on. He and Edrich brought up the 50 stand in 87 minutes and the Australians must have been frustrated at being held up by what they will have considered to be Dad's Army. It began to look as if Cowdrey might go on to make the big score which so many people were hoping for when he played back to a ball from Thomson which skidded through and had him lbw. He had batted 229 minutes and faced 171 balls and had managed just those three boundaries. For all that, it was one of the truly brave and heroic innings I have been lucky enough to see. Edrich obdurate, determined, unglamorous and chewing gum, was given out caught behind at the same score when Marsh appealed for a leg-side stumping off Mallett, and the innings subsided to 176–7 by the end of the first day and we all walked back past Captain Cook's cottage musing on what might have been.

England finished with 242. After being given a start of 65 by their opening pair Australia were dismissed for 241 with Bob Willis turning in a typically untiring performance which brought him figures of 5–61, his best to date in Test cricket. In an innings which was remarkably similar to the first two, Amiss and Greig were the two principle run scorers in taking England to 244 in their second innings. This time Cowdrey scored just eight before edging Lillee off the back foot and being well caught one- handed high to his left by Greg Chappell. On the last day Australia needed 246 to win and at the end thanks to the bowling of Fred Titmus and Tony Greig they had to be content with 238–8. It has always been said that some of the best Test matches have ended in draws and this was one of them. It was also a remarkable comeback by the Englishmen although the placid MCG pitch suited their cause much better than either of the other two.

This was a six-test series and England were back at the MCG for the final encounter. They won by an innings and four runs, but it was not the shock result which it may at first sight appear to be. During the fifth Test in Adelaide both teams had gone up to Yalumba for the rest day which was for many years the tradition in the Adelaide Test. During the afternoon Jeff Thomson had taken to the tennis court and succeeded in badly damaging his right shoulder which ruled him out of the rest of that game and the sixth Test match too. Australia won the toss at the MCG but splendid bowling by Peter Lever who took 6–38 bowled them out on the first day for 152. Joy was less than unconfined when, in the first over of the England first innings, Amiss played back to Lillee and was palpably lbw. But after bowling his sixth over of the innings the next morning Lillee pulled up with a leg injury and left the ground, and therein lies the story of the match and indeed of the series. It would have been nice if it had been Cowdrey who made the runs, but it was Denness who made 188, the highest score ever made by an England captain in Australia, and Keith Fletcher who contributed 146 and England were all out for 529. It was all slightly unreal, though, for without Thomson and Lillee it was really only a token attack although Walker strove manfully for his eight wickets. It was as clear a demonstration as you could hope for of the difference between the two sides. Australia had also won the rubber and so it was hardly surprisingly if after these two blows their main players did not summon up the effort they might have done earlier. One nice touch was the sign strung over the boundary railings: 'MCG fans thank Colin – 6 tours'.

In 1975–76, Thomson and Lillee were back at their best when the West Indies came to the MCG with the series nicely poised at 1–1. The inexperienced West Indian batsmen who were later to cause such havoc round the world had no answer to them. Watching these two bowlers in full flow was one of the most exciting spectacles I have ever seen on a cricket field and they seemed even more dramatic than the West Indian fast bowlers of the next decade. I cannot believe there has ever been a better fast bowler than Lillee, while the primeval power which Thomson put into his bowling was awe-inspiring. It was sad for the occasion that Thomson was not fit to take his place in the Australian side when England came on to Australia from India and Sri Lanka the following year for the Centenary Test to celebrate the first-ever game of Test cricket which had been played at the MCG in 1877 starting on 15 March. This match began on 12 March and set the pattern for a great many Centenary or Jubilee Test matches over the next decade and it is greatly to the credit of the authorities in Melbourne that this first celebration has remained the best of them all.

Every living cricketer who had played in a Test between the two countries in Australia was invited to Melbourne and for ten days, wherever you went it was like walking through the pages of a dusty old *Wisden*. One could only feel that the gods were prepared to smile on the occasion for we had as good a Test match as anyone could have dared hope for, and at the end of five days' cut and thrust Australia won by 45 runs – exactly their margin of victory in that first Test match a hundred years before. The occasion was graced by the visit of the Queen and the Duke of Edinburgh. The teams were presented to them during the tea interval on the last day when Dennis Lillee, ever the larrikin, produced a pen and paper from underneath his sweater and asked the Queen for her autograph. The Queen does not sign autographs but I believe Lillee later received a signed letter.

Tony Greig won the toss and he put Australia in to bat on a pitch which held enough moisture to gladden the eye of the seam bowlers. After seven overs Bob Willis and John Lever had reduced Australia to 23–3. Ian Davis was lbw playing half forward, Rick McCosker hooked and top edged the ball into his face and it fell on the stumps, and Gary Cosier hooked and was caught off the top edge. The considerable contingent of English supporters could scarcely believe their eyes and it got better and better, to the dismay of the rest of the 61,000 crowd. After a few flailing left-handed strokes, David Hookes went back to a good bouncer from Chris Old at which he had to play and was easily caught by Greig at second slip. Only six more runs had been scored when Doug Walters cut wildly at Willis and Greig held the skyed catch running back from second slip. Greg Chappell was batting with great composure and now with Marsh adding a thumping blow or two of his own they put on 51 for the sixth wicket in the only stand of note before Marsh cut at Old and Alan Knott held a brilliant catch off the under edge, changing direction with great skill as the ball flew from outside the off stump down the leg-side. Chappell was ninth out bowled middle stump swinging across the line at Underwood and Australia were all out for 138. There was still time before the close for Lillee to have Bob Woolmer caught at first slip as he aimed to drive and England were 29–1 at the end.

England's joy was short lived, for the following day Lillee, living up to the occasion, produced one of the great spells of his career, taking six wickets in all. He was well backed up by Max Walker who had the other four. With another vast crowd, of 62,000, chanting 'Lilleeeee, Lilleeeee, Lilleeeee' as he ran up to bowl, he was a glorious sight with that lovely controlled run-up bursting like a firework into one of the most perfect actions the game can have known. His rhythm was wonderful, his control extraordinary and he moved the ball both ways: in the first over of the second day Mike Brearley could not avoid a lifter; in the second over Walker accounted for the nightwatchman, Derek Underwood. That made it 34–3 and at 40 two more wickets fell. Amiss drove at Walker without any footwork and was caught in the gully and Derek Randall got an edge playing back to another short one from Lillee. England had lost four wickets for eleven runs in 51 balls that morning.

Tony Greig now played a couple of heroic off-drives but Walker brought the ball back and bowled him between bat and pad trying a third. The noise which greeted this wicket was extraordinary and it was as if the whole ground had gone mad and I daresay most Australians had, with glee. On the other hand English faces were decidedly glum as they saw the apparent advantage of the first day being thrown away, although even the most partisan must have realized they were seeing a truly great piece of fast bowling. Marsh then caught Fletcher quite brilliantly, diving far to his right when the batsman pushed forward to a wide one from Walker. When Old tried to draw away from Lillee he was too slow and was caught behind. Knott offered sterling resistance but was lbw trying to turn Lillee to leg, and Lever was Lillee's sixth victim as he waved at one outside the off stump.

After all this everyone in the ground was feeling limp and still there was time for Australia to lose Kerry O'Keeffe who was promoted to open as a result of McCosker's injury, Greg Chappell who was bowled through the gate by a beauty which Old brought back into him, and Cosier before Ian Davis and Doug Walters took Australia to 104–3 by the close. Walters had been dropped in the gully by Old when he was 16 to the great dismay of the English, for this was clearly a match where any and every dropped catch was going to be potentially decisive. The third day was much the most uneventful of the five. The pitch had dried and was playing more easily and Australia went solidly about the job of consolidating their position. Davis and Walters both got into the sixties and the only real excitement came from a brief and much publicized flurry of strokes from the left-handed Hookes. Suddenly, Underwood, of all people, dropped short and was pulled for two 4s, and then Hookes faced Tony Greig. First, he drove him over mid-off for 4, he swept the next ball to the square-leg boundary, cover-drove the one after that with a stroke of great beauty and then pull-drove the next ball wide of mid-on for his fourth successive 4. Perhaps the one major problem that Hookes has had in his career has been trying to live up to that moment. He was a brilliantly talented batsman who never allowed himself to make the most of what he had; a great pity, for I can think of few more entertaining batsmen when he was going well. He reached 50 but was then out to a brilliant diving left-handed catch by Keith Fletcher at square short-leg.

While all this was going on Marsh had been contributing handsomely in his own slightly foreshortened left-handed way. He was a most uncomplicated striker of the ball and his driving was a joy. He received good support for a while from both Gary Gilmour and Dennis Lillee and was only 5 runs short of becoming the first Australian wicket-keeper to make a hundred in a Test match against England when play ended that day with Australia 430 runs ahead at 387–8. At the fall of the eighth wicket Rick McCosker had come in with his broken jaw strapped, and with great bravery and no little skill had scored 17 by the close and had already put on 34 invaluable runs with Marsh for the ninth wicket. Marsh reached his hundred the next

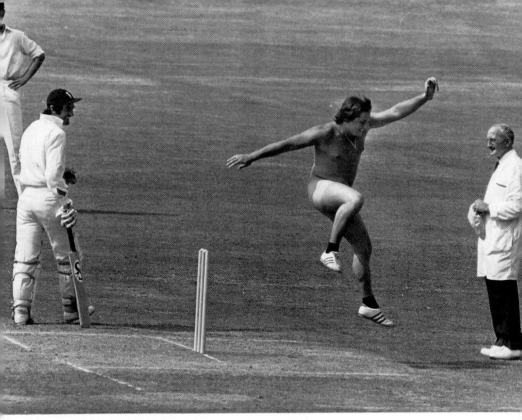

ABOVE: *The first of an extraordinarily tiresome species. Alan Turner, hands on hips, Alan Knott and umpire Tom Spencer find Test cricket's first streaker, the Marylebone merchant seaman, an object of amusing curiosity at Lord's in 1975*

LEFT: *The bank clerk at war. David Steele's well known impersonation of a Centurion Tank, this time on behalf of Derbyshire, whom he served briefly after a long career with Northamptonshire*

RIGHT: *More a royal command than a request. This is the invitation the author received from the patrons of the Hill at the Sydney Cricket Ground*

BELOW RIGHT: *A half-miracle achieved. Ian Botham, bent on self-preservation, eludes the fans when he returned to the pavilion with 145 not out on the fourth evening at Headingley in 1981*

BELOW: *The home of the White Rose. But nowadays crowds like this only turn up to watch England. The trees to the left of the pavilion have all sadly succumbed to Dutch elm disease*

A king comes home. Geoffrey Boycott acknowledges the applause on reaching his 100th first-class hundred against Australia at Headingley in 1977 after his self-imposed exile from Test cricket

Jubilation personified. Bob Taylor hangs on to the edge from Geoff Lawson off the bowling of Bob Willis at Headingley in 1981. Australia are 75/8. Taylor and Ian Botham go into their own dance routine

OPPOSITE TOP LEFT: *The guru and his pupil.*
'What about bringing long on in to short extra?'
Or is it the other way round, as Mike Brearley
and Ian Botham discuss field changes at Headingley
in 1981

OPPOSITE TOP RIGHT: *A master in repose. Geoffrey*
Boycott in India contemplating a new world record
or maybe a month or two with the rebels in South
Africa

OPPOSITE BELOW: *Calm, dignified and friendly.*
The pavilion at Trent Bridge as Australia destroy
England for the fourth time in 1989

LEFT: *Fast bowler and playboy. The training*
session captures the feline grace, the irresistible
determination, the good looks and the golden halter
of Imran Khan

BELOW: *No, not giant Catherine Wheels. Two of*
the floodlights in full bloom, the electronic
scoreboard and a huge crowd for a day/night match
at the Melbourne Cricket Ground

RIGHT: *Two of a kind! Derek Randall (on the left) and a curious and sympathetic kangaroo. Their paths crossed in Adelaide in 1982*

BELOW LEFT: *The most perfect setting of all. Test cricket's most famous seagulls in the shadow of its most famous cathedral as the sun continues to shine at the Adelaide Oval*

BELOW RIGHT: *Perhaps the greatest action of them all. Dennis Lillee, showman and never a saint, in full flight as he approaches the stumps. Has any fast bowler ever been a more inspiring sight?*

LEFT: *Biggles and Algy on the Gold Coast. David Gower (left) and John Morris embark upon their much publicised Tiger Moth escapade during England's game with Queensland on the Gold Coast in 1990/91*

BELOW LEFT: *It's easy if you know how. Rodney Marsh shows off his latest conjuring trick with mild disbelief*

BELOW RIGHT: *A study in concentration. Cricket's newest Knight, Sir Richard Hadlee, watches intently and applauds a deserving colleague*

ABOVE LEFT: *The very essence of West Indian cricket. This square cut by Gary Sobers sums up the spirit of the Caribbean and the incredible flair of the man himself.*

ABOVE RIGHT: *No, not a movie or a Graham Greene novel. Viv Richards and Allan Lamb trying to look relaxed at Sabina Park, 1989/90*

RIGHT: *'BOAC' dates this photograph. Colin Cowdrey, with bat, shepherds his illustrious flock up the steps at the start of their journey to the Caribbean in 1967/68*

morning and after McCosker had swung Old to mid-wicket, Greg Chappell declared with Australia 462 runs ahead at 419–9 and the scene was set for the final innings. I don't think many people gave England much of a chance to score more runs than had ever been made in the fourth innings to win a Test match, but at least the pitch was now playing more easily than at any time in the match.

But England made an anxious start and Woolmer played and missed twice in Lillee's first over. There was a cheerful air of resignation among those who had been hoping that England might win and the hope was that the side would not disgrace itself in this final innings. The festivities over the previous few days had been so splendid that most people were in a nicely comatose condition. England's score moved along slowly to 28 before Woolmer played half forward to Walker and was lbw when the ball came back into him. The siege was relieved when Gilmour's first three overs after lunch cost 23 runs with Derek Randall, who was as jumpy as ever and doing nothing for one's nerves, and Mike Brearley playing some good strokes. When O'Keeffe came on to bowl his leg-breaks Randall produced a glorious cover-drive and he and Brearley had put on 50 in 51 minutes with some highly entertaining batting. Randall was now batting better than I had ever seen him and Brearley too was playing one of his better innings for England although at this level he never looked the epitome of permanency.

There was something marvellously cheeky about the way Randall went for his strokes, and when he hooked Lillee for 4 in the first over of his second spell it gave one the pang of pleasure one normally gets from an excellent dry martini. There was an anxious moment later in the same over when he cut and O'Keeffe failed to hang onto a hard chance to his right in the gully. At this point Brearley walked down the pitch in scholarly fashion and had a word with Randall, whose response was to square-cut Lillee over gully's head for another 4. The stroke prompted a return visit by Brearley. Randall's 50 arrived in 116 minutes with a nudged single off O'Keeffe who was then pulled for 4 by Brearley, and at tea England were 113–1. The interval did the trick for Australia for Brearley played a half-cock stroke at Lillee's fourth ball afterwards which nipped back and had him lbw. Our hearts were in our mouths as Dennis Amiss turned his first ball uppishly past square short-leg for 2. In Lillee's next over they were back there again as he steered a short one through Hookes's hands at third slip for 4. It took Amiss a while to settle down and then he began to play pretty well while Randall kept hitting the ball beautifully at the other end. There was a gorgeous cover-drive off Walker and a couple more hooks against Lillee, one of which went square for 4 and the other in bizarre fashion past mid-off for 2, and these two had put on 50 in 69 minutes. When bad light stopped play for the day a quarter of an hour early England were 191–2 and still breathing in a happily militant manner. Randall had batted for more than three and a half hours for 87 and Amiss had managed 34 in just over an hour and a half.

Although the odds were still overwhelmingly in Australia's favour there was a healthy degree of anticipation round the MCG on the final morning and the Poms had certainly not let the occasion down. Lillee, all fire and brimstone, bowled the first over of the day, but nothing much happened until Randall swept O'Keeffe fine for 4 in the day's third over. Later in that same over he survived an appeal for a catch off bat and pad at forward short-leg and promptly square-cut for 3. In the following over he late-cut Lillee in the air for 4 and then turned him to leg for the single which brought him to his hundred which was rapturously applauded. Randall was batting better than anyone knew he could, and he was always the most entertaining of players whatever he was doing. He is a naturally funny man and even his walk brings a smile. I don't think he was particularly amused when he aimed to hook Lillee, checked his stroke and was hit on the head and the ball flew back to Lillee who appealed loudly for a catch.

When Amiss, who was giving that comforting impression of solidity, flicked O'Keeffe off his pads for 4, England were 216–2 and it began to seem possible that they might actually win. By now, everyone was sitting a little further forward in their seats and for a change I detected a fair amount of Australian anxiety. Amiss's 50 came next and the first hour's play which produced 47 runs from thirteen overs – a scandalously low over rate – ended with Randall hooking Greg Chappell for 4. Two overs later Lillee took the second new ball. He ran in as furiously as I can ever remember and his very first ball drew Randall forward and beat him outside the off stump and there was a loud appeal for a catch behind which was turned down. Lillee immediately threw a tantrum and volleys of words were exchanged between him and Randall. On these occasions with his moustache bristling Lillee always looked marvellously bad-tempered and the histrionics which followed were extremely tiresome but of course the crowd of more than 30,000 loved every second of it. Randall seemed fairly relaxed, and relieved whatever his feelings may have been by cover-driving Walker in the next over. When he repeated the stroke, which he plays with a feline grace, two overs later an all-run 4 ensued and the 250 was up. By now, everyone hoped or feared according to their allegiance that history was in the making. When the players went in to lunch after eleven overs had been bowled with the second new ball, 76 runs had come in the morning session and England were 267–2 needing another 197 to win, Randall having made 129 and Amiss 63.

There was another splendid joust between Randall and Lillee in the second over of the afternoon and it was won hands down by Randall. First, he drove Lillee in the air through extra-cover for 4 and Lillee behaved as if he had never been so badly done by in his life. He was then square-cut for 2 and when he retaliated with a bouncer he was brilliantly hooked for 4. But in the third over after lunch Amiss played back to a ball from Greg Chappell which kept horribly low and bowled him. Once he had committed himself to the back foot he had no chance, for the ball scarcely left the ground. This wicket was greeted with the sort of applause which suggested that a war had been won – which in a way I suppose it had. Amiss had batted nearly four hours for his 64 and had put on 166 with Randall. It had been an outstanding innings and really given England a chance of winning the match.

Randall was as cheerfully undeterred as ever and in the next over drove Lillee through the covers for 4 off the back foot. He played the next ball off his legs and was dropped by Cosier to his left at forward square-leg and Lillee was most definitely not amused. It was a catch which Cosier should have held. In Lillee's next over a pushed cover-drive brought Randall to 150, but, at the other end, Keith Fletcher was in all sorts of trouble which immediately took one's mind back to the 1974–75 tour when he was given such a torrid time by Thomson and Lillee. Lillee also made no secret of the fact that he did not like Fletcher and when later he was asked if there was a personality clash between the two of them, he replied that Fletcher had no personality, which was not only insulting but quite untrue for Keith Fletcher is one of the nicest people one could wish to meet. Lillee's answer spoke more of his own personality than Fletcher's. However in the same over that Randall reached his 150, Fletcher pushed defensively at Lillee and Marsh held a straightforward catch. This brought in Tony Greig who was always ready to take Lillee on as he had done in the first Test at Brisbane in 1974–75 when he made 110 in one of the most courageous innings I have ever watched and which I have compared with Dexter's 70 against the West Indies at Lord's in 1963. Greig promptly drove Lillee through extra cover for 4 and will not have had the worst of the verbal exchanges that followed.

The 300 came soon afterwards and the scene was set for a wonderful end to a fabulous occasion. One thing you have to allow Lillee is that he never gives up, but he now received a fearful hammering from Randall, who played two handsome drives through the covers off the back foot. Fourteen came from the over. There was a dreadful moment for England when Greig called Randall for a single off Chappell, sent him back and Randall collided with the bowler who threw the ball at the stumps and missed. The comparative figures of Lillee and Chappell since lunch were interesting. In four overs Lillee had taken 1–41 while Chappell had taken 0–7 in five. When Walker took over from Lillee, Greig drove him past cover-point for 4. In the next over Randall played forward to Chappell, got an edge, appeared to be caught low down by Marsh and was given out. Randall, who was 161, started to walk to the pavilion when Marsh realized that the ball had not carried to him and called Randall back. It was a wonderful gesture especially coming at such a crucial stage for it might well have meant that Randall would go on to win the match for England. No one was a fairer player than Marsh and I am afraid that a number of other players on both sides would have been only too happy to see a batsman depart in similar circumstances. It was at the MCG in 1980–81 that Marsh was the one player on the Australian side to register obvious disgust when Greg Chappell instructed his brother Trevor to bowl an underarm grub to Brian McKechnie when New Zealand needed six runs to tie a one-day international off the very last ball.

Randall celebrated his recall by cover-driving both Chappell and Walker for 4s and runs were coming too fast for Australia's liking. Chappell now took himself off after taking 1–13 in ten overs since lunch and turned to Kerry O'Keeffe's leg-breaks. In his first over Randall played forward and Cosier diving to his left at forward short-leg held a fine catch. The noise that greeted Randall's dismissal almost brought the pavilion down and I have never seen eleven such relieved cricketers as the Australians were now. The triumphant Australian applause turned to a less frenetic but almost equally resounding congratulatory appreciation for Randall as he made his way into the pavilion. He had batted for 448 minutes facing 354 balls and hitting twenty-one 4s in one of the most memorable innings ever to have been played in contests between England and Australia. Almost single-handedly he had turned a contest which looked as if it might have had a boringly one-sided end into one of the great games of cricket. It was appropriate that this should have been done by such a rich character, but sadly Randall never played so well again. His main problem was perhaps the inability to concentrate for long periods and there was also a looseness about his play which gave bowlers plenty of hope. It cannot have helped him either that he was always on the move back and across his stumps as the bowler launched into his delivery stride, for it meant that his head was not still at the moment of delivery. Randall was one of the game's great enigmas, but no one can ever take away from him what he did for English and Australian cricket on those two days at the MCG. What a pity it was that he could not go on doing it.

England now needed 117 in 130 minutes. They had a lucky escape when Alan Knott who had taken Randall's place pushed forward to O'Keeffe and was dropped by Greg Chappell at silly-point, and in the same over he swept a full toss impishly for 4. At tea, England were 354–5 and immediately play restarted Greig glanced O'Keeffe fine for 4 and square-cut him for another, but later in the same over O'Keeffe had the last word when Greig plunged forward and was caught at second attempt by Cosier at forward short-leg; 369–6 and 95 more wanted. Knott now took up the attack, hoicking Lillee wide of mid-on for 4 and then with a lovely delicate touch late-cutting him for another. But Chris Old did not stay for long and was seventh out at 380 slashing at Lillee and being caught at first slip. By now it was obvious that England were going to be beaten, but it was of little account as it had been such a glorious match. Knott carried on the fight, but he soon lost John Lever who pushed myopically forward to O'Keeffe's googly and was lbw. It was now an all-Kent partnership of Knott and Derek Underwood which produced 25 runs in five overs and had just begun once more to give England real cause for hope when Underwood was yorked by Lillee, and 7 runs later it all ended when Knott was lbw trying to turn Lillee to leg. As a final word on a quite remarkable game of cricket I can only say that the pleasure of being there and seeing it far outweighed any worries about the result. It was one of those rare games where the result did not matter.

The Centenary Test was an impossible act to beat, but in the following years I was lucky enough to watch any amount of exciting and dramatic cricket at the MCG. At the start of 1979 Rodney Hogg with his crimpy fair hair, his deadpan, almost sullen appearance and his long run up, took 10–66 in the only match which Graham Yallop's side managed to win in that series. These ten wickets took Hogg's tally in his first three Test matches to 27. The following year when England were again back at the MCG they also lost but to a stronger Australian side for the players who had joined World Series Cricket had by then returned. The Australians were kept waiting until the fifth day only because of a thrilling and magnificent hundred from Ian Botham. He took them from 92–6 when they were still 79 behind, to 273 which meant Australia had to score 103 to win. There were many Australians who did not know what all the fuss was about with Botham. They had a fair idea after this.

In December 1980 Doug Walters was allowed to make his fifteenth, and last, Test hundred because one of the umpires, Ray Bailhache, who sometimes seemed to relish controversy, called a no-ball after Australia's last man, Jim Higgs, had been caught behind the wicket off a bouncer from New Zealand's Lance Cairns on the grounds of intimidation although it was the first bouncer he had received. Walters was 77 at the time and the last wicket pair then took their partnership to 60. The match was drawn on a pitch which, in typical Melbourne fashion, had a desperately uneven and low bounce. Australia were back at the MCG five weeks later for a Test against India which they lost by 59 runs after they had been left to score only 143 to win. Kapil Dev, who had pulled a muscle in his thigh, and left-arm spinner Dilip Doshi, with a broken bone in his foot, were the main executioners. Another reason this match will be remembered is for Sunil Gavaskar's reaction when he was given out lbw in India's second innings. He was so angry with the decision that he ordered his partner, Chet Chauhan, to leave the field with him. The manager, S. K. Durrani, met the batsmen at the gate leading off the field and instructed Chauhan to return to the middle where the umpires must have been considering awarding the game to Australia with India apparently forfeiting the match.

At the end of 1981 Pakistan beat Australia for the first time by an innings, in a match which brought more complaints about the wicket and also included an all-run 7. Majid Khan square-cut Lillee almost to the boundary and the batsmen ran 4 before Bruce Yardley who caught Dirk Wellham's throw, hurled the ball at the stumps and gave away three overthrows. With two touring sides in the country Australia played the West Indies at the MCG in a Test which began eleven days after they had been beaten by Pakistan. Australia won the match by 58 runs thanks largely to another command performance by Dennis Lillee. On Boxing Day evening Lillee produced an amazing four-over spell after Faoud Bacchus had been caught at fourth slip in Terry Alderman's first over. With the crowd baying at his back Lillee had Desmond Haynes caught at second slip as he drove in his second over. Colin Croft, the nightwatchman, immediately shuffled across his stumps and was lbw and in the last over of the day Viv Richards drove at Lillee and played the ball into his stumps. The West Indies were 10–4 and it was all very reminiscent of the Centenary Test match. The next afternoon at five minutes to three, Lary Gomes played back to Lillee and was caught by Greg Chappell at first slip and this gave Lillee his 310th Test wicket thereby beating Lance Gibbs's record. Lillee took ten wickets in the match.

The Englishmen were back at the MCG on Boxing Day in 1982 for a most exciting game in which both sides were out twice and the four totals were all within eleven runs of each other. England made 284 and 294, Australia 287 and 288. Needing 292 to win, Australia lost 9 wickets for 218 before Jeff Thomson joined Allan Border. Bob Willis, captaining England, decided that he would set the field deep for Border and allow him a single any time he wished so that he could attack Thomson, but this plan came very close to failing for Thomson batted pretty well and Border still managed to find some gaps in the field. When the fourth day's play ended Australia were 255–9 and on the fifth morning Willis continued to use the same tactics and Border and Thomson inched their way towards victory. Thomson had played a couple of maiden overs from Norman Cowans most capably and when 4 were needed to win Botham was bowling to Thomson from the Southern end. The tension was unbearable and it really did look as if England had thrown the game away. Botham's first ball was short and Thomson played back and edged it at waist height to Chris Tavaré's right at second slip. He got both hands to it but could not hold on and the ball jumped out, but Geoff Miller at first slip was already moving behind Tavaré and the ball flew straight to him and England had won by three runs.

There were no complaints with the pitch in 1983–84 when Pakistan were involved in a high-scoring draw with Mohsin Khan playing well for 152 and Graham Yallop going on to reach 268 in 716 minutes which had the rather gruesome merit of being the seventh longest innings ever played in first-class cricket.

There was a double century the following year from Viv Richards which contained its usual number of wonderful strokes and a hundred by Andrew Hilditch which saved the match for Australia and was a most impressive exercise in concentration. This match produced one most unhappy incident. On the fourth day which was Boxing Day – Christmas Day was the rest day – Geoff Lawson appealed most belligerently for lbw against Gordon Greenidge in the first over of the West Indies second innings. The umpire Steve Randell gave him not out and Lawson's dissent was embarrassing to watch. When he eventually decided to get on with the over, he took off his sleeveless sweater but refused to give it to Randell and Border who was fielding at mid-off had to take it to the umpire. At the end of the over Lawson refused to take either his cap or his sweater from Randall who called over Border who had to carry them to Lawson at fine-leg. It was a ghastly performance by Lawson who was fined A$500 by the ACB and put on a good behaviour bond of A$1,500.

A thunderstorm which burst over the MCG during the tea interval prevented India from beating Australia in December 1985. India were 59–2 needing another 67. A marvellous knock of 163 by Border had kept Australia alive in their second innings; even so, their ninth wicket fell at 231 when they were only 48 ahead before Dave Gilbert and he added 77 for the last wicket which were in the end decisive runs. In the first innings Gilbert had stayed in for 49 minutes which allowed Greg Matthews the 41 he needed to complete a hundred. The Boxing Day Test match in 1986 was exciting only if you were an Englishman. Australia's batting collapsed pathetically in each innings and after Chris Broad had scored his third hundred of the series England won by an innings and Mike Gatting became only the fourth England captain after Percy Chapman, Len Hutton and Mike Brearley successfully to defend the Ashes in Australia.

The New Zealanders who played at the MCG the following year will all insist to their dying day that the ball in the penultimate over of the match from Danny Morrison which cut back and hit Craig McDermott just above the knee would have knocked his middle stump out of the ground. Umpire Dick French did not agree, however, and the match which was extremely hard fought but seldom had us right on the edge of our seats was drawn. The following year there was the element of excitement which the West Indies fast bowlers bring to cricket, but the batting was for the most part laboured as the West Indies won massively. The eighties ended at the

MCG with some rather dubious umpiring which sent the Pakistanis to defeat just when it looked as if they might win the first of their three Test matches.

One of my favourite commentary box stories comes from the MCG. For the 1983–84 season, Radio 3AW in Melbourne covered all the games at the MCG and their principal commentator was Harry Beitzel who had made a great name for himself on Melbourne radio. Australian Rules Football was his main game and one which he understood far better than cricket. Brian White, the general manager of 3AW, had asked Harry to come up with a different method of commentating on cricket, to try to break the traditional mould which may have begun to seem a trifle boring. Harry decided that most casual listeners were bamboozled by the traditional field placings, such as long-leg, extra-cover and silly mid-off or wherever, and did not have the faintest idea of what they meant. He decided to call the game in relation to the face of the clock. Accordingly, a cover-drive became a drive through half past two, a straight drive went to twelve o'clock and a hook would often end up at half past seven. Needless to say, it became inordinately complicated because it was far from being an exact science and I would have thought that the listeners would have had considerably less idea of what was going on than in the good old days when they dealt with good old extra-covers, although I doubt if Harry would agree.

During one game at the MCG, Harry described at some length an off-drive which ended up as a brilliant catch at half past twelve. He then had a bit of an argument with himself as to whether it was really half past twelve or whether it might just have been a quarter to one and I think he agreed with himself that 12.45 won the day. Having sorted this out he handed back to the studio for the news bulletin. The announcer in the studio thanked Harry for his graphic description of the catch at a quarter to one and then told his listeners that he was about to read the deep fine-leg news.

Cricket at the MCG has not often been dull and it is a ground which I am sure will continue to produce both incidents and excitement. Over the years I have found that it has most certainly lived up to the reputation it brought with it over the airwaves all those years ago. I shall never tire of that walk past Captain Cook's cottage. I am finishing this chapter on a day when after lunch I shall make the journey once again to see Australia play New Zealand and also to see the huge gap where the Southern Stand used to be. It has been pulled down prior to being rebuilt.

6

ADELAIDE:
Close to the Cathedral

I would hate to miss the Adelaide Test match more than any other. If there is a prettier Test ground in the world I have yet to see it. As a social occasion it even manages to upstage Lord's and I shall go to my grave remembering the sumptuous picnics on the lawns behind the main stand. The crayfish and the prawns are washed down with the most delicious white wine from the Barossa Valley, the girls grow steadily more beautiful and so does the ground itself. The new Bradman Stand at the River end is an architectural masterpiece which blends in so well with the rest of the ground, that it might have been there for ever. The only people ever to suffer heartbreak at the Adelaide Oval are the bowlers. The pitch is easy-paced and full of runs and, at Test match time, there always seems to be a hot sun burning down from a cloudless sky. The traditional Test match in Adelaide always used to be held over the long weekend at the end of January which incorporates the Australia Day public holiday on the Monday. In recent years the Test has been moved to accommodate the heavy programme of one-day internationals which has become such a feature of the Australian season. This has not been popular with the locals who have found it more difficult to leave their farms or whatever in December. The Australian Cricket Board has, as a result, rethought its fixture planning and for the 1990–91 Ashes series the Adelaide Test was restored to its rightful place and the one–day matches were played earlier in the season.

The cathedral with its twin spires sticking up behind the scoreboard and the rich foliage of the Moreton Bay fig trees in the left-hand corner of the ground as you look out from the main stand makes the Adelaide Oval what it is. The view from the George Giffen Stand looking across the ground is magic. The wrought iron Victor Richardson

Gates are directly across on the other side, and then stretching into the distance is the lush green parkland and the Botanical Gardens. In the far distance stand the foothills of the Mount Lofty Ranges. It is a view which has never changed and yet each time I see it there always seems to be something that I have not seen before. The long, low members' stand with the players' dressing-rooms at the back has the most delightfully discreet terracotta coloured roof which is matched by the roof of the Bradman Stand and there is nothing anywhere that offends the eye.

The other two grounds with views which compare with Adelaide are Newlands in Capetown which stands, ringed with oaks, in the shadow of Table Mountain, and Queen's Park Oval in Port of Spain looking out from the pavilion to Trinidad's North-Eastern range of mountains. Queen's Park is at its best when the flamboyant trees are flowering in the hills, but neither is in such a tranquil setting as the Adelaide Oval. One of the joys of the Adelaide Test is the walk down from the city past the Festival Theatre and the grass slope which goes down to the river Torrens. The road bridge takes one over a river which has been made by man rather than nature. One turns left over the bridge and a short walk through more parkland and past the statues of Keith and Ross Smith, the South Australian brothers who were the first people to fly from England to Australia, brings one to the Memorial Drive tennis courts where many Davis Cup battles have taken place and to the entrance to the Oval at the back of the Bradman Stand.

Before the Bradman Stand was built the press used to sit in the main stand just below the players' rooms, which may not have been the ideal place from which to watch cricket for it was square with the wicket, but it gave one a great sense of involvement. While the main broadcasting boxes were perched on stilts of scaffolding on the grass mounds at each end of the ground, the box which belonged to one of the local commercial radio stations in Adelaide, Radio 5DN, was right at the back of the main stand and this was presided over by the former South Australian cricketer, Ken Cunningham or KG as he was always known. For some years 5DN co-opted my services for the Test match and we had an awful lot of fun producing a programme which was certainly different and, I hope, entertaining for the Adelaide audience. One year we had to sit at a table in the stand rather than in the box and we were joined by Derek Nimmo and for some reason which was probably to do with the rights 5DN had bought from the Australian Cricket Board, we were allowed to talk about anything except the cricket in that we were not allowed actually to commentate on what was happening. I doubt any of it made much sense but Derek was, as always, brilliantly funny and I only hope the audience appreciated him. KG, who each day ran a two-hour sports programme in the early evening, was a law unto himself. He was and still is a fierce Australian and South Australian patriot and whenever things were going badly he always managed to inject a ray or two of piercing hope into his listeners' minds. I remember he was never particularly sympathetic to an umpire who gave an Australian out and if a South Australian was given the finger he almost choked with righteous indignation. KG was a physical fitness freak and on occasions when he felt the commentary was in safe hands or when we were off the air, he would disappear for a five-mile run. There was one splendid occasion when he returned from his run to find that the score had not changed. In the fullness of time 5DN bought an FM licence and dropped all sport and after presiding over the breakfast show with, I am sure, the same frenetic enthusiasm he brought to his cricket commentary, KG moved stations.

The first Test match I saw in Adelaide was the fourth against West Indies in January 1969 which turned out to be the highest-scoring Test match ever played in Australia with the two sides amassing 1,764 runs. It was also one of the most exciting Tests I have been lucky enough to see, and when the last ball had been bowled Australia were 21 runs short of victory while the West Indies needed just one more wicket. Australia's tenth wicket pair of Paul Sheahan and Alan Connolly hung on for the last 26 balls of which 16 were bowled by Charlie Griffith and Gary Sobers with the second new ball. The first day saw a brilliant hundred from Sobers but apart from him the West Indies batted badly and were out for 276. When Sobers was at his best it was difficult to imagine that it was possible to bat much better. He had such lovely footwork, supple wrists, a glorious high backlift and an innate sense of timing, and his bat always gave off that delicious mellow noise which suggested it was all middle and no edge. There has never been a more joyful stroke played than Sobers's flowing off-drive.

The Australian batsmen then made their West Indian counterparts pay for their carelessness and with Doug Walters making an entertaining hundred and almost everyone else making a contribution, they reached 533 and a lead of 257. When the West Indies went in again their batsmen appeared to be in an entirely different frame of mind. This time it was Basil Butcher who played the principal innings and was the only one to reach three figures but four others passed 50 and everyone except Lance Gibbs, the last man, made a few. They reached 616 which left the Australians 360 to win. They set off at a great pace and for a long time it looked as if they would score the runs. Lawry, Stackpole, Ian Chappell and Walters all passed 50 and the bowling was reduced to tatters. Australia went past 200 for the loss of only two wickets and at 215 there occurred one of those unhappy incidents which in the best regulated circles would never happen. The Australians were up against the clock and were doing their best to steal every run they could. Ian Chappell was facing Griffith who was bowling from the River end and Ian Redpath was the non-striker and when backing up he had in his enthusiasm been guilty of leaving his crease before the bowler had let go of the ball. Griffith was obviously aware of this and when he now ran in to bowl he did not deliver the ball but broke the wicket and appealed with Redpath stranded a yard and a half up the pitch. The time-honoured behaviour in these circumstances is for the bowler to hold the ball against the stumps the first time and to warn the batsman that if he continues to do this he will be run out. Griffith had given Redpath no such warning and the umpire, Lou Rowan, had no alternative but to give Redpath out. He was out according to the letter but not the spirit of the law. It was an incident which caused a great outcry and probably cost Australia the match for their batsmen now lost their way. There were three more run-outs and at the end Australia were 339–9.

The next day all the Australian papers strongly condemned Griffith's action with the exception of two former Test cricketers, Bill O'Reilly and Keith Miller, both of whom wrote that Redpath was trying to gain an unfair advantage and that it was right that he should pay the penalty. This incident happened on the last day but when Jack Fingleton, whose pithy remarks were no less a feature of the Australian press box than Bill O'Reilly's, next bumped into O'Reilly he strongly chided him for his defence of Griffith adding, 'You'd never have done a thing like that yourself in a million years, Tiger.'

'When I was bowling I never met a batsmen that keen to get up the other end,' was the response. And there was no answer to that.

When I was back in Adelaide in 1974–75 Thomson and Lillee continued to bludgeon the life out of the English batsmen after Denness had put Australia in to bat, which is seldom the wisest course of action in Adelaide as another England captain, Bob Willis, was to discover eight years later. Superb bowling by Derek Underwood brought him the first seven wickets to fall in Australia's first innings and he finished with eleven in the match. England were asked to score 405 in the fourth innings and even though Australia were without Thomson who had injured his shoulder playing tennis on the rest day, they found that the combination of Lillee and Max Walker was almost as unpleasant.

On the rest day of the Adelaide Test match, both teams and their friends and the press corps and many others were invariably invited by Windy and Helen Hill Smith to spend the day at the Yalumba Winery. It was one of the great days of any tour of Australia and was always most eagerly awaited. The weather was more than kind for I can only remember it when it was scorching hot. The food was delicious to say nothing of the wine and we were able to go round the winery, play tennis or swim or simply sit and drink ourselves into the corner which rather too many people did. Windy himself played cricket for Western Australia and South Australia and was a man of great good cheer. He loved having people around him and he told incessant stories of the past most of which ended in a lovely throaty chuckle. If you were very lucky, which I once was, you were asked after lunch to go and join him in his den and I have seldom passed such an entertaining afternoon anywhere in the world. It was probably just as well that I had drunk enough to have had no chance of remembering any of some splendidly slanderous stories.

One of the sad side-effects of the new regime when World Series Cricket and the Australian Cricket Board came together was that Test matches in Australia no longer contained rest days. A reason for this may have been that it added considerably to the cost of Channel Nine's television coverage if the crews and cameras had to be fed, watered and maintained on a blank day. I have no doubt that the charm of a Test series in Australia suffered when rest days were done away with. There is still an occasional day off when England tour Australia, for the Test and County Cricket Board always try to have them reinstated but with only partial success, and there has not been a rest day in Adelaide for many years now. Windy Hill Smith sadly died in 1990 taking a massive chunk of unwritten Australian history with him, but Rob, his older son who now runs the winery would, I am sure, continue this brilliant day should the opportunity ever again arise. Australian seasons which sometimes include six Test matches as well as fifteen one-day internationals can develop into a treadmill after the New Year and it is days out like this which make it all rather easier. I feel that by cancelling rest days the Australian authorities are planning their seasons according to the letter rather than the spirit of the game. It was playing tennis at Yalumba that Thomson injured his shoulder so maybe their argument is that their cricket is healthier without rest days.

When the West Indies came to Adelaide the following year they were 3–1 down in the series and their young players had been unable to rediscover the form which had enabled them to trounce Australia in the second Test in Perth, and Australia won a fairly uneventful game with some ease. The only significant piece of cricket was the century by Viv Richards in the West Indies second innings. Richards had not had at all a happy series and before coming to Adelaide the West Indies had played a three-day game against Tasmania in Hobart. Clive Lloyd had arranged for Richards to open the batting in that game and he made a fast hundred and acquired some confidence. When the side came to Adelaide Lloyd sent him in first with Roy Fredericks and in the second innings when the West Indies were set to score an impossible target of nearly 500, Richards hit his second hundred in Test cricket. Although the result was a foregone conclusion, it was an innings that contained all the magnificent strokes which were to become the hallmark of any innings by Richards. He again opened the innings in the sixth Test and made 50 and 98, but when he returned home he batted at number three in the first Test against India in Barbados and made 142. It was the hundred in Adelaide which put him back on course.

I visited Adelaide early in 1978 to see the last four days of the fifth Test against India. Both sides had won two matches each and we had a most exciting finale. These four days came in the middle of the most intensive few months' cricket watching I have ever experienced. I set out from England in November to watch the start of World Series Cricket in Melbourne before flying to Pakistan to cover the short England tour. Then, it was on to Perth for a couple days of World Series Cricket at the Gloucester Park trotting track on the other side of the road from the WACA ground, to Adelaide to watch Bobby Simpson's Australian side for these four days before rejoining the Englishmen who had already begun their tour of New Zealand. When that ended I flew back to London and straight on to the West Indies again to watch the non-WSC Australian side.

My first memory of that trip to Adelaide was of the flashing wrists and bat of Gundappa Viswanath who was always the most delightful

101

player to watch. With WSC in competition with the official series there were one or two strange names in the Australian side and one highly romantic one. The ACB had decided that as their best players had almost all gone across to WSC, they would ask Bobby Simpson who had last played for Australia ten years before in January 1968 and was now almost forty-two to captain the side. He was superbly fit and still playing Grade cricket in Sydney for Western Suburbs and was happy to accept the challenge. He had made 176 in the second Test in Perth and had made another hundred over the first two days in Adelaide when he helped take Australia to 505. In spite of Viswanath's innings of 89, India were then bowled out for 269 and it looked as if the series would peter out into a dull ending.

Simpson did not enforce the follow-on, he himself made another neat fifty picking up most of his runs from nudges and deflections in his usual style. He hit only one 4, a fierce pull off Prasanna which brought him to his fifty after nearly three hours at the crease. No one worked harder for his runs than Simpson. Australia were bowled out for 256 in their second innings which meant that India had to score 493 to win which was more than had ever been made in the fourth innings to win a Test match. For a long time it looked as if they might pull it off, too. All the batsmen made runs although none stayed on to play the big innings which they so badly needed. Australia were seriously handicapped when Jeff Thomson pulled a hamstring muscle during his fourth over in India's first innings and was unable to bowl again.

Because the series had still not been decided, this final Test was, according to the rules then operating, played over six days to try and ensure a decision. Such good progress was made that when India began their second innings fourteen hours of the match remained and time was, therefore, not a problem for them. Both the Indian openers, Gavaskar and Chauhan, played careless strokes on the fourth evening, but the next day Viswanath and Mohinder Amarnath batted extremely well and India passed 200 with only two wickets down and Australia's bowling resources were made to seem slender in the extreme. These two batted through the morning session and made a good start after lunch taking the score to 210 when, for no very good reason, Viswanath drove a trifle airily at Wayne Clark who was not the most frightening of seam bowlers, and was beautifully caught by Simpson low at first slip falling away to his right. Vengsarkar now took up the running and played some of those glorious cover-drives, but at 256 Amarnath was caught at deep square-leg sweeping at Bruce

Yardley. This pattern continued to the end of the match just after lunch on the sixth day. Two batsmen would settle in and India would look as if they were in with more than a chance of victory when suddenly a careless stroke cost a wicket. To be realistic, I suppose their chances went when, at 348, Vengsarkar was sixth out driving an off-break from Yardley to long-on. In the end, India were out for 445 which was the second highest fourth innings total ever made in a Test match. It was appropriate that Simpson should have taken the final wicket when he had Chandrasekhar caught behind for it was his forty-second birthday.

When England came to Adelaide early in 1979, the first day of an undistinguished Test match nearly saw the death of one of the Australian openers, when Rick Darling, who came from Adelaide, was hit over the heart by a lifter from Willis in the first over. He collapsed unconscious and only quick thinking by umpire Max O'Connell and John Emburey saved him for he had to be given the kiss of life. He was carried off still unconscious but was able to continue his innings the next day. England won the match by 205 runs and the only real excitement was whether Bob Taylor would score a hundred, but in the end he was caught behind off Rodney Hogg when he had reached 97.

I shall never forget in 1979/80 the furious assault which Viv Richards launched on the Australian bowlers before lunch on the opening day of the first Test in Adelaide not to include a rest day. He hit Lillee, Dymock and Pascoe for 76 runs off 68 balls and I have seldom seen a cricket ball hit harder. There were thirteen 4s from a selection of drives, hooks and square-cuts played with an almost arrogant disdain after the West Indies had been put in to bat by Greg Chappell. They won the match by 408 runs and with it their first-ever rubber in Australia.

The 1980s have left me with an extraordinary kaleidoscope of memories from the Adelaide Oval and most of them concern massive scores both individually and collectively, but there was a strange low-scoring one-day match played there between Pakistan and the West Indies in 1981. One-day cricket has made almost no appearances in these pages for the simple reason that I am unable to remember one-day matches in the way that Test matches come back to me. This particular game was an obvious exception. Clive Lloyd put Pakistan in to bat and with only Zaheer Abbas – what a marvellous player he was – and Sarfraz Nawaz making much sense with the bat, they were bowled out for 140 at which point it looked like a spectacular non-contest. But soon the West Indian batsmen were having problems. Gordon Greenidge chopped Sarfraz into his stumps, Richards, almost certainly thinking that it was all too easy, was caught behind trying to glance the same bowler and when Haynes was caught behind pulling at a fairly gentle offering from Tahir Naqqash the West Indies had lost three wickets for 38 before Lloyd and Bacchus began a solid partnership which took the score to 85. When Lloyd was dropped at mid-on by Javed Miandad off Tahir it looked as if any chance Pakistan had of beating the West Indies had gone. Two runs later, at 85, however, Lloyd swept at Ejaz Faqih and was brilliantly caught by Tahir at square-leg. It was now that Miandad who was captaining Pakistan made an inspired decision and brought on Wasim Raja to bowl his leg-breaks. Immediately Dujon played back and all round one and was bowled which made the score 88–5. With Marshall taking two 4s through mid-wicket in the same over against Ejaz, the West Indies will still have felt they were going to win. In his fourth over however Wasim Raja gave one a little more air than usual and Bacchus came down the pitch to drive, was beaten in the air and bowled. When later in the over Deryck Murray was lbw on the back foot, the West Indies were 107–7 and Wasim had taken 3–8 in four overs. At 120, Marshall became his fourth victim when he also played back and was bowled off his pads. Imran now came back and quickly disposed of Roberts and Holding and Pakistan had achieved a most unlikely and exciting victory by 8 runs. Because Australia were not playing there was only a small crowd to enjoy this extraordinary game.

One incident at the Adelaide Oval I shall not forget was the splendid sportsmanship of Jeff Crowe who captained New Zealand there in December 1987 on a featherbed of a pitch which produced a mountain of runs. Andrew Jones and Martin Crowe made hundreds for New Zealand and Allan Border then made his first double century for Australia. Just before tea on the third day, Border who had made 66, on-drove a ball from Dipak Patel and Crowe appeared to make a brilliant diving catch at mid-wicket, rolling over in the process. Border was satisfied that he was out and set off the pavilion but Crowe realized that he had not taken the catch cleanly and promptly called him back. It was a fine gesture, for Crowe was the only person on the field who could have known that he had not held the catch.

The 1982–83 season produced two rather weird, not to say macabre, games against England. The third Test match was played in

Adelaide beginning on 10 December which was a long way from that weekend at the end of January, although three one-day games were to be played then. Putting the opposition in to bat at the Adelaide Oval can be one of the most unrewarding courses of action as we have seen when Mike Denness went this way in 1974–75. This time Bob Willis was in charge and he too put Australia in and paid the penalty. It was discovered afterwards that this had been the result of a consensus decision, which implied that the entire group of tour selectors were utterly barmy. I am not sure whether this piece of information was produced as an excuse for what happened or merely as an explanation. Without ever being in the slightest difficulty, Australia compiled 265–3 on the first day with Greg Chappell making an inevitable century in his usual neat and composed way. His cover-driving that day was as good as any I have seen. He was entirely relaxed, he saw the ball with so much time to spare and it was almost as if he was giving coaching lessons, for he demonstrated the entire art of batsmanship. If there was one criticism it was that he got himself out, as he sometimes did, soon after reaching his hundred. This time it was to a brilliant diving left-handed catch in the gully by David Gower off the persevering and perspiring Willis. As it happened, it did not matter that he did not go on and score the double century which was there for the taking, for a score of 438 was more than enough for Australia's needs. England were bowled out most ignominiously for 216 and although a delightful hundred by David Gower enabled them to avoid an innings defeat, Australia had to make only 83 to win and the game was over before lunch on the last day. So much for consensus decisions.

It was no happier for England when they returned to Adelaide at the end of January for a one-day match against New Zealand. This time Willis decided to bat when he won the toss and the first half of the day could hardly have gone better for England even if Chris Tavaré did spend twenty overs making 16. Happily, Ian Botham had gone in first with him and was in thunderous form. Only two fielders are allowed on the boundary for the first fifteen overs of these games and Botham took full advantage of this. Sixteen runs came in one over from Martin Snedden and Euan Chatfield was destroyed in similar fashion. When in the sixteenth over of the innings Botham was bowled having another swing at Chatfield, he had made 65 from 51 balls with four 6s and seven 4s and had scored his runs out of only 75. It was one of the most dramatic displays of hitting I can remember. After that, David Gower made a hundred too gracefully for words. Trevor Jesty, who had joined the tour as a reinforcement, and Derek Randall made useful contributions and England amassed a score of 296–5 which should effectively have decided the contest.

The New Zealanders lost a couple of early wickets including Glenn Turner whose style of play was never much suited by the needs of one-day cricket; one got the impression that he played it only reluctantly. John Wright and Martin Crowe now built up an impressive momentum and New Zealand reached 100 in the 23rd over. Wright was run-out which let in Lance Cairns, one of the biggest hitters of a cricket ball that the game has known. He made 49 now and his runs, which included four massive 6s, came in eight overs. When he and Crowe were both out with the score 166 Jeremy Coney and Richard Hadlee managed to maintain this dizzy rate of progress against some very ordinary England bowling, and amazingly New Zealand won by four wickets with seven balls to spare. In 100 overs 593 runs had been scored and I doubt there will ever be a much more entertaining day's cricket. I don't know whether Willis attributed this defeat to collective captaincy, but it was, to say the least, clumsy to lose a fifty-over match after making 296 runs. It is a curious coincidence with the huge amount of one-day cricket that is now played, that the two best games I can remember were both played out in the shadow of Adelaide's cathedral.

Adelaide Test matches have seldom failed to produce huge scores and over the years I have seen a great many centuries scored on the ground. Any hundred from Clive Lloyd was an enjoyable experience even if his 121 in 1979–80 was eclipsed by Viv Richard's extraordinary hitting which I have mentioned earlier in the chapter. The following year the unhappy, enigmatic Kim Hughes made 213 against India and because he raised such strong feelings in people his batting ability may not have been appreciated as it should have been. In 1979–80, he had succeeded Graham Yallop to the captaincy of the non-World Series Cricket Australian side and had captained them on the tour of India. The disagreements between World Series Cricket and the Australian Cricket Board were then sorted out and WSC players were again available to play for Australia. Hughes was never a favourite with these World Series players and it is fair to assume that if he had been, he would have been asked to join WSC. Now, he was as it were the champion of the Establishment side although the captaincy went back to Greg Chappell. Chappell remained in charge in Australia but he grew less inclined to go on tour and Hughes then took over as he did for the tour of England in 1981 although Chappell reassumed command the following season in Australia, and so on.

This did not make life easy for Hughes who had become captain by default and by no means all of those playing under him had a great respect for him. When Chappell finally retired from the captaincy before the 1983–84 season in Australia, Rod Marsh was the popular choice to succeed him, but it was Hughes who was given the job and he can only have been an uneasy figure in the dressing-room throughout the home series against Pakistan at the end of which Chappell, Lillee and Marsh retired, which may have made him feel better. But it left Australia a much weaker side and they now had an unhappy tour of the West Indies, not that Hughes's side was alone in that. At the start of the next season in Australia when the West Indies were again their opponents, Hughes was under a great deal of pressure and many influential people wanted him to be removed from the captaincy. The West Indies won the first two Test matches by big margins and Hughes did not help himself by failing with the bat. After the defeat at Brisbane in the second Test, he tearfully resigned from the captaincy at a press conference immediately after the match.

There was something of the little-boy-lost about Hughes with his fair hair and boyish appearance. His main problem was perhaps that he wanted the Australian captaincy for the wrong reasons, for reasons of personal aggrandisement rather than simply the determination to put his side first and to help them win cricket matches, which is all his successor Allan Border ever wanted to do. But there was no doubt that Hughes was a most capable and attractive batsman.

Border was another who hated to waste the flat Adelaide pitch and he made a most resolute hundred against the West Indian fast bowlers, and Michael Holding in particular, in 1981–82. Holding was perhaps the best fast bowler of all to watch for he had that marvellous, almost liquid run-up and he ran in such a way as to suggest that his feet never really touched the grass. He took eight wickets in that match, in which Larry Gomes made the first of two excellent hundreds at Adelaide. In 1983–84, six hundreds of varying quality were made when Pakistan were the visitors. Kepler Wessels, at times an unconscionably boring batsman, made a relentless 179 while Border and Hughes provided better entertainment. Mohsin Khan, Qasim Omar and Javed Miandad then replied in kind for Pakistan in what was a tedious game of cricket.

The bowlers found the going more helpful the following year and Geoff Lawson took eleven wickets and Malcolm Marshall ten in a match which the West Indies, as usual away from Sydney, won easily. In 1985–86 Sunil Gavaskar carried his bat right through India's first innings. This was the stage of his career when he was looking to go for his strokes more and it was a glorious innings although he was overshadowed at the start by Srikkanth's 51. David Boon and Greg Ritchie, a good cricketer but whose character did not always allow him to rest easily in the Australian dressing-room made hundreds for Australia. The pugnacious Boon with his bristling moustache is always good value to watch and he was one of four batsmen to make hundreds the following year when the Englishmen were back. Border kept him company, and Chris Broad made the second of his three hundreds in the series and Gatting collected his only one. Border went one better with his first double century the following year, but in a perverse way arguably the most memorable hundred in the decade was one of the slowest. Gordon Greenidge had toured Australia five times and had never scored a hundred there in a Test match. When he came out to bat in the West Indies second innings it was his 32nd Test innings in Australia and in all probability his last. He had never come to terms with the extra bounce on Australian pitches and now it was grim determination which he showed rather than his customary flashing strokeplay, although when given the chance he played a few of those exhilarating square-cuts. He fought on and on and to his tremendous delight reached that elusive hundred just before the match ended in a draw. It was a game in which the West Indies equalled their own most unenviable world record by bowling no less than forty no-balls in Australia's first innings. It was also a match in which Australia had rather the better of things with Dean Jones showing that his best batting talents were not, as many felt, exclusively for exhibition in one-day matches. He batted beautifully for his 216 and his driving was a joy. Although they had beaten the West Indies in the freak spinning conditions at Sydney, this game in Adelaide confirmed a renaissance in Australian cricket which culminated later in the year with their 4–0 Ashes victory in England.

The Adelaide Test match will remain a mixture of runs, wine, picnics and sunshine. It is an occasion not to be missed and if the occasional run glut becomes too tedious there are so many other enjoyable diversions. Even the Adelaide seagulls are entertaining.

7

PORT OF SPAIN:
It Only Needs Ten Balls . . .

My first major tour as a cricket writer was to the West Indies with
Colin Cowdrey's England side in 1967–68 and I soon discovered that
the Caribbean was the most fascinating and irresistible part of the
cricketing firmament. In recent years, the powerful phalanx of West
Indian fast bowlers has turned tours to that part of the world into
unrelenting hard labour for batsmen, but for all that, the game in the
West Indies has a flavour and romance which I have never found
elsewhere. It has always surprised me that the West Indian temper-
ament should have grasped cricket as it has for I would have thought
that a faster-moving, body contact sport would have had more appeal.
Yet the West Indians bring a vibrancy and excitement to the game at
whatever level it is played which you don't find anywhere else.

   The cricketing West Indies is comprised of a string of islands as well
as Guyana at the top of the South American mainland and the main
occupation of most of them is to grow sugar cane, attract tourists, sing
calypsos and play cricket. The major industrial island, which successfully combines all four and indeed is the home of calypso is Trinidad.
It is not a holiday island in the sense of Barbados – that distinction is
left to its near neighbour, Tobago which is a part of Trinidad – but I
have always found Port of Spain the most exciting city in the West
Indies. After the recent political turmoil it is nowadays rather run
down but I don't think anything could ever dampen the spirits of a
race which for two days before the start of Lent is able to produce the
fun and excitement of Trinidad's Carnival when the entire island goes
on the most enormous musical bender. Carnival's origins go back to
the days of slavery when at this time each year the slaves dressed
themselves up to look like their masters for two days of celebration
before the austere regime of Lent began. Special calypsos were

composed for each year's festival and nowadays the bands and their supporters parade unceasingly through the streets with the entire population swaying to the rhythm as they dance the Jump-Up, which is the calypso dance. Trinidad's Carnival is second only to Rio's and even then not by much. Understandably Test matches and Carnival would not mix and so I have never been in Port of Spain for Carnival itself but preparations go on for a long time beforehand and I have enjoyed these on several occasions, visiting the calypso tents where the principal calypsonians sing their new songs each night in the build-up. When I first went to Port of Spain, The Mighty Sparrow and Lord Kitchener were the two great calypsonians and rivalry between them was intense.

The importance of cricket to the West Indies in general and Trinidad in particular will never be better explained than it was in C. L. R. James's book, *Beyond a Boundary*. Queen's Park Oval, the home of the island's cricket, is a lovely ground and also much the biggest in the West Indies. Gradually, the open terracing and the small covered stands are being replaced by more modern constructions although there is still the open seating down one side of the ground where the banter of the crowd is as entertaining as it ever was. I think the character of West Indian grounds would change if everyone was given individual plastic seats. The bubbling humour which comes from the packed popular side of the ground might then become too sanitized. West Indian crowds like to express their feelings without any inhibition and at other times groups will want to sing calypsos. I cannot see them doing that in plastic seats, and the atmosphere would be poorer without it.

That first tour of the West Indies remains the best Test series I have ever watched, and this is not distance lending enchantment. Four of the five Tests were dramatically exciting and at the end of it, against all odds, the Englishmen had won 1–0. The first and fourth matches were played at Queen's Park Oval and the first was the best of the ten I have watched on that ground. In 1963 under Frank Worrell and three years later under Gary Sobers the West Indies had won series in England. The batting with Sobers, Kanhai, Hunte, Nurse and Butcher was formidable, the fast bowling of Hall, Griffith and Sobers was devastating while the spin bowling of Gibbs and Sobers (the latter with orthodox and unorthodox left-arm spin) was as good as any in the world. England were apprehensive as they arrived in the Carribean. The captain had a certain guarded optimism, but three hard months lay ahead. Cowdrey himself was back in the job he had for long coveted but never held before other than as a caretaker. Even now he had been given the job by default, for Brian Close had captained England through a successful summer in England before being involved at Edgbaston in a game between Warwickshire and Yorkshire in which, in order to save the match, he had indulged in some reprehensible time wasting tactics which cost him the job. It was as a journalist that he now made the trip.

I have described the first Test match of this series at great length in *Cricket in Three Moods* and therefore I intend to skim only briefly over the details, most of which remain as clear to me as they were the day after it finished. I was deeply impressed by the whole paraphernalia of a Test match in the West Indies and I shall never forget the gripping excitement of arriving at Queen's Park Oval on the first morning. A crowd of 25,000 was in position long before the start. The players practised on the outfield, cheered, identified and watched eagerly by a crowd which was hungry for cricket and the success which West Indian crowds had grown to expect. The noise was tremendous and already the peanut sellers in their scarlet coats and hats were doing good business and Coca-Cola was flowing tinged, I have little doubt, with liberal doses of Fernandez rum; the Carribean is not given over to temperance. When Sobers and Cowdrey walked out to toss they were clapped every inch of the way. The crowd held its breath while Sobers spun the coin which glinted momentarily in the sun as it fell to earth. The captains bent down. Cowdrey had guessed right and decided to bat, they shook hands and the crowd, perhaps mildly peeved that Sobers did not get it right, quickly drew in its breath before continuing the burble of noise which is ever-present at a full West Indian Test ground.

England batted well, better than we had dared hope. Edrich and Boycott gave us a good start before Cowdrey and Barrington, who indulged in his favourite party trick of reaching a personal landmark, this time his 50, with a 6, took England to 244-2 at the close. Twenty minutes before the end Wes Hall took the second new ball when ninety overs had been bowled. It is a long time now since the West Indies have bowled their overs at this rate, but then it is a long time since they have had three spinners in the side, Gibbs, Holford and Sobers. The proceedings throughout the first day were watched from the open terracing by a gentleman who was dressed in a grey morning suit, a top hat and an elaborate watch chain with small silver shields hung from it.

The second day saw Tom Graveney play the most beautiful innings I have ever seen. He was now well into his 'late' period as an England player and was batting better than he had ever done. He always had a penchant for West Indian bowling and somehow one sensed something was up when he emerged from the pavilion after Cowdrey had been caught behind in the first over. He announced himself with as lovely a straight drive as one could wish to see and while Barrington ducked and weaved at the other end, Graveney stood up and dismissed the bowlers to all parts of the ground. He hooked Hall and Griffith off the front foot, he shook his bat in anger at Griffith when he retaliated with a beamer. His touch against the spinners was magic and he repeatedly drove Gibbs through the covers with the finesse and the footwork which Rudolf Nureyev once brought to *Swan Lake*.

Barrington distracted us only once when he drove Gibbs for 6 over long-on to reach his hundred, allowed himself a slight smile, and continued chewing. A straight drive off Griffith took Graveney to *his* hundred and when he was bowled trying to drive Gibbs off the back foot one sensed that one might never see the like of it again. He hit twenty 4s in his 118 and I can see each one of them still. England batted into the third day and were finally dismissed for 568. Three West Indians were out for 195 that night and by the end Kanhai was at his best and a very tall, rather gawky looking young left-hander who batted in glasses and was in a high class as a gum chewer had made us all look up when he drove Titmus over mid-off for 6. His name was Clive Lloyd. He reached a fine hundred the next day but wickets fell too often at the other end for the crowd's comfort and the West Indies were all out just before tea for 363, Jeff Jones having taken the last three wickets, including that of Lloyd, for six runs in four overs. They had failed to save the follow-on by five runs. During the tea interval the heavens opened and probably saved the match for them.

The last day was thrillingly tense as the West Indies made a good start and then began to lose wickets, and when suddenly Kanhai and Lloyd were out in mid-afternoon within three runs of each other, England had a chance of victory. Shortly before tea with the score 180 David Brown in perhaps his best spell in Test cricket took three wickets. Butcher shuffled across his stumps to one which nipped back and had him lbw. In the same over Murray played back, the ball kept low and he too was gone lbw. Griffith stretched forward to the first ball of his next over, it was outside the leg stump but it hit his toe and went into the stumps. The crowd were silenced, which is not something that often happens in the West Indies, and with the new ball to come soon after the interval an England victory seemed assured, but Sobers was still in. He was joined by Wes Hall who kept pushing his left leg far down the pitch to everything. The new ball was survived, the innings defeat saved and suddenly the game was safe. While this stand was going on a group of spectators to the right of the press box gathered behind the fence and gave their own rendering of Calypso Rose's hit of that year, 'Fire in Your Wire'. It was not the least memorable part of a match in which, for me, the spectators and the players had been equally entertaining.

For England, it was so near and yet so far, and one wondered if they would ever get such a good chance again. Yet the West Indies had clearly reached the stage where advancing years were taking their toll. Wes Hall, all sweat and gold chain, was no longer terrifying, Graveney could hook Charlie Griffith with impunity off the front foot and now the great West Indian batsmen actually got themselves out. Even the crowd had shifted uneasily in its seats.

There is nothing sadder in cricket than watching once great players find that they can no longer do it. Suddenly they have to struggle like ordinary mortals, and this was what was happening to Sobers's side.

We were back at Queen's Park Oval in the middle of March after three drawn Tests. Again there was a huge crowd to watch the toss. Sobers spun the coin, it fell on the pitch and rolled towards the other end. Playfully Cowdrey bent down and beckoned it on. It stopped and fell and Cowdrey won't have liked what he saw. Sobers batted and to the hysterical delight of the usual vast and colourful crowds, the West Indies made 526–7 declared with Kanhai reaching 153. In the 1960s the rest of the West Indian side walked in the shadow of Gary Sobers who was probably the most versatile cricketer of all time. Yet there was a time when Kanhai was an even better batsman than Sobers and never received the credit he should have done. He was not quite the same easy-going, good-natured chap as Sobers but he had an awesome ability with the bat. He was a small man and it was extraordinary how he was able to find the power he put into his strokes. In one respect he would have suffered in any comparison with Sobers in that he was a right-hander while Sobers was lucky to be a left-hander who by some quirk of nature have been endowed with a greater degree of natural elegance. But Kanhai's driving and cutting, his footwork and his wrists, his judgement of length and his ability to drive the ball off the back foot which is rare in so short a man set him apart from everyone else. Then, of course, there was that famous sweep which ended with Kanhai flat on his back in the crease and the ball smashing into the fence. That stroke was really his trademark. In his innings I remember thinking that his greying hair added to the distinction of his strokeplay. He batted with his sleeves down but kept them unbuttoned and he had a white handkerchief knotted round his neck.

England were then taken to safety principally by an outstanding innings of 148 by Colin Cowdrey who remained substantial, cheerful and efficient throughout this entire tour. At his best, Cowdrey made batting seem one of life's easier occupations. He was blessed with that lovely innate sense of timing which made it appear as if he never really hit the ball in anger but simply caressed it through the gaps which he found with a beguiling ease. On his good days it seemed inconceivable that he could ever have a bad one. Yet he did, and then his batting became deep, dark and mysterious, not to say utterly inexplicable.

Boycott and Barrington gave him good support but Alan Knott in his first Test of the series produced a most delightful innings and in so doing showed the selectors that they had been wrong to keep Jim Parks in the side for his batting. Always cool and in control, Knott batted in that impish way of his we were to come to know so well. His sleeves were buttoned tightly to his wrists and against the full might of the West Indies he looked so terribly young and frail and defenceless. He helped Cowdrey add 113 for the sixth wicket and stayed to the end.

The West Indies had a lead of 122 and there was only time for two overs on the fourth evening before bad light intervened, and with one day left a draw was surely inevitable. A negligible crowd turned up on the last day but even with only a handful of people in the ground, it still looked as lovely as ever with its luscious and ever-changing backdrop of that mountain range. As the clouds blew overhead the shadows swept over the green foilage, now lighting it all up with bright sunlight and then in the next moment plunging the mountainside into deep shadow. It formed a magical frame for what was to develop into one of the most surprising cricket days I have ever seen. There had been rain in the night and David Brown had to call for some sawdust in the first over of the day which took all of ten minutes to bowl. After that, John Snow and Brown took about four minutes an over and it was less than riveting stuff. Two girls in shocking-pink trousers in the stand at the mountain end attracted more attention than the cricket. Stephen Camacho, fair-haired and bespectacled and looking for all the world as if he was a biology student sitting through

114

a particularly difficult examination paper, was a picture of perplexed concentration until he drove Snow to mid-off just before lunch when the West Indies were 68–1. To heighten the gloom it rained during the interval. When, just before the restart, Rohan Kanhai was asked why the West Indies had made such slow progress during the morning, he replied, 'What can you expect if they keep the quicks on?' It was that sort of a day, and it was with less than enthusiasm that the players once more took to the field. A few more runs were scored and then Joey Carew called Basil Butcher for a quick single to mid-wicket and Snow's direct hit ran-out Butcher. Ten more runs were scored in the next fifteen minutes which hardly suggested urgency and then at a quarter past two, Gary Sobers stood up on the players' balcony, clapped his hands and waved his batsmen in. England had been left 165 minutes in which to score 215 to win and Charlie Griffith who had pulled a muscle after bowling three overs in England's first innings was unfit to bowl.

The West Indian supporters seemed shocked by the declaration and certainly it was not the normal gesture that captains make on the last afternoon of a Test match, for in Test cricket everything had to be earned and nothing given away. Against that, Sobers was always a most fair captain who liked to make a game of it when he could. When the post mortems were held all sorts of theories were put forward as to the reason for the declaration. The most likely seemed to involve Everton Weekes who was the West Indies team manager. He was very keen to beat the Englishmen and was sure that it was right to give them a target they would go for and on a wearing pitch he felt that the West Indies could bowl them out. He is purported to have said to his captain, 'It only needs ten balls to win the match.' Sobers obviously agreed and so the scene was set.

In Charlie Griffith's absence Sobers shared the new ball with off-spinner Lance Gibbs. With Sobers running in off only those twelve loping paces and Gibbs taking not much more than a couple of minutes to bowl an over, it meant that the over rate was alarmingly fast from the West Indian point of view. In fact 38 runs came in the first half an hour of the innings and we were already in the eleventh over; when Edrich swept leg-spinner Willie Rodriguez for 4, the 50 had arrived in 42 minutes, and to general West Indian horror England appeared to be winning the match fast. Edrich was bowled pushing forward in that brave-Horatius-saved-the-bridge way of his which made it 55–1, but Colin Cowdrey started in on Rodriguez as though

115

he had been licking his lips in anticipation. He pulled a googly for 4 with a stroke which said most clearly, 'You'll have to hide it better than that', and then with that inimitable paddled sweep he dispatched him off the middle of the bat to fine-leg for 4 more and England were 73–1 off 27 overs at tea after 75 minutes' batting.

The target was now 142 in 90 minutes and England's cause was helped by the first four overs after tea which produced seven 4s. There were four leg-side full tosses in Butcher's first over of leg-breaks which brought three boundaries, and at the other end Rodriguez was if anything rather worse. Butcher, who had been allowed six overs in his previous 31 Test matches, had taken 5–34 to finish off England's first innings. Now, 50 was scored in the first 25 minutes after tea and when Gibbs and Carew took up the attack they were unable to stem the flow. Cowdrey was lazily elegant. His bat cut a lovely curve when he square-drove Butcher for 4 and it was with an almost apologetic air that he swept Carew over square-leg for 4 from outside the off stump. Although he did not possess Cowdrey's felicitous timing, Boycott was also batting splendidly and there was one most satisfying square-drive off Gibbs. Eighty-two were needed from the last hour and Boycott's 50 came in 108 minutes from the next over. When Cowdrey lofted the very next ball, from Gibbs, over mid-wicket for 4, he had reached his 50 in 55 minutes with seven 4s. The 150 came up in 120 minutes and 65 were needed in the last three quarters of an hour, but by now Cowdrey and Boycott had built up such a momentum that although it was incredibly tense, it began to look as if England would get there.

Sobers bowled to Cowdrey. The first ball went wide down the leg-side for four byes, the ball after that was glanced exquisitely for 4 with a stroke that Ranji might have envied, and later in the over Cowdrey came onto the front foot and drove magnificently to the extra-cover boundary. It was exhilarating cricket. At the other end, that left leg of Cowdrey's advanced and Gibbs was on-driven to the fence, but in the same over he swung Gibbs off the front foot to mid-wicket where Sobers threw up the catch. Cowdrey's last 42 had come in 34 minutes and his 71 had taken 76 minutes and had included ten 4s. It may be because of the result but I think I shall remember this innings of Cowdrey's longer than any other I saw. That day, he was a wonderfully reassuring sight. It was an innings which made those occasions in county cricket when he struggled for, say, two hours for 30 runs on an innocuous pitch with a perpetual frown on his forehead, unaccountable. Each time it was as if the Royal Mint had turned out a dud threepenny bit.

Nine runs later Tom Graveney was yorked by Gibbs and again there was a flutter of doubt in English stomachs which intensified when a furious lbw appeal greeted Basil D'Oliveira's attempts to play his first ball. He received the benefit of the doubt and he and Boycott, whose unflappability did wonders for our nerves, scampered two leg-byes. Then Seymour Nurse, the Sidney Poitier lookalike, threw down Boycott's stumps when he went for another quick single. Again the umpire ruled in the batsman's favour. The 200 came when Boycott swung Gibbs to mid-wicket for 4 and then late-cut at the next ball and got 4 more off the top edge. Fifteen were now needed in eighteen minutes and when D'Oliveira glanced Gibbs for a single the score-board showed 215–3 and England had won by seven wickets with three minutes to spare.

The fuss now began. Sobers had gone from hero to something worse than a villain for making the declaration and, worse still, he was thought in some quarters to have been fooling around with West Indian nationalism. He had to be spirited out of the back of the pavilion, and the following day when he arrived with the West Indian party in Georgetown for the fifth Test he was given a police guard. In the final analysis, it was a poor declaration for although it only needed ten balls to win the match, the West Indies did not have the bowling to produce those ten balls. Amazingly, there was a certain amount of recrimination in the England camp as well. There were those all too anxious to say that Colin Cowdrey had originally felt that it would be better to settle for a draw and that it was Ken Barrington and John Edrich who had been responsible for changing his mind. Perhaps Cowdrey was at times too timid in pursuit of victory but all I can say is that he never for a moment batted like a man who had thoughts of safety-first uppermost in his mind. This was only the fourth occasion that a side had won a Test match after a second innings declaration by the side batting first. I suppose it is small wonder after watching two such Test matches at Queen's Park Oval on my first tour of the West Indies that I have a strong and, who knows, exaggerated respect for the ground and that lovely mountain range.

As far as I was concerned, the magic of Queen's Park Oval did not end there. I was back in the Caribbean in January 1972 for the first series that New Zealand had ever played in that part of the world. I don't think even the New Zealanders would have given themselves much chance of surviving that series and yet in another extraordinary rubber they managed to draw all five Test matches and indeed in the third, in Barbados, were within two dropped catches of winning after Bruce Taylor, moving the ball away from the right- handers, had taken 7–74 on the first day with a superb piece of bowling on a pitch which held more early moisture than usual. The West Indies were bowled out for 133, but in their second innings Charlie Davis and Gary Sobers both survived straight-forward catches in the slips to make big hundreds and save the day.

New Zealand came to Port of Spain for the second Test after an extraordinary innings by Glenn Turner – of which we will hear more later – had saved the first for them in Kingston. Still, the West Indies were confident of subjecting their opponents to an humiliating defeat with four Tests remaining. This was my third visit to Port of Spain and it was now that I met one of Trinidad's and, indeed, the world's great characters. By a lot of curious chances which I have described in the chapter about Sabina Park, Kingston, I had commentated on the first Test match for the commercial network of radio stations in the Caribbean which runs in competition with the government-owned stations which also produce a ball-by-ball commentary on every Test; which shows how keen they are about it all in the West Indies. As soon as I arrived in Port of Spain I was contacted by the head of Trinidad's commercial station. Peter Hesketh, and was signed up to commentate first on the game Trinidad played against the New Zealanders at Guaracara Park at Pointe-a-Pierre in the middle of the island's oilfields, and then on the second Test match. I was then taken downstairs from Peter's office and introduced to the ubiquitous Raffie Knowles.

Raffie's office was all good natured chaos with papers everywhere but mostly on the floor, photographs of racehorses and pretty girls. A thin, almost raffish character, with swept back hair which had once been fair and was now receding sharply, sprang up and enthusiastically pumped my hand as a torrent of welcoming words tumbled out of his mouth. From that first moment Raffie was irresistibly warm and friendly and so highly strung as to make a high tension cable seem positively docile. He loved sport and people in any order. The population adored him and for many he *was* Radio Trinidad. His outpourings on the radio were never scholarly, seldom exact, invariably fanciful and, when commentating on a live event, they never amounted to more than a rough approximation of what was actually happening, but the one quality he had which more than made up for any technical shortcomings was an unchallengable enthusiasm for sport and for life in general which was obvious in everything he did.

His cricket commentary was, in the words of W. S. Gilbert, 'a thing of threads and snatches'. I was lucky enough to share the Radio Trinidad commentary box with him during five Test matches – in 1976 the Great Scorer knocked on his door early one morning – and I have a clear recollection of one immortal piece of commentary which just about summed up Raffie. His words were always delivered at a fearsome speed in a high-pitched voice which, when the excitement really mounted, came close to the falsetto. The Australians were touring the Caribbean and the third Test was played at Queen's Park Oval. When Australia began their second innings, Keith Boyce was bowling to Keith Stackpole and Raffie was at the microphone. It went something like this and at a breathless speed:

'And Keith Boyce comes running in and . . .' there was then an undisguised yell of squeaky triumph, followed by, 'and Fredericks is jumping all around there and Stackpole's on his way man and Australia are 31 for 1 and what about that, Gerry?'

The measured Trinidadian tones of the former West Indies all-rounder Gerry Gomes then told listeners that what Raffie had really meant to say was that Boyce had bowled one to Stackpole which had lifted from not far short of a length. Stackpole did not quite get on top of it and Fredericks held a fine low tumbling catch at forward short-leg. I don't know if Raffie's way of putting it was better but it was certainly more exciting and even had us out of our seats in the commentary box.

Gerry, by the way, apart from being the most urbane of men and another reason Radio Trinidad's commentary box was such a delight, has a unique record to his name. When the Australians toured the West Indies in 1964–65 they played the third Test in Georgetown. At that time Gerry was one of the West Indian Test selectors. The evening before the match Cecil Kippins of Guyana who was one of the umpires decided not to stand at the request of the British Guiana Umpires' Association who were objecting to the appointment of Cortez Jordan of Barbados as the other umpire. Gerry was the only alternative. He held an umpire's certificate although he had never stood in a first-class match, and according to none other than the Australian captain Bobby Simpson, he did a good job. When play ended each day he had to take

119

off his white coat and slip round to the Radio Demerara commentary box and give a lengthy summary of the day's events. So, he selected the West Indies side, umpired the match and summed up the play on the radio. It says a great deal for the respect in which he is held in the Caribbean that his efforts in none of these roles were questioned, but then I doubt if there is a much fairer man on earth.

Raffie owned some racehorses and occasionally one of them won but I cannot vouch for the quality of the races. The ultimate danger was that Raffie – who would have turned Tossing the Caber into a major sporting entertainment if he had ever been allowed to get to grips with it on the radio – sometimes had to commentate on a race in which one of his own horses was running. Dave Lamy, who was Raffie's number two before succeeding him on his death, played me the tape of one such occasion.

Even by his own considerable standards, Raffie was in a fair lather of excitement before the off. We followed his animal step by step to the start although, it is true, one or two others got a mention. But when the race began it was all too much for him and now his voice did reach the falsetto, and without pause or much that resembled coherence it went on while the horse covered the distance which was about a mile. I frequently caught the name of his own horse but as far as I could tell none of the others got a touch and at the end I gathered that his horse had romped home, so fair enough. It was only after the tape had been turned off that I discovered from Dave that it had finished eighth. Nonetheless, it had been a considerable sporting experience.

Raffie had one party trick which was reserved for television at the weekend when he had a ten minute slot in which he went through all the major sporting results of the two days interspersed with just a touch of comment. It was always a question of trying to get a quart into a pint pot but fifty-two times a year – he never had a holiday – he managed too magnificently for words. He never had a note of any sort or used a teleprompter, and the only difference each week was that he got quicker and quicker so that he could get more information into those ten minutes. Whenever I saw him perform, there was never even a stutter. My only doubt was whether anyone could actually understand what he was saying, but it was such a *tour de force* that you certainly couldn't turn it off. Raffie had played hockey for Trinidad and I daresay the island has never had a greater patriot in its entire history. I last saw him, and indeed shared a microphone with him, on

England's tour of the Caribbean in 1973–74. By then we had become great friends. I had always found his mixture of friendship, humour, excitement and total chaos quite irresistible. I was deeply touched, therefore, when at our last meeting he presented me with the tie which is given to all Trinidadians who represent their country on the sporting field. It was, he told me, his only one – and money couldn't buy it off me.

To return to the New Zealand tour of the West Indies, the second Test was another extraordinary game of cricket. New Zealand were put into bat and midway through the first afternoon Vanburn Holder and Gary Sobers had reduced them to 99–6. With four and a half days to go there surely could be no escape from that. Bevan Congdon, a vastly underrated cricketer who was to take on the captaincy when illness forced Graham Dowling to go home after this Test, had already been dropped twice but was still there. He and Bruce Taylor added 69 and then Bob Cunis, of whom Alan Ross once wrote in *The Observer*, 'His bowling, like his name, is neither quite one thing nor the other', had helped Congdon add another 43 by the close when New Zealand were 211–7.

At lunch the next day New Zealand were 284–7 and when at ten past two Cunis pushed the first delivery of the second new ball gently back to Holder, they had put on 136 in just over three hours and New Zealand were 304–8. Although Hedley Howarth did not last long, the 41-year-old leg-spinner John Alabaster, the most delightful of men, helped add another 41 for the last wicket and when New Zealand were all out for 348, Congdon was 166 not out. It had been a marvellous piece of batting for not only had he managed better than anyone when the seam bowlers found enough moisture to move the ball around on the first day, but he also coped splendidly with the back-of-the-wrist left-arm spin of Inshan Ali, the leg-breaks of David Holford, the off-breaks of Lance Gibbs and the all-sorts of Gary Sobers himself. He never forgot the importance of keeping the scoreboard ticking over, either. He is a small man who at times hit the ball as hard as Kanhai. His most exciting stroke came when he jumped out and straight-drove Inshan Ali into the pavilion. There was any amount of delightful driving and it was one through extra-cover off Inshan which brought him to his hundred after 366 minutes at the crease. Congdon is a tough man, an immense trier and unrelenting in his determination to wear the other chap down first. This was an innings of immense character and so too were those of Taylor and Cunis, for they showed all the qualities a captain would like to find in every one of his players.

Thanks to Taylor who took four wickets and Howarth and Congdon who had three each, New Zealand even gained a first innings lead of seven runs. Congdon bowled in the same way that he batted. Nothing was given away. His control at a gentle medium pace was superb, he moved the ball in the air and off the pitch and he had a cleverly disguised slower ball which now accounted for Lawrence Rowe. Howarth's left-arm spin was crucial to the New Zealanders' efforts too, and he was at his best on this tour although it is probably true to say that by the end he was being used as the stock bowler in the side and was therefore pushing the ball through too much. He never regained the looping flight he had shown in the first half of the tour and this was especially true in Australia's first innings now, when he had the figures of 53–17–102–3. He wheeled away for hours on end and never forgot that concentration is as important to a bowler as it is to a batsman. He is the most genial of men, always relaxed, more so than his brother Geoff who went on to captain New Zealand. Hedley now runs the family fishing business at the top of the North Island of New Zealand but still finds time for the occasional visit to Eden Park in Auckland. He filled a most important role for New Zealand in the West Indies.

The second Test caused the West Indies even more embarrassment before it was over. The New Zealanders reached 288–3 in their second innings and then on the last afternoon, when Alabaster had the ultimate triumph of bowling Sobers, took five West Indies second innings wickets for 121. The Kiwis were proving to be a little bit better than anyone expected and the West Indies had still failed to win a Test when they came back to Queen's Park Oval for the fifth Test which proved to be yet another exercise in cliff hanging and nail biting. The West Indies won the toss and made 368 and then bowled out New Zealand for 162. Sobers did not enforce the follow-on and after the West Indies had been bowled out a second time for 194, the New Zealanders had to score 401 for victory or to bat for 605 minutes for a draw. With important help from the weather which claimed almost two and a half hours on the fifth afternoon – it was a six-day match – New Zealand just managed to hang on. Turner and Congdon made obdurate fifties and late on Bruce Taylor and Ken Wadsworth, so tragically to die of cancer four years later, batted out the last hour and three quarters with New Zealand seven wickets down. I shall never watch a more exciting series in which all five Test matches were drawn and if ever a side took a moral victory home with them it was New Zealand now.

The following year when Australia were their opponents in the Carribean, Rohan Kanhai had taken over the captaincy from Gary Sobers and the sides came to Queen's Park Oval for the third Test after the first two had been drawn. It was memorable first for a brilliant hundred by Doug Walters who reached three figures on the first day in only two hours and, driving, cutting, pulling and hooking, he was in brilliant form until he failed to spot Inshan Ali's Chinaman; and then for the leg-spin bowling of the restless and insecure Terry Jenner who took four wickets in the first West Indies innings, and the beguiling Kerry O'Keeffe who picked up four in the second. Australia won by 44 runs and as they won the fourth Test in Georgetown I did not stay for the fifth in Port of Spain with the series already decided.

England went to the Caribbean in January 1974 with a new captain just as they had done six years before. After the home series against the West Indies in 1973, Ray Illingworth had been cast aside and Mike Denness had taken his place. By now, the West Indies side was less of a threat. Hall and Griffith had not been replaced; Sobers and Kanhai were on the point of retiring and Lance Gibbs was still wheeling away with his off-breaks, bent on beating Fred Trueman's record of 307 Test wickets. England arrived at Queen's Park Oval for the first Test match in a state of mind which approached equanimity.

It did not last for long. Rohan Kanhai put England into bat and his fast bowlers cut through the batting. Queen's Park has a reputation for favouring spin but the damage there has usually been done by the seam bowlers. There was a happy amount of surface moisture in the pitch for the seamers that morning although the first wicket to fall was a gift. Geoff Boycott had been caught on the boundary hooking at Keith Boyce in the Test at Lord's the previous August and he repeated the stroke now for Bernard Julien to take the catch at long-leg. England were bowled out on the first day for 131 and although the West Indies then lost half their wickets for 146, an innings of great maturity from Alvin Kallicharran, helped by the more flamboyant Julien, took them to 392. Kallicharran's innings was a lovely blend of watchful defence interspersed with those delightful wristy strokes which always made him such a joy to watch. When he was going well there was just a touch of magic about his batting. Because he was so small and had a charming and rather naive smile underneath a thick crop of boyish hair, he gave the impression of being an innocent in a man's world. It was this innocence which so nearly cost him his wicket at the end of the second day in an incident which at the time threatened the very existence of the tour.

England never had a much more competitive cricketer than Tony Greig and he now bowled the last over of the day to Julien who played it back down the pitch and turned for the pavilion, for the hands of the clock were just beyond half past five. At the bowler's end Kallicharran had been backing up in the normal way and when he saw that Julien had negotiated the ball safely he continued to walk to the pavilion. Greig picked the ball up, spun round and, seeing that Kallicharran was not in his crease, threw the stumps down and howled an appeal. Umpire Douglas Sang Hue had no option but to give Kallicharran out and the bemused players came off the field as the enormity of what had happened began to sink in to the spectators. Greig was booed off and with his South African connections was even more villified than he might otherwise have been. That evening hurried consultations took place between the worried officials of both camps and telephone calls were made to Lord's. Eventually, after the captains and the umpires had been called together by the administrators, it was decided that in the interests of the tour, for which read 'peace', the appeal would be withdrawn and Kallicharran would continue his innings the next morning. The burning question which remains unanswered is, did Greig know that it was the last ball of the day and was he being opportunistic or was he simply caught up in the battle and acting on instinct? Had the decision to give Kallicharran out remained, there is little doubt that the rest of the tour would have been played in an atmosphere of great bitterness. The decision to bring Kallicharran back, which will have been strongly advocated by Jeff Stollmeyer who was then the president of the West Indies Board of Control, was the best for all concerned. That evening in the old Queen's Park Hotel on the Savannah was one of the tensest I can remember and George, the barman, was deeply concerned. The next morning before play began, Greig and Kallicharran shook hands out in the middle. (Stollmeyer, the most gentle of men, was murdered in 1989 when he surprised robbers who had broken into his house.)

When England batted again, they were given a wonderful start by Boycott and Amiss who matched each other run-for-run, reaching their fifties in successive overs. When play ended on the third day England were 210 without loss, Amiss 92 and Boycott 91. Boycott scored only two more runs the next day. He was out a fair number of times in the nineties in Test cricket, maybe wanting the hundred rather too much for his own good. At 328–1, England were in a wonderful position to save the match and Denness was playing probably his best innings of the series when Amiss drove Gibbs almost to the boundary. They ran two easily enough but then there was a slight hesitation before they embarked upon the third and Kallicharran's brilliant throw to wicket-keeper Deryck Murray from the cover boundary ran out Denness. Soon after tea England were all out for 392 leaving the West Indies with more than a day to score 132 to win, which they achieved for the loss of three wickets.

England had collapsed against the off-spin of Lance Gibbs who had bowled quite beautifully throughout. Coming in from the mountain end with that high stepping run and fast arm action, he had worried all the batsmen with his clever variations of flight and his changes of pace. Soon after the start of the fourth day he had Boycott caught at shortleg playing forward a fraction too soon and at the end the lower order were no match for him and he took 5–13 in his final spell. Watching Lance Gibbs bowl was always one of the great pleasures, for his style was in such contrast to most English off-spinners who rely mostly on spin which comes from a more deliberate and pronounced delivery stride and action. Gibbs, reared on hard and uncompromising pitches, had learned to make the subtleties of flight his main weapon.

When England returned to Queen's Park for the fifth Test of that tour this first Test was still the difference between the sides although England and most particularly Keith Fletcher had had to fight hard to earn a draw in Barbados. As the series was undecided the fifth Test was played over six days and this charming ground produced yet another sensational cricket match in which Tony Greig and Geoff Boycott played the leading roles for England. This was to be Sobers's and Kanhai's last Test match.

England won the toss and ground their way through the first day with Boycott at his most obdurate, taking 220 minutes to reach his fifty and at one stage going for 50 minutes without scoring. He was 97 not out at the end, when England were 193–4, and just as had happened in the first Test he was out after scoring two more runs the next morning, brilliantly caught behind the wicket by a diving Murray when he glanced Julien. His 99 had taken him all but six and a half hours. One could only wonder if it might not have been better for his and England's cause if he had attempted rather more than he dared.

125

England's final tally of 267 was made to seem even more inadequate when the West Indies had reached 174–2 by the end of the second day.

In the fourth Test in Georgetown which had been ruined by rain, Tony Greig had started to bowl off-breaks, had picked up a couple of wickets and had not been played at all easily. By the close on this second day he had, after sharing the new ball with Geoff Arnold, reverted to off-breaks, and had again instilled doubts, but little did we know what was to come. But first, more than an hour of the morning session on the third day was lost to rain and in between the showers Lawrence Rowe and Clive Lloyd took the West Indies to 224–2. Then Lloyd went onto the back foot to try and force an off-break which of course turned away from the left-hander and was caught behind. Gary Sobers pushed forward three balls later to one which spun away from him, also took a thick edge, and was caught by Jack Birkenshaw in the gully. There was something strangely mesmerizing about the tall figure of Greig as he bounded in mostly round the wicket with fielders all around the bat. In his next over Kanhai was beaten by one which Greig held back a fraction and I have never seen a bowler accept a return with greater enthusiasm. Six runs later Deryck Murray, always such a useful batsman in a crisis, drove too soon and was caught by Pat Pocock high up at wide mid-off. When, at 270, Julien played forward and was picked up at backward short-leg, Greig had taken 5–21 in 8.3 overs.

Meanwhile Rowe was still soldiering on at the other end and had reached his hundred after batting for six hours, but after Boyce had skyed Greig to mid-off, Rowe could only pull the next ball, a full toss, to mid-wicket. Inshan Ali was lbw on the back foot and the West Indies lead had been restricted to a mere 38. Greig had taken 8–86 with his off-breaks and these are the best figures by an England bowler against the West Indies.

England's second innings was again all Boycott in an innings of great technical perfection and which contained rather more imagination than he had shown in the first. He won a fascinating duel with Gibbs until he too was beaten in the air and bowled by the first ball after lunch on the fifth day. By then he had made 112 and, with Fletcher and Knott being the only other worthwhile contributors, England were all out for 263 which left the West Indies the seemingly easy task of scoring 226 to win. This time Greig began to bowl off-breaks with the new ball, but Fredericks and Rowe kept their heads scoring 30 before the close and took their stand to 63 on the sixth morning before Rowe was lbw playing back to one from Birkenshaw which turned but desperately slowly. In the next over Kallicharran stretched forward to Greig. The ball turned away from the left-hander, found the outside edge and flew off Knott's pad to Fletcher at slip. This brought in Clive Lloyd who seemed uneasy about the situation, to say the least, while Roy Fredericks at the other end had been playing with great confidence. In the very next over after Kallicharran's dismissal, Fredericks played Birkenshaw off his pads to mid-wicket and they ran an easy single. As Boycott picked the ball up just inside the wire netting fencing on the open side of the ground, Fredericks started back for the second. But Lloyd stopped. So too did Fredericks. Then Lloyd started again, stopped and finally ran past a totally bemused Fredericks who was hovering in mid-pitch. Fredericks was run out and the West Indies were 65–3.

After a short break for rain, Lloyd thumped Underwood for a couple of 4s but Kanhai was never relaxed in his last Test innings and at 84 drove wildly outside the off stump at Greig and was caught at slip. One run later Lloyd was beaten in the air and drove frantically and too soon at Greig who somehow held a quite brilliant diving right-handed return catch and the West Indies were 85–5. It was an extraordinary turnaround and once again Queen's Park Oval was producing a remarkable game of cricket. It was clear by now that Greig was exerting some sort of spell and England were on the threshold of a remarkable victory.

Gary Sobers and Deryck Murray then joined forces and they began to bat pretty well. In that lovely languid left-handed way of his, Sobers drove Greig through extra-cover for 4 and then swept him for another, strokes which seemed to ask what the fuss was all about. Murray then got in on the act, cover-driving and straight driving Greig for two more 4s and the only alarm came when Sobers was 19 and he played back to Pocock and Fletcher missed a hard chance at slip when the ball turned and lifted. But Sobers scored only one more run before he drove over the top of a slightly quicker ball from Underwood and was bowled. With the fall of Sobers's wicket I think everyone knew that England were going to win. Three runs later, at 138, Julien, never the most resourceful of batsmen in this sort of crisis, played a great heaving drive at Pocock and skyed the ball to Denness at cover. Murray's was now the wicket England needed most, but he continued to bat with shrewd common sense, picking up runs where he could but taking few risks. The score had reached 166 when he too succumbed to Tony Greig, driving at one which went straight on and

Fletcher accepted the chance at slip. English nerves grew tense again as Boyce threw his bat about to good effect and Inshan Ali played some suprisingly good strokes although he was dropped by Frank Hayes at forward short-leg off Greig. Soon afterwards, at 197, he drove at Greig who had taken the new ball hoping for more bounce and was caught at a deepish mid-off. Two runs later a yorker from Arnold removed Lance Gibb's leg stump and England were home by 26 runs five minutes into the last hour of another unforgettable Queen's Park Oval Test match. Tony Greig had taken 5–70 in the second innings which gave him match figures of 13–156, also the best by an England bowler against the West Indies and, strangely, he hardly ever bowled his off-breaks again. This result meant that England had drawn the series and had still only lost one series in the Caribbean since the war and that was the first when Gubby Allen's side which was not much more than a 'B' side lost 2–0 in 1947–48. All of that was soon to change.

The next time I returned to Queen's Park Oval it was at the time the Packer revolution had split cricket. The Establishment Australian side, led by Bobby Simpson, was playing a series against the West Indies who began the rubber by playing their WSC players in the first two Test matches which they won easily. Then, for the last three, the West Indies Board banned the WSC players, which of course, weakened them. Australia won the third Test in Georgetown and in the chapter about Bourda, the Test ground in Guyana, I shall talk about all the political to-ings and fro-ings that took place just before that match.

The fourth Test of the series, like the first which I did not see and which the West Indies won on an awkward pitch, was played in Port of Spain and surprisingly the 'new' West Indies won by the huge margin of 198 runs with more than a day to spare. Simpson put the West Indies in on a moist pitch and before a scant crowd – for the West Indian public had not been impressed by a decision which had robbed them of the opportunity to watch their principal heroes in action – will have been pleased to have dismissed them for 292 early on the second day. Basil Williams, an unknown from Jamaica who would never have played a Test match if it had not been for the political situation, and Alvin Kallicharran, one of the few who had apparently resisted the blandishments of WSC, were the only two to make runs. Australia got to within two of this total and had looked like taking the lead before Vanburn Holder finished things off, taking 6–28 in all.

Holder played 40 Test matches for the West Indies in which he took 109 Test wickets and he owed this to the fact that he came along at exactly the right time: after Hall and Griffith and before Roberts and Holding, when the West Indies did not have any great fast bowlers. A tall man, he had a great heart, a longish run, an ungainly action and a lovely smile. He did yeoman service for Worcestershire but was just a little bit short of ability at the top level. Given a helpful pitch he could be spiteful in the extreme but with Test pitches becoming more and more uniformly flat he was too plain to disturb the best of batsmen. For all that, he was a credit to every side he played for and was another of that rare brand who so obviously enjoy themselves while playing.

Thanks to Greenidge, (Alvin, not Gordon), and Derek Parry, neither of whom would have played Test cricket in normal circumstances, the West Indies made 290 in their second innings which left Australia to make 292 to win. In Australia's second innings eight wickets had fallen to spin and now by the time Australia began their second innings the ball was turning a long way and the bounce was increasingly uneven. Parry (off-breaks) and Raphick Jumadeen (orthodox left-arm spin) took eight wickets between them and Australia were bowled out for 94. It was not a particularly exciting Test match but it was all part of a fascinating situation in which the game's established authorities and World Series Cricket did everything in their power to humiliate and destroy each other.

Political sanity had returned to the game when England visited the Caribbean in 1980–81 under Ian Botham, not a leadership experiment that worked. They lost the series 2–0 although there was no second Test as the Guyana government declared Robin Jackman, who had come out as a replacement for Bob Willis after the first Test in Port of Spain, *persona non grata* because of his South African connections and England rightly refused to play in Guyana. Only one Test was played in Port of Spain because a Test had been given to Antigua for the first time and the fourth was played on the Recreation Ground in St John's. In the first Test the West Indies made 426 before that unstoppable fast bowling combination of Roberts, Holding, Garner and Croft bowled them to victory by an innings and 79 runs. It was thrilling for West Indian supporters but as a contest it had little to offer for it was all so inevitable.

It was even more so four years later when David Gower's side was swamped 5–0 in the series. This time, it was Holding, Marshall, Garner and Patterson who did the damage and the West Indies won by ten wickets at Queen's Park in three days. It was an extraordinary game for statistics. Ian Botham took his 26th haul of five or more wickets in a Test innings regaining his own record temporarily from Richard Hadlee, while Richards reached 6,000 runs in Test cricket, Gordon Greenidge 5,000 and Larry Gomes 3,000.

This was a tour which was bedevilled by various allegations of curious off-the-field behaviour which were levelled at Ian Botham, and also by a campaign mounted against the Englishmen especially in Trinidad because of the decision of some players and Gooch in particular to join the England rebel tour to South Africa four years earlier. The players concerned had all been banned from Test cricket for three years for taking part in that tour which at the time had been agreed as sufficient and just penalty by the Boards of all the Test-playing countries. On coming to Trinidad, Gooch had said that he refused to go on to Antigua for the fifth and final Test because of certain remarks made about South Africa by Lester Bird, the Foreign Minister of Antigua. Donald Carr, the secretary of the Test and County Cricket Board flew out from London and after some hours of intensive discussion Gooch was persuaded to change his mind.

In Barbados, a former Miss Barbados, apparently with wads of tabloid newspaper cash in her back pocket, if that's where she kept it, had been telling stories of romps with Ian Botham, of broken double beds in the team hotel and of the partaking of illegal substances sniffed, as far as one could gather, off the bathroom floor in Mick Jagger's house. It was all fearfully diverting and it hardly made for a peaceful atmosphere in which to try and sit down and work out how the West Indies cricketers might be held in check. Botham was in the spotlight again in Trinidad for his then manager, former Hollywood disc jockey Tim Hudson, had said at a party in Malibu when told that his client had been accused of taking drugs, 'So what, doesn't everyone take drugs?' Hudson then decided to fly out to Barbados, Botham talked to him by telephone from the Queen's Park Oval press box without mincing his words and Hudson, perhaps wisely, flew straight to London's Gatwick Airport and soon afterwards relinquished his commission as the great man's agent. Add to this the fact that although all was falling down around him, Gower had instituted a system of voluntary nets which meant more deep-sea fishing for those who were less than enthusiastic about the main job in hand, and it will be seen that chaos could hardly have been more confused. I felt sorry for Tony Brown, the manager, who found himself hopelessly out of his depth.

Sadly, I was in New Zealand and not Port of Spain when England came within a whisker or, to be precise, a shower of rain, of beating the West Indies in the Third Test in 1989–90 and taking a 2–0 lead in the series. By all accounts, they also suffered from some reprehensible time-wasting tactics by Desmond Haynes who was captaining the West Indies in the absence of the injured Viv Richards. But the next time I am lucky enough to watch a Test match there I know it won't be dull although I shall still miss Raffie Knowles and continue to look a real idiot when trying to dance the Jump-Up to that year's crop of calypsos.

8

GEORGETOWN:
"Land of my Fathers" and a Maiden Over

Guyana is perched on the tip of the South American mainland and was once British Guiana, which explains why it has embraced the game of cricket. In recent times it has led a somewhat troubled life and some of the problems have spilled over onto the cricket field. While George-town – its canals a hangover from the days of the Dutch – and the sugar fields are essentially West Indian in feel and spirit, the interior with those huge rivers, the Demerara, the Essequibo and the Berbice penetrating deep into the continent, is the essence of South America.

Georgetown, the capital, boasts the tallest wooden building in the world, the cathedral. It also has spacious streets and sprawling mansions which tell of a former prosperity; Starbroek Market with its intriguing Dutch architecture and which is one of the most fascinating centres of trade I have ever come across; and Bourda, which is the most delightful cricket ground. It is almost as if it was a big ground built in miniature, and as we shall see it has had its fair share of excitement in recent times. The interior of the country boasts the Kaiteur Falls which are the tallest in the world even if only a trickle compared to the Victoria or the Niagara. The interior is also peopled by indigenous AmerIndian tribes, and a two-hour journey down the Kimuné tributary off the Demerara brings one to Santa Mission which is the closest AmerIndian settlement to the capital. Guyana provided the final home for the Reverend Jim Jones and his crazed followers at Jonestown where one day they all followed his example and drank deadly poison with predictable effect. Georgetown is also the home of the redoubtable Luckhoo family, of whom more later.

132

Since gaining independence, Guyana has had a series of left-wing rulers of whom Cheddi Jagan and Forbes Burnham have been the best known. Neo-Marxism has not worked there any better than it has elsewhere although the nearness of Barbados and other islands has enabled the country's leaders to keep their own larders stocked and their glasses full. In some ways it is curious that an autocracy should tolerate the game of cricket which is surely a supreme throwback to colonialism and all the capitalistic values that stands for, but like all the best traditions it has survived all the changes. The Guyanese love their cricket just as they do in the West Indian islands in which it is played. Sadly, Guyana, for all its posturing over the South African issue, is far from a multi-racial society. It is ruthlessly run by Negroes while the considerable Indian segment of the population is given second-class status. The Negro population has been drawn to the cities, while the Indians work the cane fields.

Bourda itself is very much a reminder of a colonial past with its small but stately pavilion and Ladies Stand in one corner of the ground and the small covered one-tiered stands which go on all round this small ground. There is a touch of old world elegance about the wooden pavilion although, like so much of Georgetown, it always seems to be in need of a coat of paint. On the other side of the ground the back of the football pavilion which serves the needs of those who play soccer on the neighbouring ground rises above the stands and is not nearly so easy on the eye. Whenever I have been to Bourda it has been plastered with advertisements which proclaim the merits of certain types of booze, most of which are probably unattainable in Guyana. Bourda's strong individual flavour is helped too, by the police horses ridden by officers in full uniform which stand on either side of the sightscreen at both ends of the ground and in the four corners. They add a lovely touch although again it is not necesarily what one would expect to find in that political climate.

I first went to Guyana in 1968 when the cricket was presided over by Berkeley Gaskin who was the most delightful of men and a gloriously, if slightly overstated, throwback to the past. He was highly cultured, extremely well read and he spoke in rounded tones which suggested that he had spent a large part of his life at both Eton and Oxford. He had bowled at medium pace and with scant success for the West Indies against England in 1947–48 and now administered with a light hand and an avuncular manner. He was married to the Minister for Education in Forbes Burnham's government. Win was of a considerable size and Berkeley remained somewhat in awe of her, and was quick to tell you that he had perfected the role of the prince consort. He and Win were most hospitable and it was always a delight to go round to their house and listen to Berkeley discourse about cricket, politics, his own adventures as manager of West Indies sides overseas, and life in general. His conversation was always liberally interspersed with Shakespearian quotations. In his quiet way he was one of the great characters I have met in my endless journeys round the cricket world and whenever I think of Georgetown, he is always the first person who comes to mind. His Australian-inspired nickname of Ghastly Backspin was, I suppose, inevitable.

He managed the West Indies side in India in 1958–59 when he had the doubtful distinction of being the manager who sent home Roy Gilchrist for using beamers as a regular weapon against Sarawanjit Singh. He also managed Frank Worrell's team in England in 1963, and in 1968–69 he was in charge of Gary Sobers's side which went to Australia and it was on that tour that I collected my favourite Gaskin story. The West Indians went from Sydney to Brisbane to play Queensland then the first Test Match, but Sobers himself did not make the trip and went instead to Adelaide to meet the future Mrs soon to be Lady, Sobers who had returned from a visit to England. At one of those hastily convened press conferences which always seem to take place on a flight of stairs, I asked Berkeley if he thought that with the series about to start it was the wisest course of action for Sobers to take. He turned to me and with a charming smile said, 'Dear Boy, what you do not understand (Berkeley would never have said don't) is that our captain has gone on a mission which will be of great benefit to the side.' To have doubted it would have been rather like accusing the prophet Job of losing his temper. As it happens, Sobers returned in plenty of time for the Test match, took six wickets in Australia's second innings and the West Indies won the match by 125 runs. When I next saw Berkeley he smiled, inclined his head slightly to one side in a gesture of mock sympathy and said, 'I told you, dear boy.' It goes without saying that he was always immaculately dressed and groomed.

This first Test I ever saw at Bourda was unquestionably the most exciting and dramatic I have been lucky enough to watch there. It was the fifth in that exciting 1967–68 series against England and it came in the same week that Sobers's declaration at Queen's Park Oval had allowed England to win the fourth and go one up in the series. But because the series had not been decided and it was still possible for the West Indies to level it at 1–1, the last Test was given an extra day so that there was every chance of achieving a result. This would have been fair enough if the series was drawn when the sides came into the last match but when one side was a match up, it seemed unfair to penalise them in this way.

The weather on the first day was glorious with just enough of a breeze to keep us all from getting too hot and the gates were shut with 13,000 inside long before the start. Already the palm trees behind the press box at the southern end of the ground were full of people. The pitch was dry. What grass was visible was straw-coloured and one police horse champed a trifle impatiently on its bit to our left, for the press box was in the low stand next to the sightscreen. The sun was gleaming off the shining silver dome of the Queenstown Mosque at the far end of the ground. There were huge colourful advertisements on the east side of the ground one of which proclaimed in huge letters, 'Basil Butcher says Diamond Club', another gave out the message, 'Watneys Extra Milk Stout gives me my extra energy says Rohan Kanhai'.

The tension was terrific. It was as if a saucepan was about to come to the boil, the steam already bursting out from the sides and the lid clattering up and down.

When the two captains, Sobers and Cowdrey, walked out in their blazers to toss, waves of noise burst round the ground. The toss is always more of an event in the West Indies than anywhere else, and when with a gesture Sobers indicated that he had won it the crowd roared its approval.

The next concerted roar greeted the arrival of the umpires. Cortez Jordan from Barbados, a short man, was wearing a panama hat and his colleague, Cecil Kippins from Guyana who was much taller, was resplendent in a white topee. They walked purposefully to the middle and half the crowd were probably betting on who arrived first for West Indian crowds will bet on anything. The applause was more muted when Colin Cowdrey led out England but there was nothing inhibited about the noise that greeted Stephen Camacho, a Guyanese, and Seymour Nurse when they came out to open the West Indies innings. The crowd that day were wearing red giveaway paper hats which bore the legend Bulmers Cider, across the peak, and somehow rows and rows of spectators wearing identical hats heightened the sense of anticipation. There was a gasp when Nurse played at and missed Snow's second ball and another when he did likewise at Jeff Jones's first ball. In Snow's second over Nurse played back to Snow, was hit on the knee, and umpire Jordan turned down the appeal. The West Indies had reached 29 not without a certain amount of luck when Camacho hooked at Jones who held a simple return catch. At 35, Nurse cut at Snow and was caught behind. The crowd greeted this disaster with an uncomfortable silence, and now Kanhai made an anxious start. He pushed Snow close to Edrich at forward short-leg and then snicked Jones wide of the slips. The score had reached 72 when Kanhai drove Jones to Boycott's left at mid-on. Kanhai called for the run, Butcher responded, then doubt set in and Boycott threw high to Jones who took the ball above his head and still managed to break the wicket before Butcher could get back.

Sobers, batting at number five for the first time – he preferred six – had a mixed reception for he was being held responsible for that defeat in Port of Spain, and Cowdrey began to crowd him by bringing up the close fielders. If England could have disposed of either Kanhai or Sobers before they settled they would be in charge of the match. Pat Pocock bowled two excellent overs of off breaks at Sobers, who then snicked Jones just wide of Graveney at first slip. They went into lunch grateful for the respite, with the West Indies at 94–3.

Gradually the bat took control after lunch. The score had reached 145 when Cowdrey threw the ball for the first time to Tony Lock, who had come out from Perth in Western Australia, for whom he was then playing, as a replacement after Fred Titmus had had four toes cut off by the propellers of a speedboat while bathing in Barbados. Lock had been suspected of throwing his faster ball and in his old age had completely remodelled his action, although he remained the same abrasive character who never minced his words. Sobers was extremely careful against him, and at tea the West Indies were 187–3.

Immediately afterwards Sobers came forward and edged Snow wide of second slip for 4, but the crowd erupted when Kanhai square-drove Jones for 4 and when, later in the over, he hooked for another which brought him to his hundred, pandemonium broke loose. Kanhai then swept at Lock and missed; already the odd ball was coming through low. Before the end of the day Sobers himself had been beaten on the front foot first by Pocock and then by Barrington who was allowed an over or two of leg-breaks right at the end. When the bails came off, the West Indies were 243–3, Kanhai having made 113 and Sobers 75. These two had pulled the West Indies round after their bad start and the crowd dispersed happily enough.

There were another 13,000 present an hour before the start on the second day and now there was also a crowd standing on the roof of the stand at the northern end. A hugh advertisement for Russian Bear Rum had gone up overnight in the far corner of the ground. The new ball was due and England claimed it at the start and Jones bowled from the southern end to Sobers. The last ball of that first over was fast, it pitched short of a length and Sobers went onto the back foot. The ball kept horribly low and hit Sobers on the ankle, as far as one could see, in front of middle stump. There was a riotous appeal and it was almost as if the fielders did not bother to look at umpire Kippins for the decision was surely a formality. Yet to general amazement Kippins straightened up and refused to put up his finger. English bewilderment was acute and it was Keith Miller who wrote in the London *Daily Express* the next day, 'Yes, Umpire Kippins, you were right, it would have missed the leg stump. But no, Umpire Kippins, you were wrong, it would have knocked the middle stump five yards back towards Alan Knott.' Even Johnny Woodcock writing in *The Times* was moved to say after he had described what actually happened that whatever infinitessimal amount of doubt that can have existed in his mind, Kippins gave unerringly to the batsman. His comments caused something of a stir between Woodcock and Jim Swanton when, towards the end of the match, the England manager, Les Ames, visited the press box and Swanton reached for Woodcock's airmail edition of *The Times*, turned to the offending passage and suggested to the manager that in his day responsible correspondents did not cast imputations of this nature. Woodcock and Miller were right. It was the outest lbw decision I have ever seen to be given not out.

It may not have been wholly unconnected with the fact that on the fourth evening of the match Kippins announced his retirement as a Test match umpire because of the personal threats he had received. He would not have been threatened for giving Sobers not out; the clear indication is that he might have been in deep trouble if he had raised his finger. This, of course, makes an umpire's life intolerable and who can blame anyone who shades his views in favour of the home side if he knows that he might find his house burnt down if he had given a particular decision to the visitors? It took the England players a while to get over the shock of that decision and I remember Cowdrey saying later, 'The most difficult thing is to calm yourself down afterwards.'

Sobers also seemed to be affected, for his first runs came that morning when he hooked Snow off the splice just over Lock's head at short-leg. Before he had scored another run he came forward to Jones and edged the ball at catchable height between Knott and Cowdrey at first slip. The crowd were visibly unsettled by all these goings on but were sent mad with delight soon afterwards when Sobers hooked Jones most fiercely to square-leg for 4 and in the next over Kanhai square-cut Snow for another. England must have felt their chance had gone. The 200 stand was greeted with general rejoicing and then cover-drives off Jones and D'Oliveria brought Sobers to his hundred. When, a quarter of an hour before lunch, Pocock came on to bowl the day's first over of spin, England had to face the fact that the new ball had failed and at lunch the West Indies were 317–3, seventy-four runs having come in the two hours.

In a way this was as partisan a Test match as any I can remember for England had done wonderfully well to win one Test and were determined not to throw their advantage away, while the West Indies undoubtedly felt that their honour was at risk. It was a match which saw some glorious cricket and never more so than when Sobers and Kanhai were together, but for many it was the result and only the result that mattered. When the end is all that matters, it is perhaps difficult to appreciate the means. Both men might have been out on several occasions as if to prove that they were only human after all. But they were up against some truly magnificent fast bowling from John Snow and Jeff Jones and even now, more than twenty years afterwards, I can feel something of the atmosphere of thrilling suspense which held us all that week at Bourda.

When play began again after lunch Kanhai pulled a short one from Pocock for 4, but then heaved most inelegantly at the very next ball and John Edrich, standing by the square-leg umpire clutched it to his chest. Clive Lloyd began with a thunderous straight drive off Snow. When he was 9 he should have been caught by Cowdrey two- handed at first slip off Snow but he and Sobers now brought up the 50 stand in 59 minutes and it looked as if there would be no end to England's suffering. Sobers's 150 came from a thick-edged drive from Ken Barrington but when he drove at a wide one in the same over Cowdrey took a quick catch waist high at slip and now, not surprisingly, it all became rather more manageable. David Holford played back to the first ball of a new spell from Snow and was lbw; Lloyd was seventh out at 399 when he cut at Lock and played the ball into his stumps, and one run later Murray swung at Lock and skied a catch to Knott. Snow soon shattered the stumps of King and Gibbs and the West Indies were all out for 414 which, considering that both Kanhai and Sobers had reached 150, was not at all a bad result for England.

Boycott and Edrich came out with almost an hour and a half to go and the crowd baying for the kill as Hall and Sobers shared the new ball. They received a shock when Hall bounced the fifth ball of the first over and Boycott swivelled and hooked him beautifully for 4. In Hall's second over Boycott drove a no-ball from Hall through extra-cover for 4, a stroke which brought a 'Great shot, Sir' from the policeman standing by the press box. Then came a bouncer which lacked Hall's usual pace and Boycott picked it up and hit it first bounce into the crowd at square-leg.

Sobers, who had already gone a long way towards redeeming his reputation, now bowled to Edrich who followed one outside the off stump and was joyously caught behind by Murray. It was now England's turn to hold its breath. Cowdrey pushed his first ball to mid-off for a single and then Boycott, after taking a while to take guard and then holding Sobers up halfway through his run, drove the next ball through the gully for 4. There was a lovely easy extra-cover drive from Cowdrey off Sobers which was stroked away with all the timing in the world. These two hung on and at the end England were 40–1 and we had plenty to talk about over the excellent buffalo steak washed down with Mateus Rosé at the Palm Court Restaurant alongside the old Park Hotel on Main Street where I was staying .

The third day was overcast and in the two and three quarter hour's cricket which was possible Boycott and Cowdrey, mostly uneventfully, added another 106 runs taking England to 146–1 by tea when rain set in for the day. There were a few of those lovely rippling strokes from Cowdrey when he moves so effortlessly into position and his bat seems to instruct the ball where to go and always in hushed tones. While Boycott may not have been able to match Cowdrey for grace and elegance, he was just as effective and once again he took to Hall as he several times hooked and drove. If anything, Boycott was the more solid of the two and on the only two occasions a wicket might have fallen Cowdrey was the batsman.

There were many fewer people present on the fourth day although the ground was still pronounced to be full. There were only just over 8,000 paying spectators, which suggested that all illegal means of entry had been stopped. Boycott and Cowdrey went on for most of the morning with admirable discipline. Cowdrey soon chopped

Gibbs for a couple to bring up his 50 and the 150 stand came shortly afterwards in 239 minutes. It was not a hectic rate but these two batsmen were interested only in saving the match and making sure England won the rubber. After spending twenty-five anxious minutes on 99, Boycott straight drove King for his eighteenth 4 which brought him to his first hundred against the West Indies. It had taken him 268 minutes.

Then, at 176–1, Sobers took the new ball and after one final off-drive against Hall, Boycott followed a short one and was caught behind, having done a superb job. Worse was to follow when, in the next over, Cowdrey played half forward to Sobers's first ball and was lbw after batting 275 minutes for 59. Suddenly England had two new batsmen at the crease. The excitement was intense for the crowd were sensing victory, Sobers surrounded the batsmen with close fielders and they were under seige. There was a moment's relief when Tom Graveney on the back foot drove Wes Hall past mid-off for 4, but at 194 Ken Barrington, normally so reliable in these circumstances, turned Sobers round the corner and Kanhai held a tumbling catch at backward short-leg and the players went in to lunch.

English nerves were again soothed by Graveney when, soon after the interval, he lent gracefully into an on-drive which brought him 4 runs off King and he followed this with an equally effortless stroke through mid-off against Sobers. But at 240 he tried to drive off the back foot and was caught behind. This was the start of a small collapse. D'Oliveira, Alan Knott and Snow all went and the score slid to 259–8. It looked as if the West Indies would have a sizeable first innings lead, but this was not allowing for that most formidable of cricketers, Tony Lock.

He had begun by driving Holford over the off-side field and then, with evident relish, set about attacking Lance Gibbs and with excellent judgement too as he cut and swept. When he had made 18 he had another go at Holford but this time got under the ball and it steepled up to Camacho at deep extra-cover who circled beneath it and dropped the catch. At the time it did not seem to matter but in the final analysis this miss cost the West Indies the match.

After tea Lock was at his belligerent best, playing a series of resounding strokes each one of which was accompanied by a certain amount of chatter. When Lock swept Gibbs for one to reach his 50 Pocock at the other end had still not scored although the partnership was now worth 52. When the new ball came at 347–8 they weathered it in comfort and had the satisfaction of watching the last ball of the day disappear down the leg-side for 4 byes. England were 352–8, just 62 runs behind.

Next morning the score had reached 368 when Pocock played much too soon in trying to drive King and gave the bowler a simple return catch to end a stand of 109 in 127 minutes. The end came three runs later when Lock, with Jeff Jones as his partner, swung across the line at King and was bowled. The West Indies lead had been restricted to 41 and there were almost two full days left. It had been an heroic innings by Lock who had made not only his highest score for England but also his highest first-class score.

The West Indies second innings started eccentrically with a top edge going for 6 as Nurse hooked at Snow, and this sent the crowd wild with delight. Nurse and Camacho were obviously under instructions to score fast and at lunch after 17 overs the West Indies were already 72–0. The running between the wickets had been particularly brave and there was nothing the crowd enjoyed more than the quickly stolen singles. Sanity returned after the interval when, in the second over first Nurse was yorked by Snow and departed lbw and then Camacho slashed at a short one outside the off stump and was caught by Graveney at short extra-cover. In Snow's next over Clive Lloyd flashed at one outside the off stump and was caught behind by Knott who made a lot of ground to his left and the West Indies were suddenly 86–3. Snow bowled quite beautifully.

Sobers moved to 36 to complete his 6,000 runs in Test cricket which, of course, both Barrington and Cowdrey had done for England. All the time the tension was building, for England's batsmen knew that the outcome of the match and the series was going to depend on their efforts in the fourth innings. They all went impassively about their business in the field as most of them had done since the tour began in January. Jeff Jones, with his boyish hair, walked the first six steps of his run up as if he could not wait to start running and to get at the batsman. At last, he broke into a slightly hesitant trot and then came the high stepping run and the blur of left-arm over action. Ken Barrington was expressionless in the covers, cap down over his eyes, every inch the true professional. Pat Pocock, tall and boyish like Jones and always eager even in those days for the chance to find someone to have a chat with but having no luck in the outfield. He was not wearing a cap as he sent those fine long raking throws back into Knott's gloves. There was all the enthusiasm of youth about Popock.

John Snow at fine-leg seemed lethargic and remained expressionless, poker-faced almost. When he walked in as Jones ran up it was almost as if the whole process bored him. But the ball would come in his direction and that long striding run would take him to it and the power and accuracy of his throw testified as to his true feeings. Then, there was John Edrich, browner faced than the others to look as if he had just finished getting the harvest in his native Norfolk. Colin Cowdrey at slip, always courteous of movement, looking quickly round at his field, first over his left shoulder and then his right and sometimes with a rather startled expression on his face. He may have won the captaincy on this tour by default but by this stage he made it his job as of right; but that broken Achilles tendon lay agonisingly round the corner and Ray Illingworth was waiting in the wings.

Tom Graveney, tall, angular and never capable of an ugly movement, standing at short extra-cover with the peak of his cap pointing off his forehead at an angle of forty-five degrees. Basil D'Oliveira, a fairy story in his own right, stood down at third-man, hands clasped behind his back trying to fight back the memories of a disappointing tour and hoping that even now he would be presented with the chance to reprieve himself; an impassive figure. Alan Knott was doing all those exercises which became such a feature of his wicket-keeping and showing the brilliance which was to make him England's permanent keeper for almost ten years. An impish, almost puckish figure crouching, waiting for the next edge with a pair of hands which were almost as safe as the Bank of England; a wicket-keeper who was always to be a tonic for his bowlers, just setting out on a remarkable career. He was another who was brim full of boyish spirits. Geoffrey Boycott in the covers was another who was unemotionally doing his duty. There was no obvious sign of enjoyment but rather an implied satisfaction at a job well done if that was the case. A man who had practised for incalculable hours to perfect any and every role which he had to play and one whose batting had played a big part in England's progress round the Caribbean.

Finally, there was Tony Lock, fatter and more bald than of old with a knotted handkerchief round his neck. His cap was perched on the top of his head and he was a jack-in-a-box anywhere in the field who never hesitated to tell an opposing batsman or a colleague a few home truths if he felt in the mood. When he chased the ball it was with surprisingly short strides but even at the age of 38 he had no peer as a catcher of a cricket ball. This was the side fighting for the honour that would come with survival in this last crucial Test Match.

Lock held a catch off Butcher's glove when he swept at Pocock just as yells of delight announced the arrival of Sobers's 50 in the same over. The 200 arrived and then Murray pulled Pocock to deep mid-wicket where Boycott held a good catch over his right shoulder. All the time it was thrust and counter-thrust. Holford swept at Lock and was bowled off his pads and King retaliated with a remarkable stroke when he drove Jones back over his head for 6. In the next over King was bowled off his pads by Snow, who quickly finished things off by bowling Hall and Gibbs which left Sobers stranded at the other end five runs short of his second hundred of the match after another memorable innings. Snow stalked off to the pavilion, sleeveless sweater slung over his shoulder and with figures of 6–60 which had taken his tally for the series to 27 and his figures for the match to 10 for 142.

There was no time for England to start their innings that evening and they had to bat through the next day for safety and the series or to score 308 to win and settle it all beyond doubt. The pitch was worn, the West Indies, especially Sobers, were ready for the kill and it was always going to be agonizing, but I am sure that none of us could have guessed at the way in which it was to unfold.

The dramas were not slow in starting, for Edrich pushed defensively at the third ball of the first over which was bowled by Sobers and it rolled agonizingly about half an inch past the leg stump. The next ball was snicked through the slips for 4 while the one after that was snicked along the ground and stopped in the slips. Another big crowd was already in a frenzy and I do not remember a much noisier day's cricket. But Boycott temporarily restored order when he square-cut Hall for 4 and Sobers for another before square-driving Sobers for 4 and 2. In Sobers's next over he glanced and turned the ball off his legs for two more 4s but then pushed forward and edged the ball to Kanhai's right at first slip. He dived, got a hand to it but could not hold on. Seventeen overs were bowled in the first tension-charged hour and at the end of it England were hanging on at 33–0. The openers did not survive much over the hour. Five minutes later Edrich played forward to Sobers and Gibbs hung onto the catch at backward short-leg. When Cowdrey faced his first ball from Gibbs in the next over he played it with his pads into the short-legs and there were screamed appeals from both crowd and players. Another single accrued, Boycott now faced Gibbs and cut at one which pitched wide of the off stump but turned back a long way and bowled him. That was 37–2 and from the noise you would have been forgiven for thinking that the West Indies had already won the match. Gibbs now bowled to Graveney with two short-legs, a slip and a silly mid-off. Graveney came forward and turned his second ball round the corner. It flew off the middle of the bat, hit Sobers at backward short-leg and rebounded back to Murray behind the stumps. This made it 37–3 and the pandemonium grew worse ten minutes later when Barrington thrust forward to Gibbs and Lloyd threw himself forward from silly mid-off and scooped up a fine one-handed catch off bat and pad. In the press box, not surprisingly we were all convinced that England had lost and even the police horses by the sightscreen found it difficult to stand still. Two runs later Gibbs threw one up most invitingly to D'Oliveira who drove it straight back to the bowler and England were 41–5 and surely doomed. Gibbs, in a truly great spell of off-spin bowling had taken 4 for 4 in nine overs and yet except for the odd quick, almost nervous grin, showed no emotion.

As impassive as ever, Cowdrey had watched the carnage from the other end and one can only guess at his feelings as he saw all England's hard won advantage being thrown away. Alan Knott was now his partner and paradoxically there was something almost consoling about Knott as he got down immediately to the business of combating Gibbs and making it seem possible after all. Cowdrey relieved his feelings with a lovely off-drive against Sobers. When Gibbs bowled a quicker ball Knott's wrists rippled as he late-cut it for 4 and then he went onto the back foot and off-drove him for another, but when he cut again he got an edge and Murray dropped the catch. Lloyd's agony at silly mid-off suggested that he had had a vision about the future.

England were 68–5 at lunch and three and a half long hours remained. Soon after the restart, Cowdrey drew away from the stumps and refused to continue because the noise and shouting from the spectators had reached such a pitch. At first, this made them even noisier but after a loudspeaker announcement sense prevailed and play continued. Our hearts were again in our mouths when Knott came forward to Holford and Kanhai, falling to his right at slip, missed a low catch. Cowdrey pulled and hooked Holford for 4s before refusing once again to continue as the air was split with the noise of rhythmical clapping all round the ground. Gradually it subsided and Sobers rang the changes. He took over from Gibbs, Gibbs replaced Holford at the other end and then King relieved Sobers. Gibbs threw one up to Cowdrey who produced a rippling cover-drive and when Holford succeeded King, Knott square-cut for 4. The all-Kent partnership was doing England proud and the hundred was up. Next came an unusually productive over from Gibbs. Cowdrey drove off the back foot with all the time in the world and with an irresistible and almost sympathetic elegance, he pulled the next ball, a full toss which showed that Gibbs was human after all, to mid-wicket, and after a single Knott pulled the last ball of the over for 4; the over had produced thirteen runs. The hour since lunch had seen seven bowling changes and suddenly the West Indies began to grow a trifle tense and the crowd became quiet.

When Cowdrey pulled Sobers for 4 to reach 50 it was greeted with near silence. The hundred stand had a similar reception. One run later the new ball was taken and Cowdrey off-drove Hall for a most satisfying 4 and then Sobers bowled to Knott. He had three backward short-legs, two slips and a gully and Knott all but played one ball into his stumps in what was a superb maiden. But Cowdrey and Knott were still together at tea. The score was 153–5 and England had been given another chance of survival. Sobers and the West Indies returned full of worry while Cowdrey and Knott gave an impression of resolute determination. As he strode to the middle, Cowdrey's head was bowed and his tread was slow for he realized that the result of more than three months' solid endeavour was going to be decided in the next ninety minutes – play finished in Georgetown at half past five. Beside him, Knott, much smaller and slimmer, was lighter and quicker on his feet but his jaw too was etched with determination.

In the first over Cowdrey turned a full toss from Hall to the mid-wicket boundary and then Knott faced Gibbs. Sobers and Holford were close in at short-leg, Fredericks, on as substitute, stood at slip and Lloyd's long form was curled up at silly mid-off. Knott played a maiden over while Cowdrey stood between balls at the bowler's end with his legs crossed and his left hand on his hip leaning on his bat with his right hand. He looked wonderfully reassuring. Knott now glanced Gibbs's quicker ball for 4 and then late-cut him for another, which prompted Cowdrey to shake his head, for the ball was turning on to the off stump. Knott pushed at the next ball and it rolled back towards the stumps before he knocked it away with his bat and passion spilled over in the crowd.

All day, Cowdrey had been playing the off-spin of Gibbs with his pads, stretching forward and letting the ball hit him on the front pad. The West Indies had yelled themselves hoarse appealing for lbw and yet Messrs Jordan and Kippins had religiously said not out. If the umpiring had been anything but scrupulously honest on this last day the West Indies would have won with ease. But now Cowdrey tried it once too often. He came half forward to Gibbs and umpire Jordan put up his finger. England were 168–6. The pavilion stood to Cowdrey as he returned and England's last 4 wickets had to hold on for another 73 minutes. Snow took Cowdrey's place and the crowd were back in full voice. Sobers took over from Gibbs bowling fast left-arm over and Snow played out two anxious maidens.

Knott was altogether more skittish and pulled a full toss from Holford through mid-wicket for 4 to reach his 50 and then he square-cut and pulled him for two more. Snow, bare-headed and almost unconcerned, now began to play Gibbs with his pads while Knott, shirt sleeves buttoned to his wrists, and dark hair sticking out beneath the back of his cap, stroked Butcher off the back foot through extra-cover for 4. It was five minutes past five with the West Indians taut with tension and just twenty-five minutes remaining when Snow came forward to Sobers, played no stroke and, after batting for forty-six minutes, was given out lbw by umpire Kippins. Six minutes later Lock pulled a rank long-hop from Sobers straight to King at mid-off and stalked off trying to hide his feelings of shame with a look of murderous belligerence. England were 200–8 and nineteen minutes remained.

Knott took a single off Gibbs's last ball to keep the bowling but trying to do the same off Sobers he made the mistake of hitting it for 4. Gibbs now bowled to Pocock with six men round the bat, three on each side of the wicket. Pocock played a maiden, Knott did likewise with Butcher and then appealed against the light. In the good old days this was allowed, but the appeal was hastily turned down and the umpires did not even meet to discuss it. Gibbs bowled again to Pocock and now there were seven men around the bat. It was 5.24 (six minutes to go) when Pocock came forward to Gibbs and played the ball to Lloyd at square short-leg. The batsman thought it was a bump ball and stood his ground, there was a huge appeal, up went umpire Jordan's finger and it was down to the last man Jeff Jones. Hemmed in so that he was almost invisible, he played the last remaining ball of the over. Knott now survived a maiden over from Sobers, unable to get the single which would have given him the strike, and Gibbs turned to bowl the last over of the match with the series depending upon it.

I don't suppose I shall ever again watch an over like this one. Before it began, Knott and Jones met in mid-wicket to make sure that there would be time for only one over. I asked Alan Knott on the aeroplane back to England the next day what they had talked about. With a twinkle in his eye he told me that they sang the first verse of 'Land of My Fathers'. Jones played each torturous ball. He took three deliberately on the front pad, the second time surviving a loud appeal. When he had pushed the sixth along the ground into the short legs, the umpires took off the bails, the crowd poured onto the field and one huge West Indian picked up Alan Knott and carried him into the pavilion. What a way to win a series! By the end we were not so much on the edge of our seats as out of them altogether.

Not surprisingly, Bourda has never again managed anything as exciting as this although the cricket there, when not interrupted by rain, has always been interesting. I was next there in March 1972 with that first New Zealand side to tour the Caribbean. The two weeks' cricket began with a game between New Zealand and Guyana which was memorable for the huge number of runs scored on a pluperfect pitch. Guyana won the toss and made 493–4 declared with Clive Lloyd, Alvin Kallicharran and Roy Fredericks scoring hundreds, and New Zealand replied with 488. Bevan Congdon who had by now taken over the captaincy from Graham Dowling who had returned to New Zealand, made a good hundred, but Glenn Turner – was there ever a more acquisitive batsman? – scored his third double century of the tour, reaching 259 after spending a small matter of 602 minutes at the crease. There was then time for Lloyd to complete his second hundred of the match in as exciting a display of hitting as one could wish to see before this particular run spree came to an end.

Three days later another Test began when the West Indies won the toss although carelessness cost them their first five wickets when all the batsmen were set. Only Kallicharran, who was playing in his first Test match, reached three figures to the immense delight of the locals and Sobers declared when he got there at 365–7. For the next day and a half the West Indians toiled under the hot sun while Glenn Turner and Terry Jarvis compiled 387 for the first wicket. It was slow progress for by now the New Zealanders realized that with only one more Test to come they had a great chance of drawing the series and so set about cutting the West Indies out of the match. Turner's powers of concentration were legendary while Jarvis, who batted 540 minutes for 182, showed that he was a willing pupil. After Jarvis had driven David Holford to Gordon Greenidge at cover late on the fourth day,

Turner late cut off-spinner Tony Howard for 4 to reach 200 in 553 minutes. New Zealand carried on batting into the fifth day and curiously Turner was out for 259 at Bourda for the second time in eight days when he was lbw trying to work Howard to leg. New Zealand eventually declared at 543–3 at the end of what had become a statistician's delight.

When Guyana played the Australians a year later the excellence of the pitch had in no way diminished. Bad batting cost Guyana the match, but not before Greg Chappell had made a big hundred and Roy Fredericks had hit a hundred in each innings for Guyana. Guyana's second innings was the only time that Bob Massie looked anything like the bowler who had swung the ball like a boomerang the previous June at Lord's when he took eight wickets in each innings of the Test match. He now took 7–53 but it was not enough to win him a place in the side for the Fourth test. The West Indies, now being captained by Rohan Kanhai, won the toss and batted and an innings of 178 by Clive Lloyd, which contained some marvellously powerful strokes although it took him getting on for six hours, enabled them to reach 366. The Chappell brothers and Walters then made important contributions taking Australia to 341. The West Indies were three for no wicket at the start of the fourth day but then collapsed in remarkable fashion to the fast medium seam bowling of Max Walker and Jeff Hammond. They were bowled out for 109 which was their second lowest total in a home Test match after the 102 they had made against England at Bridgetown in 1934–35.

Hammond and Walker were most competitive bowlers. Walker, off the wrong foot and hence his nickname, 'Tangles', was always attacking the stumps as he brought the ball back into the right-hander, while Hammond, dark haired and terrier-like, moved the ball predominantly the other way. They were supported by some splendid fielding although the West Indians succumbed to some woefully careless strokes and the Australians who had to score 135 to win, did so by 10 wickets and won the series as well, being two up with one match to go.

A year later Roy Fredericks, as was customary, made a hundred in each innings for Guyana and Dennis Amiss and Geoffrey Boycott made hundreds for what was still in those days called MCC, and the match was drawn. When England won the toss in the Test match, Amiss and Greig made centuries but rain then washed out almost all play on the last two days and the game was hopelessly drawn. This was Greig's second century of the series and Amiss's third and they had both in their very different ways established an ascendency over the West Indies which in Greig's case was as much as anything psychological. It was in the short West Indies first innings that Greig began to bowl off-breaks and he took a couple of wickets although he did not hint at the mastery he was to build up in the fifth Test when he took those thirteen wickets. Greig was an extraordinarily versatile cricketer and not only with his bowling, for no batsman could have produced two such dissimilar innings as he played at Brisbane in 1974–75 when he took on Thomson and Lillee and made 110 of the most dramatically exciting runs you could wish to see, and at Calcutta in January 1976, when on a pitch ideal for the three Indian spinners, Bedi, Prasanna and Chandrasekhar, he batted for 413 minutes to reach 103, the fourth slowest hundred ever made for England. When the respective merits of Greig and Botham as all-rounders come up for discussion, it is worth remembering that Botham could never have played an innings like this last one in a million years. I doubt too, that he would ever have taken 13/156 bowling off breaks against the West Indies while, on the evidence of Brisbane, Greig might very well have made that 149 not out at Headingley.

The cricket season which stretched from October 1977 to April 1978 was without doubt the most confused the game has ever known. World Series Cricket had been founded in 1977 by Kerry Packer and it divided the game as no other issue has. During that season I seemed to be inextricably involved with the dramas which came from the ongoing battles between the establishment and WSC and the latter's attempt to win world wide support and to gain credibility. It began for me on 24th November at the VFL Park in the Melbourne suburb of Waverley, the venue WSC had settled upon when they were refused permission to play at the Melbourne Cricket Ground, when the Australian XI played the Rest of the World. I then flew back to Karachi for the start of England's series against Pakistan in the course of which there was an attempt to reinstate three of the WSC players, Mushtaq Mohammad, Zaheer Abbas and Imran Khan, into the Pakistan side. In the end the President of Pakistan, General Zia-ul-Haq intervened and they were not allowed to take part in the series. I then returned to Australia for another glimpse of WSC at Gloucester Park in Perth before flying on to Adelaide for the last four days of the final Test between Bobby Simpson's Australian side and India. The next leg of the journey was to watch England in New

Zealand and then it was on to the West Indies where Simpson's Australians played a five-match Test series. All kinds of dramas were enacted there as the West Indian selectors began the series by including their WSC players and then, after an extraordinary few days in Georgetown which ended with the WSC players pulling out of the West Indian side in protest after three of their number, Deryck Murray, Desmond Haynes and Richard Austin, had been dropped for the third Test. Kerry Packer himself flew in saying that he had never had the chance to see Guyana and that he wanted to watch some cricket, although in the event he flew on to Barbados to entertain his WSC players and their wives at the Sandy Lane Hotel on the west coast.

It was an extraordinary period where rumour and counter-rumour flew around and it all took place in the unlikely setting of the Pegasus Hotel on the sea wall in Georgetown. I have recounted the to-ings and fro-ings at great length in *The Packer Affair*. Undoubtedly there was subterfuge and deceit, double dealing and intrigue, naivety and downright bloody-mindedness. I have little doubt that Packer and World Series Cricket wanted to assume control of West Indies cricket by making it plain that their star players could only perform with WSC's permission, and by signing up extra players they made it increasingly difficult for the West Indian selectors to come up with a representative side that was worth anything. The Australian side was, of course, much weakened by WSC and so in fact the two teams were much of a muchness with Australia winning the third Test in Georgetown, the West Indies winning the fourth in Port of Spain. Just when it looked as if the Australians would win again in Kingston, riots caused the match to be cancelled.

If anyone had doubted the bitterness which the formation of WSC had caused and how those involved with the breakaway body acted as if they were taking part in a crusade, the saga in Georgetown produced overwhelming evidence. No one was indifferent to the outcome and one could understand only too well how the participants felt. The WSC West Indians saw the chance of making a decent living and understandably went to Packer, the authorities felt deeply affronted by what had happened and became almost apoplectic with indignation having not the slightest doubt that they had right on their side. But, as they were to find out, this seldom guarantees victory and there is no doubt that Kerry Packer's cheque book won the day in his confront-ation with the game's Establishment. With the advantage of hindsight, how much simpler it would have been if the Australian Cricket Board had been prepared to negotiate with Packer when he first came to them in an attempt to buy the exclusive rights to televise Test cricket in Australia. But then, it is hard to blame them for failing to realize the determination and the single-mindedness of Packer himself, and what began as an attempted business deal was soon to become a crusade.

The principal participants in that week in Georgetown were Fred Bennett who was the manager of the Australian side, Bob Simpson the captain, while commentator Alan McGilvray was never far away. The West Indian Board of Control relied mostly on Jeff Stollmeyer, the Chairman of the Board, Peter Short from Barbados, while from Guyana, Berkeley Gaskin was much to the fore as was the notable legal family, the Luckhoos. Sir Lionel Luckhoo was legal adviser to the Prime Minister, Forbes Burnham, and it was in his house that the most far-reaching decisions were taken by the Establishment side after various members of the Board of Control had flown in late one evening. The West Indies selectors, Clyde Walcott, Joey Carew and 'J K' Holt were also very much in evidence. On the other side, Clive Lloyd played a big part as did Deryck Murray who never emerged from Trinidad although he was the WSC representative in the Caribbean and the telephone lines burned hot between his house and the Pegasus Hotel. Later, Austin Robertson, who had been instrumental in the formation of WSC, flew in with Kerry Packer. Another big part player was Guyana's Minister for Sport, Shirley Field Ridley, and finally the assembled cohorts of the press made up the numbers and for a whole week it seemed as if a permanent press conference was taking place round the swimming pool of the Pegasus Hotel, which was pronounced locally as the Pegassus Hotel.

The five WSC players in the original West Indies side refused to play and like all such pieces of news it broke most inconveniently late at night. We had dined at Lionel Luckhoo's house before being asked to leave when the main members of the West Indies Board of Control arrived from the airport so that they could have a private meeting. The next day after breakfast Jeff Stollmeyer read out the unlikely list of players who formed the revised West Indian side for the third Test. It was rather like living in the middle of the most complicated detective story and I am quite sure that even now there are some parts of the story that I do not know and that there are other parts which the participants will always tell differently.

151

The third Test itself could only be an anti-climax after all this. The young West Indian side captained by Alvin Kallicharran, who had been asked to join WSC but apparently had refused, were bowled out for 205. Thanks to a most determined and patient 67 by Simpson and fifties by Graeme Wood and Steve Rixon, Australia replied with 286. Larry Gomes and Basil Williams then made hundreds for the West Indies who compiled 439 to leave Australia the considerable task of making 359 to win on an excellent Bourda pitch. They lost three wickets for 22 thanks to a brilliant opening spell by Sylvester Clarke but then Wood and Craig Serjeant made hundreds and the Australians won a superb game of cricket by three wickets.

Even by then, the main concern was the whereabouts of Kerry Packer and the likelihood that he had signed additional players. This quite unforgettable fortnight was enacted around Easter which in Georgetown is the time of year for kite-flying, and along the sea wall by the hotel the sky was for days as full of kites as the Sydney harbour was of boats on the day of Australia's bi-centenary in 1987. This made it all seem even more bizarre.

My next visit to Guyana for what would have been the second Test between the West Indies and England in late February and early March 1981 was even more completely swamped by politics and this time the issue was of the Guyanese government's making. England had lost the first Test in Port of Spain by an innings and 79 runs and at the end of it Bob Willis, who had been unable to play because of a knee injury, had to return to England for an operation. As a result the tour selectors sent for a replacement who turned out to be Surrey's Robin Jackman. We all arrived in Georgetown, back at the good old Peg*ass*us before going up to Berbice for a one-day international which the West Indies won by six wickets. On our return to Georgetown we found that the pot was boiling. A radio commentator in Jamacia had queried Jackman's right to be in the West Indies because of his South African connections. He had married a South African and spent most English winters in the Republic playing and coaching cricket. The Burnham government took up the issue with alacrity and before we knew where we were Jackman had been declared *persona non grata* in Guyana which meant that he would have been unable to play in the Test.

The to-ing and fro-ing round the Georgetown pool and indeed back to the Luckhoo house in Bel Air Park was strongly reminiscent of all that had happened three years before. Whispered meetings took place in the hotel corridors and groups of three and four spoke behind their hands by the pool. Meanwhile the Pegassus's lift had ceased to function and so we had the daunting prospect of walking up twelve floors or so to our rooms every time we wanted to make a private telephone call. I did my best to persuade the management to install an impromptu bar on the sixth landing but my pleading fell on deaf ears. The long and short of it all was that England rightly refused to play the Test in Guayana and we all flew off to Barbados and the Rockley Resort where the future of the tour was decided by the foreign ministers of the islands in which the remaining matches were to be played. The first-ever Test match was due to be played in Antigua and one of the ministers was Lester Bird, the son of the Antiguan prime minister, who was himself a cricket commentator and who would for the first time become a Test commentator when the match began in Antigua. I would like to think that the possibility that this might not have happened will have prompted him to vote for the continuation of the tour and, if so, it says something for the power of cricket in the region.

No one felt the political worries and the failures of England's cricketers on that tour more than the cricket manager, Ken Barrington, who after the second day's play of the third Test at Kensington in Bridgetown had a massive heart attack and died. English cricket had lost one of its greatest servants and friends.

The next time England toured the West Indies, in 1985–86, there was no Test match scheduled for Georgetown but on the tour after that Graham Gooch took his side there although rain prevented a single ball being bowled in the Test. By then, Forbes Burnham had gone the way of all flesh which may have made it easier for normal service to be resumed. Whatever it may have been, Guyana, Georgetown and Bourda have never in my experience been dull. I have seen some wonderful cricket there as well as having to endure the most insufferable political posturing both by cricketers and politicians. But when I think of Bourda my mind will always go back to Alan Knott and Jeff Jones, the first verse of 'Land of my Fathers' and that final over bowled by Lance Gibbs to Jones. So, it is cricket and not politics which has the last word.

9

KINGSTON:
Tear Gas in a Cockpit

Jamaica is the largest and most intriguing of all the islands which form part of the cricketing West Indies. It is an extraordinary paradox too, for the north coast is everyone's idea of the perfect tropical island. From Montego Bay to Port Antonio, there stretches mile upon mile of glorious sandy beaches and swaying palm trees with irresistible pale blue seas reaching to the horizon and a non-stop procession of waiters carrying planter's punches. The north coast is one of the world's favourite holiday resorts. Amazing hotels abound; there are also the rambling villas which are the playthings of the enormously wealthy and each one looks like a rarified Hollywood set. The names conjure up visions of leisure which has been developed almost to the point of decadence: Runaway Bay, Half Moon Bay Hotel, The Casablanca, Ocho Rios with the Jamaica Inn and Sans Souci and the Dunn's River Falls not far away and that bewitching drive down Fern Gully into the small town, and so on down to Port Maria and beyond. Small wonder that Ian Fleming and Noel Coward both had houses on this idyllic stretch of coastline where the 'Yankee dollar' reigns supreme.

The south of the island, Kingston and Spanish Town, could hardly be more different. Poverty, overcrowding, dirt and all the unhappy side effects of slum dwellings abound. Crime is an industry, gunfire is a common occurrence and although Montego Bay may be only 109 miles from Kingston by signpost it is several worlds apart. The country in between with its bananas and its breadfruit and its citrus fruit is sometimes mountainous, always hilly and never less than beautiful from the moment you climb out of Kingston up to the Blue Mountain Inn where they still serve a banana flambé which defies description. It is an island of staggering contrasts and if one remembers the north coast with that beguilingly named banana port,

154

Oraccabessa, where Harry Belafonte found that most lilting of calypsos, 'The Banana Boat Song' (Day-o and all the rest), you cannot avoid memories of the less savoury south which in ways is just as intriguing. A journey past Palisadoes Airport on that thin peninsula out of Kingston to Port Royal where that most famous of all pirates, Morgan, once presided over every possible sort of skullduggery, is not to be missed.

Test cricket in Jamaica is played at Sabina Park in Kingston while the island also plays a number of matches as do touring sides at Jarrett Park, the delightful ground in Montego Bay. Sabina Park is, for me at any rate, just about the most vibrantly exciting Test ground in the world. When I first went there in February 1968 it was also the smallest in the world, a real cockpit of cricket. Recently, neighbouring land has been bought and the ground has been considerably enlarged without detracting in any way from the fiercely exciting atmosphere. It has been a ground too, which almost every time I have been there has produced extraordinary games of cricket which have more than lived up to the title of this book. It is a ground which is redolent of the city of Kingston itself. It has an unforgiving atmosphere and the crowds there give the impression of wanting to win even more desperately than in other parts of the Caribbean. There is a starkness about the game at Sabina Park which I have not found anywhere else.

It was in Jamaica in rather curious circumstances that my own Test match broadcasting career began. I went to the West Indies in 1971/72 to watch New Zealand in their first ever tour of the West Indies. The tour began in Jamaica with two first-class games, against the island and the President of the West Indian Board of Control's XI and then the first Test match. On the day before the island game I had lunch with Alan Richards who was covering the tour for Radio New Zealand and according to the Commonwealth Agreement this meant that he would be commentating for local consumption in the Caribbean. This had been agreed before he left New Zealand.

The problem was that in each island there were two networks, both of which broadcast ball-by-ball commentaries on the international cricket. The day we had lunch Richards had been approached by a local broadcaster who had asked him to join his station's commentary team and, thinking that it must be the one Radio New Zealand had already been in contact with, he agreed to do so. A little later he discovered that there were indeed two stations in Jamaica, the government station and the private enterprise network owned by Rediffusion, and that he had agreed to commentate on both of them.

155

At lunch, Richards asked me if I had ever done any commentary and, lying through my teeth, I assured him that I had and he said he would put me in touch with a certain Winston Ridgard who ran these things for Radio Jamaica. I met Winston and perpetuated the same lie, as a result of which he took me on to commentate for the three games in Jamaica. Accordingly, I joined Peter Bailey who played for Guyana and toured England with the West Indies in 1939, Jackie Hendrick, the former West Indian wicket-keeper, and Laurie Foster, our splendid scorer who was at other times a customs official at Kingston's Pallisadoes Airport. I had listened to the BBC commentaries all my life and was sure that I would be able to do it without any problem. It transpired that I did not make too many howlers and I was used on that tour all round the Caribbean. The next year I was back in the West Indies for the Australian series and I was again asked to commentate and so, by the time I came to do my first commentary for the BBC, I had already cut my teeth and made my major mistakes during those two series in the Caribbean. Thank goodness I was a well-established and fluent liar.

I have written earlier that the first tour I covered in the West Indies with Colin Cowdrey's side in 1967–68 produced the most consistently exciting cricket of any that I have been on since, and at the time of writing that must reach around forty. Queen's Park Oval and Bourda have already given ample evidence of this, but any personal essay about Sabina Park would not be complete without an account of the second Test match of that tour which was no less dramatic and exciting than any of the others I have described. Sabina Park was tiny in those days and I can so well remember Wes Hall starting his run from the old press box or southern end of the ground and almost pushing himself off the white wall which did duty as the sightscreen. The huge new pavilion stand has now taken over that end of the ground but in those days we all sat in the noisy air-conditioned chaos of a tiny press box which was on two levels. Because of the air-conditioning it was sealed and therefore the noise of the crowd did not penetrate and it was what I imagine watching cricket through a periscope would be like, for the sound was not so much turned down as turned off.

The old, flaking green-painted pavilion stood square to the pitch away to our left as we peered out at the action. The players inhabited the ground floor and there were two more tiers upstairs. The first combined a dining-room and bar with a long balcony and on the floor above there was open air seating. The colonial architecture was a throwback to the past, and just like the green-roofed pavilion at the Sydney Cricket Ground or the small wooden pavilion tucked away in the corner at Bourda, there was a rather charming Victorian modesty about it which was happily matched by the wives of the members of the Jamaican Cricket Association who came along to watch – at least they did in February 1968 – in a splendid array of colourful hats and dresses. It was a long scramble to get to the ground in the morning because the traffic jams went on for ever and tempers often became frayed as the assembled multitude of taxi drivers fretted at the enforced inactivity. A constant cacophony of angry horns did nothing for anyone's ear drums or their peace of mind either. Eventually we arrived and were shown where we had to sit by the doyen of the Sabina Park press box, Jack Anderson, whose grey hair and avuncular manner masked a formidable temper. Jack's affectionate relationship with the rum bottle had stood the test of time and later in the day he was seldom in the mood to argue logically or to listen thoughtfully to any differing point of view. He came to the saddest of ends, for after reporting a day's Test cricket at Sabina Park in the early seventies, he returned home and later that evening found a burglar in his house who shot him dead. Jack was one of those characters that cricket produces and so richly deserves and who one will always remember.

For this particular press box I was positioned in the front row on the ground floor next to the formidable figure of Jim Swanton, the famous *Daily Telegraph* cricket correspondent who even to this day is hard to keep out of print and who manages still to maintain the standards of his earlier days. It was my first tour and part of my duties were to act as Jim's runner which meant taking notes for him when he was having lunch with the committee or the Governor General or maybe the Prime Minister, taking his copy to the cable office and running errands generally. He was an exacting taskmaster, one who was never in his life known to have suffered fools gladly. He was too, the most brilliant describer of a day's cricket, and of course, having a holiday house at this time in Barbados, the West Indies was rather more than just spiritually his home. Whether we are conscious of it or not, I daresay all of us who write about cricket learned a certain amount about the business from the example of Jim Swanton and certainly the game has never had a greater friend.

In those days the visiting team to Kingston always stayed in the lovely old Courtleigh Manor Hotel, although Jim Swanton may well have found a billet with a local governor or a retired Admiral of the

Fleet. The England players viewed the second Test of this series with some apprehension. They had come to the Caribbean probably thinking that they were unlikely to win and then had to suffer the agony of having come so close to victory in the first Test in Port of Spain. I can well remember Cowdrey shaking his head on the evening of that drawn match and saying that he wondered if England would again have such a good chance to win a match. I don't think he or perhaps anyone realized that age had taken the West Indians past their best. If you had played against them in England in 1966, maybe this was understandable.

The pitch at Sabina Park, for a long time the fastest surface in the world, had been relaid and no one was certain how it was going to play. There had been some heavy rain during the night three days before the match began; there had been no covers on the pitch and so it was still damp on the first morning, which brought another unknown factor into the equation. When I arrived at Sabina almost an hour and a half before the start, it was already packed to the point of overflowing. There cannot have been more than 10,000 there but from the noise and the excitement it seemed that most of the population of Jamaica had found their way to Sabina. To a man, they were all wearing bright orange-red sun shades which were being given away as an advertising gimmick by Shell. The noise was helped by the melodious intervention of a 56-man police band which marched up and down. The drama was increased by the numerous spectators who had climbed up the palm trees at both ends of the ground, behind the press box and at the Blue Mountain end as well. They too were wearing their Shell hats and as the palms swayed in the wind it looked as if they had grown a most extraordinary blossom. At the north end, a wall also acted as a sightscreen and already one spectator was sitting on the top of it with a most unlikely mauve parasol to give him shade. Behind him the Blue Mountains were covered in haze. Away to our right, on the popular side of the ground behind the high wire-netting fencing there was open ground and a number of small skeleton-like trees which were filled far beyond capacity by eager spectators. There were also four floodlight pylons at the corners of the ground and the two on this side were also being used as vantage points for spectators who had climbed to the very top and were sitting in among the lights. Goodness knows what happened when they wanted to spend a penny for you may be sure that the moment they had vacated their perch it would have been filled by those beneath.

Action started when the captains, Sobers and Cowdrey strode out to the middle to toss. Cowdrey won it and chose to bat, for even on this new pitch it was the obvious choice. Sobers, with three buttons of his shirt undone, ambled out of the pavilion with his troops at his heels. Geoff Boycott and John Edrich came next, two supremely phlegmatic opening batsmen, as they needed to be. Wes Hall marked out his thirty-yard run at the press box end and the crowd roared its approval as he did so. He started no more than ten yards from where I was sitting. It was windy and the flags were blowing out fiercely as blue sky and cloud intermingled overhead; one moment the ground was in shadow which was almost immediately chased away by bright sunlight.

Boycott took guard from umpire Jordan, looked round the field and settled over his bat and an ear-splitting roar went up as Hall began his long-legged run: all the excitement of the Caribbean bowling to the impassive imperturbability of Yorkshire. An ever-increasing roar accompanied Hall and he was about two thirds through his run when, with a tremendous explosion which even penetrated the press box, a thunder flash went off. Hall stopped and with a broad smile trudged his way back, the gold cross dangling round his neck gleaming in the sunshine as it spilled out of his shirt.

Boycott edged the fifth ball of the first over in the air square between the short-legs and from the noise you could have been forgiven for thinking the West Indies had already won the match. That over was survived and so was Charlie Griffith's first from the other end. In Hall's second over Boycott on-drove for 4 which produced a subdued reaction but when this was followed by a bouncer the noise was ear-splitting. Edrich had been batting for 36 minutes when he square-drove Hall for 4 to get off the mark and followed with a cover-drive off Griffith. The first hour produced 34 runs and a shameful eleven overs. Cricket played at sixty-six balls an hour is a relatively uneventful pastime, but nothing would have stopped that crowd from bubbling and the high point of their morning came twenty minutes before lunch when Boycott tried to drive Hall through the off-side off the back foot and played the ball into his stumps. England were 49–1, but Edrich was going well and he now square-cut Sobers for 4 while Cowdrey, with perfect timing, cut Hall for 4 with a stroke which seemed absurdly easy and England had reached 62 off 25 overs at lunch.

The afternoon began with a moment of riotous disbelief when

Edrich was bowled by Griffith and it took a while to dawn on the crowd that the umpire had had the temerity to call a no-ball. Lance Gibbs was bowling with the mountains behind him while Griffith and Sobers took turns at the southern end. Edrich square-cut Gibbs twice for 4 with strokes which were fashioned by those powerful forearms and were effective rather than beautiful. His fifty arrived soon afterwards and the fifty stand was posted in 73 minutes, which was not bad progress considering the over rate. There was a gasp when Edrich lofted David Holford back over his head first bounce for 4 and then hysterical roars when Cowdrey took a short single to mid-on and only just made his ground when Clive Lloyd threw down the stumps at the bowler's end. On England went through the hot afternoon. Edrich played Gibbs off the front foot through mid-wicket, he drove Holford through extra-cover while in the same over Cowdrey paddled him to long-leg for 4 and the hundred stand arrived in 113 minutes. It was high-class batting. Then Hall and Griffith came back and the over rate again slowed and a brown parasol joined the mauve one on the far sightscreen; soon afterwards a black parasol with white edges completed an interesting trio. At tea England were 172–1 and things were going even better than they can have hoped, with Edrich 95 and Cowdrey 48.

Sobers bowled his orthodox left-arm spin after the interval and Cowdrey square-cut for 4 which took him to fifty but, after scoring another single, Edrich faced Sobers and tried to dive over the covers and was caught at extra-cover by Rohan Kanhai. After being beaten by an off-break from Gibbs which went over his middle stump, Ken Barrington soon settled in and by the close England were 222–2, he and Cowdrey having weathered six overs with the second new ball. The second day began like the first with Hall marking out his run in front of the press box. After every ball, he walked back head down, shirt open to his tummy, polishing the ball vigorously as he went and then as he turned at the top of his run he would hitch up his trousers before starting in again. Watching Hall was an entertainment on its own.

On the first morning the pitch was covered with a jigsaw of small cracks and the surface shone like a shattered mirror. Now, on the second morning, the cracks had widened and it was beginning to look like a drunken chess board and, more ominously for the West Indies who would have to bat last, two balls in Hall's first two overs kept horribly low. It was slow going at first as the bowlers were given every possible vocal encouragement by another full house crowd and only thirteen runs came in the first ten overs. To general dismay a confident lbw appeal in Griffith's first over against Barrington was turned down. Nineteen runs came in the first hour, and seventy-five minutes before Cowdrey with an apologetic air drove Sobers through extra-cover for the day's first 4. Gradually the batting became more fluent and Barrington drove Griffith for 4 while Cowdrey straight-drove Sobers and hooked Griffith and came to his hundred when he pull-drove Gibbs for 4 in the last over before lunch. Later in the same over though, he tried to cut and was caught behind after a wonderful innings. His 101 had taken him 343 minutes which was a sure indication that the pitch was nothing like so easy as he made it seem. England were 284–3 at the interval.

A late-cut for 4 off Gibbs brought Barrington to his fifty on the restart. There was then one of those golden pieces of cricket which are lost to records because they go down in the scorebook as simply a dot. Gibbs threw one up to Graveney who, in that lovely angular way of his, produced an exquisite off-drive which looked as if it was 4 runs off the bat but Sobers running at full tilt to his left at mid-off swooped on it one-handed, threw back to Deryck Murray and Graveney had a scramble to get back into his crease. The crowd lapped it up. The score was 310 when Holford gave one a little more air and when Barrington drove the bowler held onto a brilliant one-handed catch high to his left and a few minutes later Jim Parks played forward to Holford's googly and was caught by Sobers very close at backward short-leg. The score was still 318 when D'Oliveira reached forward to Holford and was quickly stumped by Murray and suddenly England found themselves at 318–6. By now, the crowd was in mid-season form, cheering everyone and everything to the echo.

Fred Titmus and Tom Graveney now took the score to 351 with Titmus, who was surrounded by five close fielders, taking three good 4's off Holford before he played back to the third ball of a new spell from Hall and was lbw. One run later Graveney was yorked off the toe by Hall and to general acclamation his off stump was knocked out of the ground. Hall and Griffith then disposed of David Brown and John Snow and England were all out for 376 which was a great deal less than had at one time seemed likely, but they will not have been too dissatisfied when Brown and Snow removed both West Indian openers before the close of play. Deryck Murray who, for some reason, was promoted to go in first with Steve Camacho, hooked at

David Brown in the second over and skied an easy catch to Basil D'Oliveira at backward short-leg. In the next over Camacho played back to John Snow and was torpedoed by a shooter. The pitch was fast but the bounce was becoming increasingly dangerous for every now and then the ball behaved as this one had and rose scarcely an inch. The crowd were in a high state of excitement, for having cheered Camacho to the echo when he drove the first ball of the second over for 4 they had been reduced to a twitching silence by those two wickets and then in paradoxical relief found voice again when Brown's first ball to Rohan Kanhai shot along the ground past the off stump for 4 byes.

The West Indies were 27–2 at the close, and on the third morning the crowd, as if sensing great deeds, was more squashed in than ever. The fun began almost at once for in the first over which was bowled by Brown one kept horribly low to Kanhai who did well to dig it out and Seymour Nurse then snicked a 4 through the slips. Kanhai and Nurse brought up an anxious fifty and then Jeff Jones took over from John Snow at the mountain end. In his first over he made one bounce at Kanhai, who is a small man, from only just short of a length and he played it most skilfully getting right on top of the ball and dropping it at his feet. In the next over Brown made one rear at Kanhai. He followed it with a yorker which Kanhai came down on just in time, and then in desperation he flung his bat at the last ball of the over which was on a length and it skyed over Brown's head and fell between him and Snow who was coming in from wide mid-on. It was a fine over which had caused Kanhai to panic.

The dividend came in the next over, however, when Nurse tried to drive Jones off the back foot and edged the ball into his stumps. Four runs later Jones should have had Lloyd's wicket when D'Oliveira running back from backward short-leg missed a sitter to the immense delight of the crowd. Lloyd seemed shaken for he now played and missed at five balls in a row in Snow's next over and the batting continued to be full of apprehension. The score had lurched to 80 when Kanhai went back to Snow and steered a lifter straight to Graveney at second slip. Gary Sobers now strolled out in that cool, relaxed manner of his, accompanied by the vocal hopes of the crowd. In leisurely manner he took guard, looked round the field and settled over his bat as if he was playing in a Sunday afternoon match. His demeanour had drained the pressure from situation. Snow ran in from the southern end with the crowd bubbling in anticipation. The ball was short of a length and on the middle stump. Sobers, in typical unhurried fashion, went onto the backfoot and, horror of horrors, the ball hit the edge of one of those ever widening cracks and shot along the ground, hitting the great man on the ankle. The volume of the subsequent appeal was in itself a declaration of war and every eye in the house turned to umpire Cortez Jordan who thought and then thought again before slowly and irrevocably raising his hand; in stunned silence Sobers began the walk back to the pavilion and the scoreboard showed that the West Indies were 80–5.

Basil Butcher, small, compact and dapper with his shirt sleeves buttoned at the wrist, always defiant and with a penchant for making hundreds at Lord's, temporarily relieved the seige when he straight drove Snow and hooked Jones for 4. Then, he forced Snow through mid-off to the boundary before playing back to the next ball which lifted and left him and was caught behind. Almost immediately Holford flashed outside the off stump at Snow and Parks threw aloft another catch. Charlie Griffith drove at Snow and D'Oliveira picked up the catch right-handed at third slip and Wes Hall was bowled pushing forward in the same over. Finally Lance Gibbs played a sketchy back stroke to Jones and was caught behind leaving Lloyd with 34 not out. Snow led the England side back into the pavilion with the brilliant figures of 7–49 from 21 overs. It had been a truly great piece of fast bowling in which he had taken every advantage of the help given him by a pitch with an increasingly uneven bounce. Snow, tousle haired and sleek, athletic, outwardly at any rate moody, alert and yet subdued, was the most intelligent of the bowlers and the most contrasting of men. He was capable of real pace with that slightly frenetic action which came so easily and yet in anyone else would have seemed awkward and out of place. I shall never forget him at Sabina Park walking slowly back to his mark at the southern end, polishing the ball on his trousers, his lips slightly apart, a figure of intense concentration, playing a mental game of chess with the West Indian batsmen.

As so often happens, a collapse was succeeded in the follow-on by more stalwart batting and by bowling which could not recapture the earlier penetration. Seymour Nurse now came in first with Camacho and decided that attack was the best method to adopt. Driving, cutting and playing off his legs brought him five most elegant 4s in his first 25 runs and he had scored them out of a total 27. The crowd bayed with audible relief. Camacho made him a safe and watchful partner and at the end of the day, having followed-on 233 runs behind, the West Indies were 81–0 with Nurse 56 and Camacho 19.

One could feel the suspense when arriving at the ground the next morning with another packed crowd already in place although one could not guess at the dramas which lay around the corner. Play began with another onslaught by Nurse who immediately square-cut and forced Snow for 4s and then square-cut Jones before a drive for 4 off the backfoot against Snow brought up the hundred and the ground erupted. The cheering had scarcely died down when Nurse went back to force the next ball, it came back into him a fraction and he dragged it onto his middle stump.

Throughout his career Nurse had been overshadowed by Sobers and Kanhai and yet was a brilliant performer in his own right, and was also the nicest of men. No one has hit a cricket ball much more crisply or elegantly from a lovely upright stance and his strokes were always glorious examples of the classical method. His twelve 4s and his general approach was a summation of Nurse as a cricketer. This innings contained the full splendour of his batting. Perhaps too, it contained the one blemish he had, which was that he did not go on to score the hundreds he should have made. But, like the man himself, his batting was always excitingly vibrant and tinged with a very real sense of humour. Nowadays he sports a beard which makes him almost unrecognisable until he smiles in that joyful Bajan way.

With his departure, Kanhai now took on the battle while Camacho provided the cement at the other end. The roars which greeted the three boundaries Kanhai took off Snow and Jones told the story, but then it was Camacho's turn to feel the venom of the pitch. He played back to D'Oliveira – on this pitch there was no excuse for getting onto the back foot, especially in defence – and the ball never left the ground and hit the base of his stumps. Camacho, bespectacled and earnest in appearance, left the ground slowly and thoughtfully, looking like the school swot who knew he had muffed the exam. Butcher took his place and hooked Jones for two resounding 4s which sent the crowd up into the clouds once again and the score had reached 163 with the deficit only 70. Jones now came back for another spell and in his first over Kanhai miscalculated the left-arm over angle of delivery, hooked and was caught by Edrich running to his left from just backward of the square-leg umpire. At lunch the West Indies were 173–3, but eight minutes after the restart, it was Lloyd's turn to go onto the back foot and he had no chance when this ball also ran along the ground and hit his off stump. Ringing applause greeted Sobers's arrival for the second time in the match. He seemed a slightly more careworn Sobers now and there was less inconsequentiality about the way in which he took guard. He played back to Brown's next ball and it popped over Fred Titmus's head at forward short-leg. The pulse-beat of the crowd had quickened considerably and for the next few minutes everyone on the ground lived anxiously on their nerves. Sobers had reached 7 of the least convincing runs of his career when Tom Graveney who had fielded brilliantly and caught everything at second slip was hit by a ball on the end of a finger and had to leave the field briefly for first aid. Basil D'Oliveira took his place and Sobers played back to the very next ball from Snow which found the outside edge – and flew straight to second slip. It was a simple enough catch, but D'Oliveira dropped it. By the time Snow began his next over Graveney was back with a piece of sticking plaster round the offending finger. He would have swallowed the catch.

The 200 came up soon afterwards and 4 runs later Butcher glanced at D'Oliveira, the ball hit the inside edge of his bat and Parks dived far to his left and held a brilliant one-handed catch and Butcher was walking off before the umpire confirmed his dismissal. The England players were jubilant and the ground was submerged in the usual silence which greeted the fall of a West Indian wicket. Butcher had gone most of the way to the pavilion when a growing noise took our eyes to the east side of the ground where towards the southern corner the crowd was beginning to seethe with unhappiness. Suddenly there was a flash of sun on glass and something bounced onto the outfield about twenty yards in from the boundary. It was followed by three or four more in quick succession and it was then I realized along with many others that they were bottles. They came slowly at first and then suddenly it was a fusilade; some of the spectators had remarkable arms and one or two bounced almost out onto the pitch itself. The England players edged nervously away from that side of the pitch and stood in a huddle just to the pavilion side of the ground. David Holford, the new batsman, had emerged from the pavilion and was uncertain whether or not to proceed while Sobers also edged away from the middle. The umpires too were figures of indecision and still the rain of bottles and shouts and taunts continued. The West Indies' batting and their likely defeat had prompted the outburst and it was now clear that play could not continue with one side of the ground littered with bottles. After a hasty conversation with the umpires Cowdrey led his players into the pavilion and the two batsmen followed. While this was all going on, the police arrived which, if anything, seemed to add to the crowd's excitement and it was clear that for a while no one had the slightest idea what to do next.

Cecil Marley, the white-haired president of the Jamaica Cricket Association, was talking anxiously to the two captains in front of the pavilion and soon Sobers and Cowdrey both walked across the ground to the troubled area. This temporarily halted the rain of bottles and they did their best to pacify the crowd, but soon the bottles began again and they were forced to withdraw and there was another period of inactivity. Then, from behind the pavilion more soldiers appeared with riot shields and tear gas canisters. They advanced across the ground until they were standing in front of the most militant section of the crowd although the bottle throwing by now had spread along the popular side of the ground. The fury of the crowd was evident from the noise and the police began to lob the gas canisters over the wire netting into the crowd. The only trouble was that they had failed to notice that the wind was blowing in exactly the opposite direction and the white clouds of gas were blown swiftly across the ground to the pavilion where the members received the treatment that was intended for the rioters. They piled into the telephone boxes and anywhere they could find to avoid the piercing acrid gas which made vision impossible and the back of the throat feel something similar to the effects of a dramatic drinking binge, but rather worse.

When the riot police appeared, Jim Swanton told me to go out of the press box onto the ground to see exactly what was happening and of course I did as I was told. When the first canisters were thrown I had a ringside pew, but as the gas blew back across the ground I was one of the first to be in the firing line and, swamped by tear gas (not something I recommend), I fled back towards the press box. As I approached the door with a handkerchief stuffed into my mouth I heard the ringing tones of Jim instructing whoever was standing by the door of the box to shut it so that the gas did not penetrate. It was a voice which brooked no dissent and when I was about a couple of steps from the door it was slammed shut and as far as I know, bolted. Anyway, no amount of pushing and shoving made any impression so I stayed where I was, rearranged my defences which consisted of one moth-eaten handkerchief, and settled down to a struggle for survival with tear gas swirling all around. After what seemed an age it blew away and the rioting section of the crowd had mostly climbed their way out of the back of the ground into the road and peace returned. Soon it was safe to venture forth from my perch just outside the press box door. The easterly side of the ground was covered with bottles, the area of open ground around the bare Lignum Vitae trees was almost empty, the police were bristling here, there and everywhere with weaponry at the ready and the members who had received the full force of the gas were being attended to. Gradually, people emerged from the pavilion and the business of clearing the bottles off the outfield started. It had all begun soon after half past two when Butcher was out and events had occupied a hectic forty-five minutes.

It did not take that long to clear the ground, the umpires reappeared just before four o'clock and the players followed them out. There was now a nasty moment for they were greeted by a series of long-range bottles which were being thrown from outside the ground and the players promptly retreated to the pavilion while the police put that situation to rights. When D'Oliveira was ready to complete an over which had been so dramatically interrupted, a net seventy-five minutes had been lost for the tea interval had been taken. There was now an air of complete unreality about the cricket which was, more than anything, an anti-climax, and anyone could forgive the players for keeping more than half an eye on the crowd. With immense tact, the West Indies did not lose another wicket that night and when Sobers glanced Snow for 2 the innings defeat was avoided. At the close the two cousins, Sobers and Holford, had taken the West Indies to 258–5 and a lead of 25.

There were all sorts of meetings and statements issued that night and an unscheduled sixth day was planned for the Wednesday to make up the lost time. It looked as if this decision had given England the chance to complete a victory which they richly deserved. In the event, it almost enabled the West Indies to win a match which now pursued an entirely different course. The dismay felt by those who ran cricket in Jamaica and indeed by all right-thinking Jamaicans was summed up in the statement issued by Cecil Marley:

'This day in the history of Jamaican sportsmanship and cricket will go down as the blackest of black days. I never thought that I would live to see the day that our public conduct and sportsmanship would reach such a deplorably low state. All right-thinking Jamaicans will for ever be ashamed of the conduct of the misguided group to Colin Cowdrey and his team. To our guests and visitors, I desire to express my most profound regrets.'

Understandably, there was a small crowd on the fifth day of the match and the low clouds seemed to produce a funereal gloom which may have been appropriate. However, the popular eastern side of the ground which had caused the trouble was well populated and the bare branches of the Lignum Vitae were full of people. They were in good voice too when after surviving hostile spells from Snow and Jones, David Holford drove Brown over mid-off for 4 and Sobers's fifty which it had taken him 143 minutes to compile was greeted with revolutionary enthusiasm. There was a brief interruption for rain and then Holford's leg stump was shaved by balls from Snow which kept horribly low but generally the cousins were in control and it was not until play had been in progress for ninety minutes that England had their first chance. Holford, who was 30, played forward to D'Oliveira and Edrich, at leg-slip, dropped a difficult catch low to his right. The hundred stand came next and suddenly England were on the receiving end of it, having been in complete control until that first bottle had appeared. It began to rain shortly before lunch when the West Indies were 314–5 although play was able to restart on time afterwards. Before he had added to his 35 Holford swept at Titmus and was lbw. In the off-spinner's next over Sobers straight drove for 6, glanced and swept the next two balls for 4 and took sixteen from the over and the trees swayed almost to breaking point with jubilation, not to say justification. At 351, Murray played back to Brown and was lbw to another which kept low. The crowd had sensed the West Indies' ascendancy and Sobers, who was at his most commanding, was causing great delight which reached a crescendo when a single took him to his eighteenth Test century. Jones then accounted for Griffith and Hall with successive balls and at 391–9 Sobers, who had reached 113, declared 158 runs ahead.

With the extra seventy-five minutes scheduled for the sixth day, 145 minutes remained. I don't know whether Sobers sensed that the advantage had swung completely round to the West Indies or whether with his great sense of fairness which always characterized his captaincy and his approach to cricket he wanted to give England a chance. Anyway, it did not seem an impossible target. At ten minutes past four, he ran in to bowl the first over to Boycott. The Yorkshireman tried to glance the fourth ball of the over and was bowled round his legs. The next ball was fast, Cowdrey played at it from the crease, it crashed into his pads and produced a huge appeal for lbw which was answered in the affirmative by the umpire and

England were 0–2. Maybe Sobers knew something after all. The crowd went wild and this second wicket precipitated an invasion of the field. When Griffith bowled the second over from the southern end, there was a loud appeal for lbw against Edrich off the last ball and England were living most uneasily. In Sobers's second over Ken Barrington drove through gully for 4, ran a leg-side single and Edrich then glanced for 4 more. In the next over Barrington hooked a couple of short ones from Griffith for 4 before playing back and being given lbw by Sang Hue to a ball which may have been going down the leg-side. England were 19–3 and the crowd were in frenzies of joy although it was nothing compared to what happened five minutes later when Edrich played a ball from Hall into his off stump. Five minutes after that, mercifully from England's point of view, bad light intervened and claimed the last forty minutes of the day. If play had been able to continue I am sure the match would have been effectively won by the West Indies that evening.

When those extra seventy-five minutes began the next morning England were 19–4 with Graveney and Parks both on 0. The atmosphere in the Courtleigh Manor the night before had been one of unrelieved gloom. England felt robbed, and justifiably so, by the riots and the West Indies were now sweeping along on an unstoppable course. It was going to take strong nerves if England were to survive. It is difficult to think of another session of cricket which progressed in slow motion quite as this one did. Not surprisingly a fair crowd had assembled and each over had six moments of total suspense. Emotions were sky high one moment and down in the basement the next and the tension was enormous. The England contingent braved a quick smile when Graveney on-drove Griffith's second ball of the day for 4. Then it was Wes Hall and not Sobers who bowled the second over. He employed four short-legs, three slips and a gully and when Parks played and missed twice the noise from the crowd suggested the world was coming to an end. Lance Gibbs bowled the third over and Graveney cut his first ball for 4. The first ball of Hall's second over flew off the pitch, hit Parks on the neck and he collapsed at the crease but recovered after a visit from Jack Jennings, the physiotherapist. Later in the same over, another short one flew almost over wicket-keeper Murray's head. When Sobers, bowling left-arm spin, came on for the sixth over, Parks snicked him over Gibbs's head at slip, but after thirty minutes he played forward to the first ball that Gibbs, who disliked bowling from round the wicket, had bowled from that side of

169

the stumps and was out lbw. Gibbs now bowled to D'Oliveira with six men round the bat, three on each side of the pitch. Suddenly, Sobers, the spinner, electrified everyone by producing a ball which was almost as quick as anything he bowled off his long run and Graveney knew nothing about it. D'Oliveira still had not scored when he played back to Gibbs and Holford dropped him at slip. At the other end, Sobers twice hit Graveney on the pads and the only respite for England came with the appearance of the drinks trolley after forty-five minutes. It was brought out at the double by two attendants and so swiftly did the West Indies deal with this unwelcome interruption that the cart with two tigers painted on each side was back in the pavilion in precisely one and a half minutes. To celebrate its disappearance, Sobers sent a shooter a millimetre past D'Oliveira's off stump. The action was non-stop and the excitement unbelievable.

It was the turn of the English to cheer when D'Oliveira square-cut Sobers for 4, but it was followed by one of the cruellest pieces of luck. Tom Graveney had been in quiet control and was giving little cause for anxiety when he now swept at Gibbs off the middle of the bat. It struck Steve Camacho on the left hip at forward short-leg and looped all the way to Charlie Griffith at mid-on who could hardly believe his luck as he threw up the catch. Graveney, in disgust, threw his bat two or three yards from him incurring the instant displeasure of Jim Swanton in the press box, but he had been making a note and had not seen the ball's route. There were twenty-five minutes to go and England were 51–6. When Gibbs ran in to bowl to Fred Titmus, Griffiths was the only West Indian who was not crouching round the bat. They were the longest twenty-five minutes in the life of any Englishman at Sabina Park that day. The score had crept to 56 when D'Oliveira drove at Gibbs and the ball flew hard and low to Holford at first slip, who dropped it. The hands of the clock on the pavilion had just reached midday when Titmus pushed forward to Gibbs and Camacho diving in from square short-leg held the catch off bat and pad and it was 61–7.

David Brown used his allotted two minutes and more to make his way to the crease and for the next twelve-and-a-half minutes we were all on something a great deal sharper and less certain than tenterhooks. The hands of the clock said 12.13 when Brown was yorked by Sobers but the umpires did a swift calculation, adding the two minutes allowed for the next batsman's arrival to the thirteen, and we all looked at one another in sheer amazement and disbelief. England had escaped with a draw.

After that sensational start to my Test-watching career at Sabina Park, on subsequent visits I have been lucky enough to watch formidable rearguard actions by such pre-eminent batsmen as Glen Turner, Dennis Amiss, Graham Gooch and David Gower. In February 1972, Turner played an amazing innings of 223 not out which coming out of New Zealand's first innings 386 was almost 60 per cent of the total. This all came after Lawrence Rowe, in his first Test match, made 214 in his first innings and later followed it with 100 not out in the second which made a unique first Test for the young Jamaican. On a glorious pitch and against a plain attack from which Bruce Taylor had been unaccountably omitted on the morning of the match, Rowe showed an infinite class which he was so seldom able to reproduce after this first series that I have to mark him down as one of the great disappointments of my cricketing life.

Rowe was barely twenty-one when he strode out in a cool, unruffled manner which immediately made one sit up and take note. He wore his maroon West Indies cap as though it had been there for years. He came in, at the worst possible moment, for three minutes before lunch on that first morning Joey Carew seemed to drive at Bevan Congdon almost as an afterthought, was hit on the back leg and was lbw. While Rowe was taking guard his bat seemed massively broad and there was not a hint of nerves as he tucked the ball away off his legs and he came into lunch with two runs to his name. At the other end, Roy Fredericks, later to become Comrade Roy Fredericks in the government of Guyana, was using those lightning wrists as dazzlingly as ever and even in that one over before the interval one could see a dramatic contrast in styles. Fredericks was all wrists, eye, not too much footwork and typical West Indian flair, while Rowe was classically composed, precise, economical and correct in every movement he made, but the greatest impression he made was of having so much time in which to play his strokes.

He came out after lunch looking more the part than ever and promptly hooked and glanced that most unlikely of opening bowlers, Murray Webb, for 4. Webb was very long haired and thoroughly modern in an early seventies way and could hardly have been further from the clean cut, short back-and-sides image of New Zealand cricket. They took a chance in picking him for their first-ever tour of the Caribbean for he was still very inexperienced. It did not pay dividends. In all he played in three Test matches in his short career and took four wickets, but none of them in the West Indies. His bowling was scarcely more disciplined than his reddish hair. Rowe went on through a hot afternoon unfolding one stroke after another as if it had been his intention to bring the coaching manual to life. He drove the persevering Bob Cunis most gloriously through the covers with a stroke which can never have been bettered: a delicate late-cut took him to fifty after 130 minutes. He went smoothly on until the close of play, timing the ball to perfection and playing with equal facility off both the front and the back foot. When he hooked, it was never a rough or a violent stroke: he rolled his wrists to keep the ball on the ground after moving unhurriedly across his stumps to make sure that he was inside the line. When he came onto the front foot there was the suspicion of Cowdrey's effortlessness and the only stroke he played with anything approaching ferocity was the square-cut when the ball was short and wide enough. Although Fredericks reached his first Test hundred shortly before the close, Rowe was never overawed by his partner and indeed long before the end of the day had begun to catch him up. When the players came in he was six runs short of a hundred. It took him fifteen minutes the next day to score them and when he was 99 he and Fredericks got into an anxious mix up over a single. Then, he pushed Cunis to cover and ran the single which brought him to a hundred.

When Fredericks reached 150 he clearly thought it was enough and the third chance he gave after reaching that landmark was accepted when he had reached 163. Rowe, however, went on and it was a delight to watch him battling with Hedley Howarth who bowled 44 fine overs of orthodox left-arm spin. Rowe had gone into lunch when he was 150 and had no intention of surrendering. Soon after the restart he came down the pitch twice in an over to Howarth and drove him through extra cover for two 4s with exquisite timing and he raced towards his 200 which arrived when he square-cut Cunis with a stroke which exhausted the lung power of the assembled company of around 10,000 Jamaicans. He then also felt he was being greedy and, after a last imperious straight drive for 6 off Howarth, he skied him to the New Zealand captain, Graham Dowling, at deep extra-cover. After Sobers's declaration, there was time for the West Indian opening bowlers, Irving Shillingford and the ferocious but uncontrolled Uton Dowe to take three wickets and the next morning the leg-spin of David Holford and the off-breaks of Lance Gibbs reduced New

Zealand to 108–5 when the follow-on seemed inevitable even though Turner was biding his time in mostly defensive certainty at the other end. He had almost fallen from grace for when he was 47 he had driven wildly at Gibbs and Carew had dropped the catch over his shoulder running back from extra-cover. At lunch when New Zealand were 128–5, Turner had scored exactly half the runs.

He was now partnered by the wicket-keeper, Ken Wadsworth, such a competitive cricketer who was most sadly destined to die of cancer at the age of thirty. He was not a beautiful batsman but he was mighty effective, taking full toll of anything loose and keeping his bat straight in defence, which is never a bad recipe. They survived the second new ball and the first fifty of their partnership came in 69 minutes and when shortly before tea Turner cut Maurice Foster for 4, his hundred had come in 320 minutes and his thirteen 4s showed that boundaries had been coming more freely in the second half of his innings. I have always felt that Geoff Boycott and Glenn Turner had a good deal in common. They were both dedicated to the business of scoring runs in the same obsessive manner. I have little doubt that Turner also regarded mammoth piles of runs as the principal justification for existence and he went about the process every bit as efficiently. Like Boycott, Turner spent his life refusing risks with the bat in his hand and maybe out of it as well. He was a superb technician whom practice had made as near perfect as it was humanly possible to be. On this tour of the West Indies he made four double centuries which argues a singleness of purpose given to few. This was his only tour of the West Indies and he was fortunate to have come across their bowling at a time when they were in a rebuilding process between their brilliance in the sixties and the irresistibility they were to find later in the seventies. But even so, his batting in the Caribbean was quite superb although if one could fault him, it was that when he had entrenched himself at the crease he was reluctant, just as Boycott was, to try and change gear and destroy the attack. This may have been dictated by his hatred of getting out and his fear of anything which might be interpreted as failure. He had all the strokes but sometimes a reluctance to use them. His method implies that he was wholly self-centred about scoring runs and his singleness of purpose may not always have made him the easiest of men in the dressing-room and the same too, could surely be said of Boycott. But as with Boycott his formidable record speaks for itself

By the end of the third day of this Test he had made 164 out of the

New Zealand total of 280–5 while Wadsworth had contributed a most valiant fifty. The follow-on was saved early on the fourth morning after the West Indies had taken the second new ball which came in for rough treatment at the hands of Wadsworth who took four 4s off the first two overs with it. He then hooked at Dowe and was caught low down by Fredericks at backward short-leg having added 220 in 285 minutes with Turner in a stand which enabled New Zealand to survive. But Turner went on, as unruffled as ever.

The West Indies continued their second innings until Rowe had completed his second hundred of the match, and Sobers's declaration left New Zealand to score 341 to win in 315 minutes which was hardly generous and in the end he must have regretted that he did not leave his bowlers more time, for New Zealand had lost 6 wickets for 236. Turner managed only 21 this time before he was out cutting against the spin at a googly from Holford, a mistake he will not have enjoyed.

It would have been unfair to have expected Sabina Park to have maintained this dizzy pace and the following year I watched the West Indies and Australia play out a formal draw which never looked like being anything else. The Jamaican crowd adored watching their local hero, Maurice Foster, make a hundred and then in Australia's second innings Keith Stackpole made a most entertaining 142. By the time the Englishmen returned to Sabina Park in February 1974, the ground and the population of Kingston had caught their breath in a cricketing sense, although I daresay they were not fully prepared for the shock of Dennis Amiss's famous rearguard action which enabled England to escape with a draw. Once again, it was real nail biting stuff. Mike Denness won the toss and England batted first on a good pitch and wasted the chance this gave them. All the batsmen did the hard work and played themselves in but none, not even Boycott whose 68 took three and a half hours, was able to go on to make a big score. Denness batted three hours for his 67 and was the only other to pass fifty. A total of 353 was never likely to be adequate especially when, by the end of the second day, Roy Fredericks and Lawrence Rowe had put on 159 for the first wicket. While Fredericks was both exciting and impudent in that dashing left-handed way of his, Rowe stroked the ball through the covers and elsewhere with all the precision of an animated geometry box. The next morning two glorious on-drives against Pat Pocock brought Rowe to his hundred and again his bat seemed at least twice as wide as anyone else's. The second new ball accounted for Fredericks when he hooked at Chris Old and edged the ball into his stumps six runs short of his hundred. Immediately after that, Rowe moved lazily across his stumps and hooked Bob Willis over backward square-leg for 6 but Willis had the last word when Rowe drove across the line and was lbw. But that provided only a temporary respite, for almost at once Clive Lloyd moved mountainously forward and straight-drove Derek Underwood for 6. Lloyd and Kanhai both got themselves out before the close of the third day when Alvin Kallicharran was 89 not out and the West Indies were 434–4. Kallicharran was seven runs short of a patient hundred when he drove Old into the gully but Gary Sobers and Bernard Julien made lively left-handed contributions before the West Indies declared at 583–9.

The lead, therefore, was 230 and when England ended the day at 218–5, they seemed certain to lose. The only problem for the West Indies was Amiss who batted with great composure. He had already hit four 4s, three of them with hooks, when Boycott was caught behind trying to pull out of the way of a short one from Keith Boyce when the score was 32. John Jameson now took guard and hooked viciously at his first ball which flew over third-man off the edge for 6. While Jameson used his bat rather as though he was wielding an axe, Amiss went smoothly on his way driving fluently off both feet and punishing leg-spinner Arthur Barrett whenever his strength erred. These two added 50 in forty minutes, but with Jameson one felt it was too good to last, and after square-cutting Sobers and Gibbs to the boundary, he drove firm footed at Barrett and was caught at slip. Five runs later, at 107, Amiss cut Barrett to cover where Clive Lloyd was hovering and Frank Hayes was run-out by his return to Deryck Murray. Denness helped Amiss take the score to 176 before he played forward to Barrett and was given out caught at slip after it had looked suspiciously as if the bowler was appealing for lbw. A lovely cover-drive off Sobers brought Amiss to his hundred and he then proceeded to pull the next ball, a full toss, for 6. Then just before the close Tony Greig was beaten in the air and bowled by Gibbs.

The decisive moment on the last day came in the very first over when Amiss, who had not added to his overnight 123, played forward to one from Gibbs which spun and he was dropped by Sobers who had moved the wrong way in anticipation at backward short-leg. The West Indies will not have been unduly disturbed because apart from Alan Knott, Amiss had only the bowlers to keep him company. It was agonizing to watch for it seemed that the nightwatchman, Derek Underwood, might go at any time, but he hung about for an hour and a quarter before driving at Sobers and being caught behind. This made it 258–6 and a draw looked a long way away. The situation was made worse when, at 271, Amiss who was not the greatest judge of a quick single, pushed Sobers into the covers and called Knott who was most comprehensively thrown out by Lloyd from cover. While throwing the ball, Lloyd fell and pulled a muscle and had to be helped off. That throw had surely ended England's hopes of a draw, but Amiss went serenely on playing some glorious strokes off the front foot and suddenly England's lead was past the hundred. Every run that England scored now counted double for it meant that the West Indies would themselves have to score them later if they were to win. By the time Old was bowled after batting for a valiant 111 minutes, England were 110 ahead. Pat Pocock now made another adhesive companion for Amiss, who posted his double century in 448 minutes. Together they took the score to 392 with every Englishman on the ground doing frantic calculations with the time left and the runs to be scored. Pocock was then caught by Vanburn Holder fielding as substitute for Clive Lloyd and England were 159 ahead. Pocock had scored four singles off 88 balls in eighty-three minutes. When he was out only ninety minutes remained and allowing for the ten minutes between innings England were surely safe, but to make sure Bob Willis stayed with Amiss, his Warwickshire colleague, until five o'clock when England had reached 432–9 and Amiss was 262 not out after batting for 570 minutes in a truly heroic innings.

As the West Indies had already won the series, I did not go to Kingston for the fifth Test of the series against Australia in 1977–78. Riots again intervened just when it seemed that Australia were going to win. The West Indies were 258–9 when Vanburn Holder had been given out caught behind and the trouble began. Thirty-eight balls of the mandatory last twenty overs were left and plans to play an unscheduled sixth day as had happened when England were similarly affected in 1967–68 were frustrated by the refusal of one of the umpires, Ralph Gosein, to officiate on the grounds that the playing conditions did not allow for the match to be extended.

My next visit to Sabina Park came in April 1981. An innings of 153 by Graham Gooch in England's first innings 285 saved Ian Botham's side from complete collapse. West Indies built up a lead of 157, then an untypically patient 154 not out by David Gower made in seven and three quarter hours guided England to safety in their second innings. For all that, it looked for a long time as if the West Indies would win for when Paul Downton joined Gower after England's sixth wicket had fallen at 215, the lead was only 58 and almost four hours remained. England had made a disastrous start to their second innings when Gooch, Athey and Boycott were all out by the time the score had reached 32. Peter Willey then made Gower a resolute partner with that extraordinary two-eyed stance combined with his usual large helping of obstinacy. Gower was dropped by Clive Lloyd at slip when he was 29 and cut at Viv Richards and on the last day when 84 Gordon Greenidge dropped him at mid-off, again from Richards's bowling and, at 107, Desmond Haynes missed a hard one at short backward square-leg off Michael Holding. It was another day when English hearts were more or less permanently in their mouths, but Downton kept Gower company to the end.

There were no such antics when England played the first Test at Sabina Park four years later on a pitch with a nastily uneven bounce which enabled yet another West Indian fast bowler, Patrick Patterson, to make his mark with 7–74 in a match which the West Indies won by 10 wickets. England were without Mike Gatting, who had been forced to return to England for surgery after being hit on the bridge of the nose when hooking at Malcolm Marshall in the one -day international just before the Test. Four years after that, of course, Graham Gooch's England side won a famous victory there, but, alas, I was watching India in New Zealand at the time and so that was one of Sabina Park's outstanding moments that I missed. It has certainly been a ground which over the years has had considerably more than its fair share of excitement.